THE
ENGLISH
YEAR

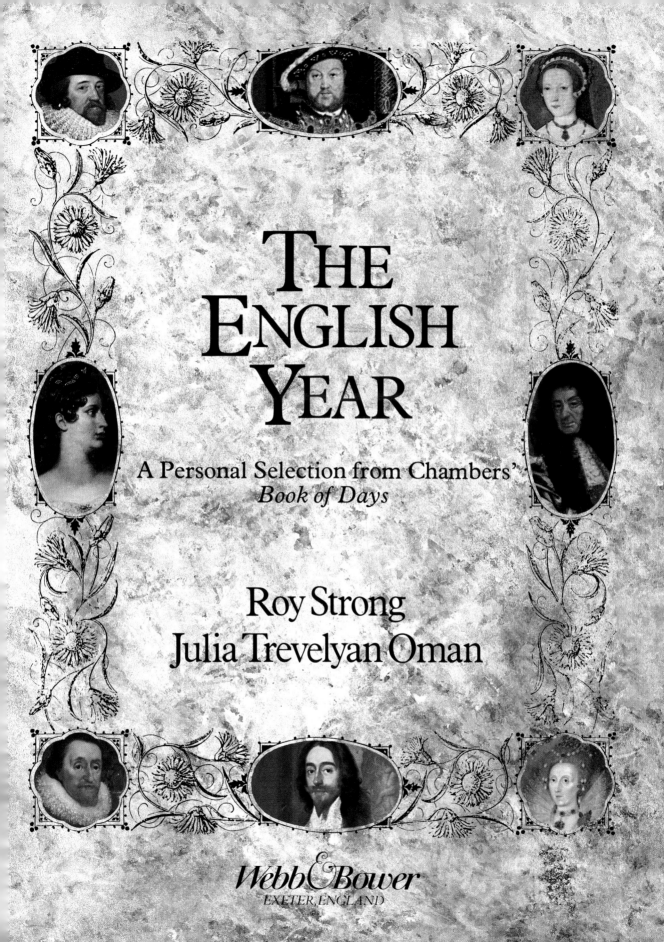

THE ENGLISH YEAR

A Personal Selection from Chambers' *Book of Days*

Roy Strong
Julia Trevelyan Oman

Webb & Bower
EXETER, ENGLAND

IN MEMORIAM
Charles Harvard Gibbs-Smith
A miscellaneous book in memory of a miscellaneous man

Note on the Zodiac Signs

The descriptions under the illustrations of the zodiac
signs are quotations from *Christian Astrology* by
William Lilly, published in London in 1647. The
astrologers of Lilly's time believed that the Sun, the
Moon and the planets—Jupiter, Mars, Mercury,
Saturn and Venus—ruled the signs of the zodiac. The
contemporary descriptions of the characteristics of a
person born under a particular sign, except Leo and
Cancer which are ruled by the Sun and the Moon
respectively, are duplicated as follows:

Gemini and Virgo
Taurus and Libra
Aries and Scorpio
Sagittarius and Pisces
Capricorn and Aquarius.

First published in Great Britain 1982 by
Webb & Bower (Publishers) Limited
9 Colleton Crescent, Exeter, Devon EX2 4BY

Designed by Julia Trevelyan Oman

British Library Cataloguing in Publication Data

Strong, Roy
The English year.
1. Great Britain—Social life and customs—
19th century
I. Title   II. Oman, Julia Trevelyan
942.081   DA550

ISBN 0–906671–29–9

Typeset in Great Britain by Keyspools Limited, Golborne,
Lancashire

Printed and bound in Hong Kong by Mandarin Offset International
Limited

PREFACE

Chambers' *Book of Days* has always been a favourite book of both my wife and myself. Published in 1862 its full title runs *The Book of Days. A Miscellany of Popular Antiquities in connection with the Calendar including Anecdote, Biography, & History, Curiosities of Literature and Oddities of Human Life and Character*. The original edition runs to almost two thousand pages of small print arranged in double columns containing an amazing and totally arbitrary miscellany of information. For us, however, its spell is cast by its encapsulation of a world that is lost, that of the seasonal rhythm of rural England in the age before the Industrial Revolution. It is a book written for city dwellers whose roots still lay in the countryside either immediately or only a generation before.

We have made no attempt to update, modernize or indeed correct the text. This would have entirely destroyed its period flavour. Instead we have extracted and abridged what we believe to be the essential Chambers. We have added to it the poetry of John Clare and the zodiacal characterizations of William Lilly. The dates of all the births and deaths, wildly inaccurate in the original edition, have also been checked throughout. From the outset the book has been conceived purely as a personal scrapbook arranged as a decorative reverie whereby to stir the memory.

ROY STRONG
JULIA TREVELYAN OMAN

Withering and keen the winter comes,
While Comfort flies to close-shut rooms,
And sees the snow in feathers pass
Winnowing by the window-glass;
Whilst unfelt tempests howl and beat
Above his head in chimney-seat.

Now, musing o'er the changing scene,
Farmers behind the tavern-screen
Collect; with elbow idly press'd
On hob, reclines the corner's guest,
Reading the news, to mark again
The bankrupt lists, or price of grain;
Or old Moore's annual prophecies
Of flooded fields and clouded skies . . .

The shutter closed, the lamp alight,
The faggot chopt and blazing bright—
The shepherd now, from labour free,
Dances his children on his knee;
While underneath his master's seat,
The tired dog lies in slumbers sweet,
Starting and whimpering in his sleep,
Chasing still the straying sheep.
The cats roll'd round in vacant chair,
Or leaping children's knees to lair,
Or purring on the warmer hearth,
Sweet chorus to the cricket's hearth.

JOHN CLARE

The deity Janus was represented by the Romans as a man with two faces, one looking backwards, the other forwards, implying that he stood between the old and the new year, with a regard to both. In the quaint drawings which illuminate the Catholic missals in the middle ages, January is represented by 'the figure of a man clad in white, as the type of the snow usually on the ground at that season, and blowing on his fingers as descriptive of the cold; under his left arm he holds a billet of wood, and near him stands the figure of the sign Aquarius, into which watery emblem in the zodiac the sun enters on the 19th of this month.'

————came old January, wrapped well
In many weeds to keep the cold away;
Yet did he quake and quiver like to quell,
And blowe his nayles to warm them if he may;
For they were numbed with holding all the day
An hatchet keene, with which he felled wood,
And from the trees did lop the needlesse spray;
Upon an huge great Earth-pot Steane he stood,
From whose wide mouth there flowed forth the
      Romane flood.

SPENSER

It is very appropriate that this should be the first month of the year, as far as the northern hemisphere is concerned; since, its beginning being near the winter's solstice, the year is thus made to present a complete series of the seasonal changes and operations, including equally the first movements of spring, and the death of all annual vegetation in the frozen arms of winter. Yet the earliest calendars, as the Jewish, the Egyptian and Greek, did not place the commencement of the year at this point. It was not done till the formation of the Roman calendar, usually attributed to the second king, Numa Pompilius, whose reign is set down as terminating anno 672 B.C. Numa, it is said, having decreed that the year should commence now, added two new months to the ten into which the year had previously been divided, calling the first Januarius, in honour of Janus, the deity supposed to preside over doors (Lat. *janua*, a door), who might very naturally be presumed also to have something to do with the opening of the year.

JANVARY

If the grass grows in Janiveer,
It grows the worse for't all the year.

A January spring,
Is worth naething.

Under water dearth,
Under snow bread.

March in Janiveer,
January in March, I fear.

If January calends be summerly gay,
'Twill be winterly weather till the calends
    of May.

The blackest month in all the year
Is the month of Janiveer.

January 1st ♍

William Wycherley   Maria Edgeworth   Francis Egerton

born: Maria Edgeworth, novelist, 1767
Edward Stanley, Bishop of Norwich, 1779
Francis Egerton, 1st Earl of Ellesmere,
statesman and poet, 1800
died: William Wycherley, dramatist, 1716

New-Year's Day Festivities

As New Year's Day, the first of January bears a prominent place in the popular calendar. It has ever been a custom among northern nations to see the old year out and the new one in, with the highest demonstrations of merriment and conviviality. It is seldom that an English family fails to sit up on the last night of the year till twelve o'clock, along with a few friends, to drink a happy New Year to each other over a cheerful glass. Very frequently, too, persons nearly related but living apart, dine with each other on this day, to keep alive and cultivate mutual good feeling.

Charles Lamb had a strong appreciation of the social character of New Year's Day. He remarks that no one of whatever rank can regard it with indifference. 'Of all sounds of all bells,' says he, 'most solemn, and touching is the peal which rings out the old year. I never hear it without a gathering up of my mind to concentration of all the images that have been diffused over the past twelvemonth; all I have done or suffered, performed or neglected, in that regretted time.'

During the reign of Queen Elizabeth, the custom of presenting New Year's gifts to the sovereign was carried to an extravagant height. The queen delighted in gorgeous dresses, in jewellery, in all kinds of ornaments for her person and palaces, and in purses filled with gold coin. The gifts regularly presented to her were of great value. An exact and descriptive inventory of them was made every year on a roll, which was signed by the queen herself, and by the proper officers. The presents were made by the great officers of state, peers and peeresses, bishops, knights and their ladies, and others of lower grade, down to her majesty's dustman. The presents consisted of sums of money, costly articles of ornament for the queen's person or apartments, caskets studded with precious stones, valuable necklaces, bracelets, gowns, embroidered mantles, smocks, petticoats, looking-glasses, fans, silk-stockings, and a great variety of other articles.

The merrymakings of New Year's Eve and New Year's Day are of very ancient date in England. The head of the house assembled his family around a bowl of spiced ale, comically called *lamb's wool*, from which he drank their healths; then passed it to the rest, that they might drink too. The word that passed amongst them was the ancient Saxon phrase, *Wass hael*; that is, To your health. Hence this came to be recognised as the Wassail or Wassel Bowl. The poorer class of people carried a bowl adorned with ribbons round the neighbourhood, begging for something wherewith to obtain the means of filling it, that they too might enjoy wassail as well as the rich. In their compotations, they had songs suitable to the occasion. What follows is an example apparently in use amongst children:

Here we come a Wassailing,
Among the leaves so green,
Here we come a wandering,
So fair to be seen.
chorus:
Love and joy come to you,
And to your wassel too,
And God send you a happy
New Year, New Year,
And God send you a happy
New Year!
Our wassel cup is made of
rosemary tree,
So is your beer of the best
barley.

January 2nd

born: General James Wolfe, major-general, 1727.
died: Alexander Wedderburn, 1st Earl of Rosslyn, lord chancellor, 1805
Dr John Mason Good, physician & author, 1827
Dr Andrew Ure, chemist & scientific writer, 1857

January 3rd

born: Douglas Jerrold, man of letters, 1803
died: George Monck, Duke of Albemarle 1607
Josiah Wedgwood, potter 1795

Introduction of female actors

Pepys relates in his *Diary*, that singular chronicle of gossip, under January 3, 1661, that he went to the theatre and saw the *Beggar's Bush* well performed; 'the first time,' says he, 'that ever I saw women come upon the stage.'

This was a theatre in Gibbon's Tennis Court, Vere Street, Clare Market, which had been opened at the recent restoration of the monarchy, after the long theatrical blank under the reign of the Puritans. It had heretofore been customary for young men to act the female parts. All Shakespeare's heroines were thus awkwardly enacted for the first sixty years. At length, on the restoration of the stage, it was thought that the public might perhaps endure the indecorum of female acting, and the venture is believed to have been first made at this theatre on the 8th of December 1660, when a lady acted Desdemona for the first time.

January 4th

born: James Ussher, Archbishop of Armagh, 1581
died: Charlotte Lennox, miscellaneous writers, 1804

Arrest of the Five Members

The 4th of January 1641–2 is the date of one of the most memorable events in English history—the attempted arrest of the five members of the House of Commons—Pym, Hampden, Hollis, Haselrig and Strode—by Charles I. The divisions between the unhappy king and his parliament were lowering towards the actual war which broke out eight months later. Charles, stung by the Grand Remonstrance, a paper in which all the errors of his past government were exposed, thought by one decisive act to strike terror into his outraged subjects, and restore his full authority. While London was on the borders of insurrection against his rule, there yet were not wanting considerable numbers of country gentlemen, soldiers of fortune, and others, who were eager to rally round him in any such attempt. His design of coming with an armed band to the House and arresting the five obnoxious members, was communicated by a lady of his court; so that, just as he approached the door of the House with his cavalier bands, the gentlemen he wished to seize were retiring to a boat on the river, by which they made their escape.

January 5th ♑

born: Thomas Pringle, traveller & poet 1789
died: Edward the Confessor, King of
England, 1066. James Merrick,
poet & scholar, 1769

Twelfth-Day Eve.

Twelfth Day Eve is a rustic festival in England. Persons engaged in rural employments are, or have been heretofore accustomed to celebrate it; and the purpose appears to be to secure a blessing for the fruits of the earth.

'In Herefordshire, at the approach of the evening, the farmers with their friends and servants meet together, and about six o'clock walk out to a field where wheat is growing. In the highest part of the ground, twelve small fires, and one large one, are lighted up. The attendants, headed by the master of the family, pledge the company in old cider, which circulates freely on these occasions. A circle is formed around the large fire, when a general shout and hallooing takes place, which you hear answered from all the adjacent villages and fields. Sometimes fifty or sixty of these fires may be all seen at once. This being finished, the company return home, where the good housewife and her maids are preparing a good supper. A large cake is always provided, with a hole in the middle. After supper, the company all attend the bailiff (or head of the oxen) to the wain-house, where the following particulars are observed: the master, at the head of his friends, fills the cup (generally of strong ale), and stands opposite the first or finest of the oxen. He then pledges him in a curious toast: the company follow his example, with all the other oxen, and addressing each by his name. This being finished, the large cake is produced, and, with much ceremony, put on the horn of the first ox, through the hole above mentioned. The ox is then tickled, to make him toss his head: if he throw the cake behind, then it is the mistress's perquisite; if before (in what is termed the boosy), the bailiff himself claims the prize. The company then return to the house, the doors of which they find locked, nor will they be opened till some joyous songs are sung. On their gaining admittance, a scene of mirth and jollity ensues, which lasts the greatest part of the night.' The custom is called in Herefordshire *Wassailing*. The fires are designed to represent the Saviour and his apostles, and it was customary as to one of them, held as representing Judas Iscariot, to allow it to burn a while, and then put it out and kick about the materials.

January 6th ♑
Epiphany. Or Twelfth-Day

King Richard II

Frederick, Prince of Wales

Fanny Burney

born: Richard II, King of England, 1367
Frederick, Prince of Wales, 1707
died: Fanny Burney, Mme d'Arblay, Novelist, 1840

Twelfth-Day

This day, called Twelfth Day, as being in that number after Christmas, and Epiphany from the Greek signifying *appearance*, is a festival of the Church, in commemoration of the *Manifestation of Christ to the Gentiles*; more expressly to the three Magi, or Wise Men of the East, who came, led by a star, to worship him immediately after his birth. In its character as a popular festival, Twelfth Day stands only inferior to Christmas. The leading object held in view is to do honour to the three wise men, or, as they are more generally denominated, the three kings. It is a Christian custom, ancient past memory and probably suggested by a pagan custom, to indulge in a pleasantry called the *Election of Kings by Beans*. In England, in later times, a large cake was formed, with a bean inserted, and this was called *Twelfth cake*. The family and friends being assembled, the cake was divided by lot, and whoever got the piece containing the bean was accepted as king for the day, and called King of the Bean.

In England, it appears there was always a queen as well as a king on Twelfth Night. A writer, speaking of the celebration in the south of England in 1774, says: 'After tea, a cake is produced, with two bowls containing the fortunate chances for the different sexes. The host fills up the tickets, and the whole company, except the king and queen, are to be ministers of state, maids of honour, or ladies of the bed-chamber. Often the host and hostess, more by design than accident, become king and queen. According to Twelfth Day law, each party is to support his character until midnight.

On Twelfth Night, 1606, Ben Jonson's masque of *Hymen* was performed before the Court; and in 1613 the gentlemen of Gray's Inn were permitted by Lord Bacon to perform a Twelfth Day masque at Whitehall. In this masque the character of Baby Cake is attended by 'an usher bearing a great cake with a bean and a pease.' Down to the time of the Civil Wars, the feast was observed with great splendour, not only at Court, but at the Inns of Court, and the Universities (where it was an old custom to choose the king by the bean in a cake), as well as in private mansions and smaller households.

Then, too, we read of the English nobility keeping Twelfth Night otherwise than with cake and characters, by the diversion of blowing up pasteboard castles; letting claret flow like blood, out of a stag made of paste; the castle bombarded from a pasteboard ship, with cannon, in the midst of which the company pelted each other with egg-shells filled with rose-water; and large pies were made, filled with live frogs, which hopped and flew out, upon some curious person lifting up the lid.

The celebration of Twelfth Day with costly and elegant Twelfth cake has much declined within the last half-century. Formerly, in London, the confectioners' shops on this day were entirely filled with Twelfth cakes, ranging from several guineas to a few shillings; the shops were tastefully illuminated, and decorated with artistic models, transparencies, &c. We remember to have seen a huge Twelfth cake in the form of a fortress, with sentinels and flags; the cake being so large as to fill two ovens in baking.

January 7th ℔

born: Princess Charlotte, daughter of George IV, 1796.
died: Alan Ramsay, Scottish poet 1758

St Distaff's Day

As the first free day after the twelve by which Christmas was formerly celebrated, the 7th of January was a notable one among our ancestors. They jocularly called it *St Distaff's Day*, or *Rock Day*, because by women the rock or distaff was then resumed, or proposed to be so. The duty seems to have been considered a dubious one, and when it was complied with, the ploughmen, who on their part scarcely felt called upon on this day to resume work, made it their sport to set the flax a-burning; in requital of which prank, the maids soused the men from the water-pails. Herrick gives us the popular ritual of the day in some of his cheerful stanzas:

"St Distaff's Day; or, the Morow after Twelfth-Day."

Partly work and partly play
You must on St Distaff's Day:
From the plough soon free your team;
Then come home and fother them:
If the maids a-spinning go,
Burn the flax and fire the tow.
Bring in pails of water then,
Let the maids bewash the men.
Give St Distaff all the right:
Then bid Christmas sport good night,
And next morrow every one
To his own vocation.

January 8th ♑

John Baskerville

died: John Dalrymple, 1st Earl of Stair, 1707. John Baskerville, printer, 1775

January 9th ♑

Thomas Birch

born: John Jervis, Earl of St Vincent, 1735 died: Thomas Birch, biographical and historical writer, 1766. Elizabeth O. Benger, historian, 1827

Touching for the Evil

On this day in the year 1683, King Charles II in council at Whitehall, issued orders for the future regulation of the ceremony of Touching for the King's Evil. Scrofula, which is the scientific name of the disease popularly called the *King's Evil*, has been described as 'indolent glandular tumours, frequently in the neck, suppurating slowly and imperfectly, and healing with difficulty.' The practice of Touching for the King's Evil had its origin in England from Edward the Confessor, according to the testimony of William of Malmesbury, who lived about one hundred years after that monarch.

Henry VII was the first English sovereign who established a particular ceremony to be used on the occasion of touching, and introduced the practice of presenting a small piece of gold. In the reign of Queen Elizabeth, William Tooker published a book on the subject of the cures effected by the royal touch—*Charisma; sive Donum Sanationis*. He is a witness as to facts which occurred in his own time. He states that many persons from all parts of England, of all ranks and degrees, were, to his own knowledge, cured by the touch of the Queen; that he conversed with many of them both before and after their departure from the court; observed an incredible ardour and confidence in them that the touch would cure them, and understood that they actually were cured.

The number of cases seems to have increased greatly after the Restoration, as many as 600 at a time having been touched, the days appointed for it being sometimes thrice a week. Indeed, the practice was at its height in the reign of Charles II. In the first four years after his restoration, he touched nearly 24,000 persons. Under the date of April 10, 1661, Pepys says: 'Met my lord the duke, and, after a little talk with him, I went to the Banquet House, and there saw the king heal,—the first time that I ever saw him do it,—which he did with great gravity; and it seemed to me to be an ugly office and a simple one.'

Touch-piece, time of Charles II

Touch-piece, time of Queen Anne

Queen Anne seems to have been the last of the English sovereigns who actually performed the ceremony of touching.

Previous to the time of Charles II, no particular coin appears to have been executed for the purpose of being given at the touching. The touch-pieces of Charles II are not uncommon. They have figures of St Michael and the dragon on one side and a ship on the other.

January 10th   VB   January 11th   VB

Mary Russell Mitford
Edward Boscowen
William Laud
Sir Hans Sloane
François Roubiliac

born: George Birkbeck, founder of mechanics
institutions, 1776
died: William Laud, Archbishop of
Canterbury, executed 1645
Thomas Erskine, first Baron Erskine, lord
chancellor, 1750. Edward Boscowen,
admiral. 1761. Mary Russell Mitford,
novelist & dramatist 1855

died: Sir Hans Sloane, physician 1753
François Roubiliac, sculptor, 1762.

The Penny Post

The 10th of January will be a memorable day in the history of civilisation, as that on which the idea of a Penny Postage was first exemplified. Let us turn our attention for a few moments to the remarkable, yet most modest man, whom his species have to thank for this noble invention. Rowland Hill, born in 1795, was devoted through all his early years, even from boyhood, to the business of a teacher. It was about the year 1835 that he turned his attention to the postal system of the country, with the conviction that it was susceptible of reform. Under enormous difficulties he contrived to collect information upon the subject, so as to satisfy himself, and enable him to satisfy others, that the public might be benefited by a cheaper postage, and yet the revenue remain ultimately undiminished. A brother of Mr Hill had, a few years before, suggested the *Penny Magazine*. Perhaps this was the basis of Mr Rowland Hill's conception, that each letter of a certain moderate weight should be charged one penny.

Plough Monday

The first Monday after Twelfth Day is *Plough Monday*. Such was the name of a rustic festival, heretofore of great account in England, bearing in its first aspect, like St Distaff's Day, reference to the resumption of labour after the Christmas holidays. In Catholic times, the ploughmen kept lights burning before certain images in churches, to obtain a blessing on their work; and they were accustomed on this day to go about in procession, gathering money for the support of these *ploughlights*, as they were called. The Reformation put out the lights; but it could not extinguish the festival. The peasantry contrived to go about in procession, collecting money, though only to be spent in conviviality in the public-house. It was at no remote date a very gay and rather pleasant-looking affair. A plough was dressed up with ribbons and other decorations—the *Fool Plough*. Thirty or forty stalwart swains, with their shirts over their jackets, and their shoulders and hats flaming with ribbons, dragged it along from house to house, preceded by one in the dress of an old woman, but much bedizened, bearing the name of *Bessy*. There was also a Fool, in fantastic attire. In some parts of the country, morris-dancers attended the procession; occasionally some reproduction of the ancient Scandinavian sword-dance added to the means of persuading money out of the pockets of the lieges.

January 12th   VB

George Villiers   Edmund Burke

born: Edmund Burke, statesman 1729
George Villiers, 4th Earl of Clarendon,
1800

January 13th   VB

John Scott

died: George Fox, founder of the
Society of Friends, 1691
John Scott, 1st Earl of Eldon, 1838

January 14th   VB

George Berkeley   Edmund Halley

St Hilary

died: Edward Bruce, Lord Kinloss, 1611
Edmund Halley, astronomer, 1742
George Berkeley, Bishop of Cologne, 1753

Great Frosts

It has become customary in England to look to St
Hilary's Day as the *coldest in the year;* perhaps from
its being a noted day about the middle of the notedly
coldest month. It is, however, just possible that the
commencement of the extraordinary and fatal frost of
1205, on this day, may have had something to do with
the notion; and it may be remarked, that in 1820 the
14th of January *was* the coldest day of the year, one
gentleman's thermometer falling to four degrees
Fahrenheit below zero.

It was at that time in 1814 that London last saw the
Thames begin to be so firmly frozen as to support a
great multitude of human beings on its surface.
Opposite to Queenhithe, where the mass appeared
most solid, upwards of thirty booths were erected, for
the sale of liquors and viands, and for the playing of
skittles. Musicians came, and dances were effected on
the rough and slippery surface. What with the gay
appearance of the booths and the quantity of
favourite popular amusements going on, the scene
was singularly cheerful and exciting. On the ensuing

day, faith in the ice having increased, there were vast multitudes upon it between London and Blackfriars' Bridges; the tents for the sale of refreshments, and for games of hazard, had largely multiplied; swings and merry-go-rounds were added to skittles; in short, there were all the appearances of a Greenwich or Bartholomew Fair exhibited on this frail surface, and *Frost Fair* was a term in everybody's mouth.

It is a phenomenon which, as a rule, appears to recur several times each century. The next previous occasion was in the winter of 1788–9; the next again in January 1740, when people dwelt in tents on the Thames for weeks. In 1715–16, the river was thickly frozen for several miles, and became the scene of a popular *fête* resembling that just described, with the additional feature of an ox roasted whole for the regalement of the people. The next previous instance was in January 1684. There was then a constant frost of seven weeks, producing ice of eighteen inches thick. A contemporary, John Evelyn, who was an eye-witness of the scene, thus describes it:

'The frost continuing, more and more severe, the Thames, before London, was still planted with booths in formal streets, all sorts of trades and shops, furnished and full of commodities, even to a *printing press*, where the people and ladies took a fancy to have their names printed, and the day and the year set down when produced on the Thames ... Coaches plied from Westminster to the Temple ... sheds, sliding with skates, or bull-baiting, horse and coach races, puppet-shows and interludes, cooks, tippling and other lewd places; so that it seemed to be a bacchanalian triumph or carnival on the water ...'

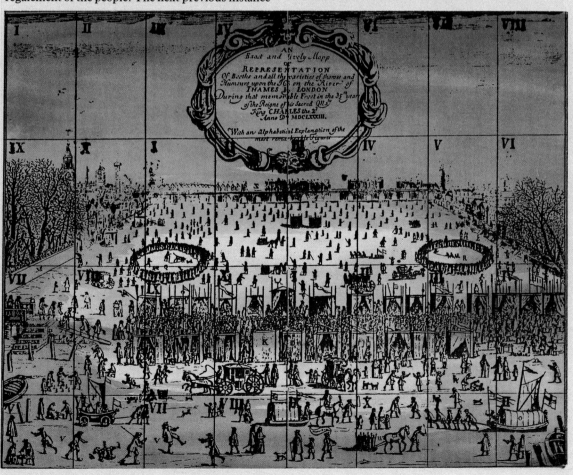

January 15th ♑

Sir Philip Warwick

died: Sir Philip Warwick, politician and historian, 1683

January 16th ♑

Edmund Lodge

Sir John Moore   Edward Gibbon

died: Edmund Spenser, poet 1599
Edward Gibbon, historian, 1794
Sir John Moore, lieutenant-general, 1809
Edmund Lodge, herald, 1839

January 17th ♑

John Ray

died: John Ray, naturalist 1705
George Horne, Bishop of Norwich 1792

January 18th ♑

Sir Samuel Garth

died: Sir Samuel Garth, physician and poet, 1719: Sir John Pringle, physician, 1782

The Peasant Countess

Died, on the 18th of January 1797, Sarah, Countess of Exeter, the heroine of a singular *mesalliance*. The story has been several times handled in both prose and verse. Tennyson tells it under the title of *The Lord Burleigh*, relating how, under the guise of a poor landscape painter, Henry Cecil wooed a village maiden, and gained her hand; how he conducted her on a tour, seeing

> Parks with oak and chestnut shady,
>   Parks and ordered gardens great;
> Ancient homes of lord and lady,
>   Built for pleasure or for state;

until they came to a majestic mansion, where the domestics bowed before the young lover, whose wife then, for the first time, discovered his rank.

The real details of this romantic story are not quite so poetical as Tennyson represents, but yet form a curious anecdote of aristocratic eccentricity. It appears that Mr Henry Cecil, while his uncle held the family titles, married a lady of respectable birth, from whom, after fifteen years of wedded life, he procured a divorce. Before that event, being troubled with heavy debts, he put on a disguise, and came to live as a

poor and humble man, at Bolas Common, near Hodnet, an obscure village in Shropshire. In anticipation of the divorce he paid addresses to a young lady of considerable attractions, named Taylor, who, however, being engaged, declined his hand. He lodged with a cottage labourer named Hoggins, whose daughter Sarah, a plain but honest girl, next drew the attention of the noble refugee. He succeeded, notwithstanding the equivocal nature of his circumstances, in gaining her heart and hand. Under the name of Mr John Jones, he purchased a piece of land near Hodnet, and built a house upon it, in which he lived for some years with his peasant bride, who never all that time knew who he really was. The marriage took place on the 3rd of October 1791, not long after the divorce of the first Mrs Henry Cecil was accomplished.

Two years after the marriage (December 27, 1793), Mr Cecil succeeded to the peerage and estates in consequence of the death of his uncle; and it became necessary that he should quit his obscurity at Hodnet. Probably the removal of the pair to Burleigh House, near Stamford, was effected under the circumstances described by the Laureate. It is also true that the peasant countess did not prove quite up to the part she had been unwittingly drawn into. Being, as it chanced, a ruddy-faced and rather robust woman, she did not pine away in the manner described by Tennyson; but after having borne her husband three children (amongst whom was the peer who succeeded), she sickened and died, January 18, 1797. The earl was afterwards created a marquess, married a third wife, the Dowager Duchess of Hamilton, and died in 1804.

January 19th ♑

William Congreve

James Watt

born: James Watt, engineer 1736
died: William Congreve, poet 1729
Isaac D'Israeli, miscellaneous
writer, 1848

January 20th ♑

David Garrick

born: Henry Cromwell, son of
Oliver Cromwell, 1628
died: Charles Yorke, lord
chancellor 1770
David Garrick, actor 1779
John Howard, philanthropist, 1790

St Agnes's Eve

The feast of St Agnes was formerly held as in a special degree a holiday for women. It was thought possible for a girl, on the eve of St Agnes, to obtain, by divination, a knowledge of her future husband. She might take a row of pins, and plucking them out one after another, stick them in her sleeve, singing the while a paternoster; and thus insure that her dreams would that night present the person in question. Or, passing into a different country from that of her ordinary residence, and taking her right-leg stocking, she might knit the left garter round it, repeating:

> I knit this knot, this knot I knit,
> To know the thing I know not yet,
> That I may see
> The man that shall my husband be,
> Not in his best or worst array,
> But what he weareth every day;
> That I to-morrow may him ken
> From among all other men.

Lying down on her back that night, with her hands under her head, the anxious maiden was led to expect that her future spouse would appear in a dream and salute her with a kiss.

On this superstition, John Keats founded his beautiful poem *The Eve of St Agnes*, of which the essence here follows:

> They told her how, upon St Agnes's Eve,
> Young virgins might have visions of delight,
> And soft adorings from their loves receive
> Upon the honey'd middle of the night,
> If ceremonies due they did aright;
> As, supperless to bed they must retire,
> And couch supine their beauties, lily white;
> Nor look behind, nor sideways, but require
> Of Heaven with upward eyes for all that they
>   desire.

Manners and Actions, when well dignified

Then he is profound in Imagination, in his Acts severe, in his words reserved, in speaking and giving very spare, in labour patient, in arguing or disputing grave, in obtaining the goods of this life studious and solicitous, in all manner of actions austere.

When ill

Then he is envious, covetous, jealous and mistrustfull, timorus, sordid, outwardly dissembling, sluggish, suspitious, stubborne, a contemner of women, a close lyar, malicious, murmuring, never contented, ever repining.

January 23rd

died: William Pitt, Statesman 1806
Sir Francis Burdett, politician, 1844

Opening of the Royal Exchange

In the sixteenth century, Antwerp had led the way in preparing a house specially for the daily assembling of merchants—what was then called Byrsa or Burse, a term of medieval Latin, implying expressly a purse, but more largely a place of treasure. The want of such a point of daily rendezvous was felt in London as early as the reign of Henry VIII; but it was not till the days of his lion-hearted daughter that the idea was realised, through the exertions and liberality of the celebrated Sir Thomas Gresham, a London merchant, who had been a royal agent at Antwerp, and ambassador at the minor Italian Court of Parma.

On the 23rd of January 1570-1, the building was opened by Queen Elizabeth. Stow relates that 'the Queen's Majesty, attended with her nobility, came from her house at the Strande, called Somerset House, and entred the citie by Temple-bar, through Fleete-streete, Cheap, and so by the north side of the Burse, to Sir Thomas Gresham's in Bishopsgate-streete, where she dined. After dinner, her Majestie, returning through Cornhill, entered the Burse on the south side; and after that she had viewed every part thereof above the ground, especially the Pawn, which was richly furnished with all sorts of the finest wares in the city, she caused the same Burse by an herald and trumpet to be proclaimed the *Royal Exchange*, and so to be called henceforth, and not otherwise.'

January 21st

James Quin

born: William Henry Smyth, admiral and scientific writer, 1788
died: James Quin, actor, 1766
Henry Hallam, historian, 1859

January 22nd

Sir Robert Cotton

Francis Bacon

Lord Byron

born: Francis Bacon, Lord Verulam, lord chancellor, 1561
Sir Robert Cotton, antiquary, 1573
George Byron, Lord Byron, 1788

January 24th

Charles Sackville   *Charles James Fox*

born: Charles Sackville, 6th Earl of
Dorset, poet 1638
Charles James Fox, statesman, 1749

January 25th

The Conversion of St Paul;
deposition of Edward II

Robert Burns

Robert Boyle   *Daniel Maclise*

born:
Robert Boyle, natural philosopher, 1627
Thomas Tanner, Bishop of St Asaph, 1674
Robert Burns, poet, 1759
Sir Francis Burdett, politician, 1770
Daniel Maclise, painter, 1811

St Paul's Day

The festival of the Conversion of St Paul, instituted by the Church in gratitude for so miraculous and so important an instance of the Divine power, 'a perfect model of a true conversion,' is mentioned in several calendars and missals of the eighth and ninth centuries.

The day has also a celebrity of another description, the origin of which has not yet been discovered. It has been an article of constant belief in Western Europe, during the middle ages, and even down to our own time, that the whole character of the coming year is prognosticated by the condition of the weather on this day; and this is the more singular, as the day itself was one of those to which the prognostication gave the character of a *dies Ægyptiacus*, or unlucky day. Fair weather on St Paul's day betided a prosperous year; snow or rain betokened a dear year, and therefore an unfruitful one; clouds foreboded great mortality among cattle; and winds were to be forerunners of war. The special knowledge of the future, which it was believed might be derived from it, were arranged under four heads, in four monkish Latin verses, which are found very frequently in the manuscripts of the middle ages. Several old translations of these lines into verse in French and English are met with; the following is one of the English versions:

> If St Paul's day be fair and clear,
> It does betide a happy year;
> But if it chance to snow or rain,
> Then will be dear all kind of grain;
> If clouds or mists do dark the skie,
> Great store of birds and beasts shall die;
> And if the winds do flie aloft,
> Then war shall vexe the kingdome oft.

Other days in the month of January enjoyed at different times, and in different places, a similar reputation among the old prognosticators, but none of them were anything like so generally held and believed in as the day of the Conversion of St Paul.

January 26th

Edward Jenner   *George Sackville Germain*

born:
George Sackville Germain, 1st Viscount Sackville,
soldier & statesman 1716
Samuel Parr, pedagogue 1747
Benjamin Robert Haydon, painter 1786
died: Henry Briggs, mathematician, 1631
Dr Edward Jenner, discoverer of Vaccination,
1823

January 27ᵗʰ

Sir William Temple

died: Sir William Temple, statesman and author, 1699
Samuel Hood, 1ˢᵗ Viscount Hood, 1816

Robert Burton

On the 27th of January 1639, there was interred in Christ Church Cathedral, Oxford, one of the most singular men of genius that England has at any time produced—the famous Robert Burton, author of the *Anatomy of Melancholy*. Though occupying a clerical charge in his native county of Leicester, he lived chiefly in his rooms in Christ Church College, and thus became a subject of notice to Anthony Wood, who, in his *Athenæ Oxoniensis*, thus speaks of him: 'He was an exact mathematician, a curious calculator of nativities, a general-read scholar, a thorough-paced philologist, and one that understood the surveying of lands well. As he was by many accounted a severe student, a devourer of authors, a melancholy and humorous person, so, by others who knew him well, a person of great honesty, plain-dealing, and charity. I have heard some of the ancients of Christ Church say, that his company was very merry, facete, and juvenile; and no man in his time did surpass him for his ready and dexterous interlarding his common discourse among them with verses from the poets, or sentences from classical authors, which, being then all the fashion in the University, made his company more acceptable.'

Christ Church Cathedral, Oxford.

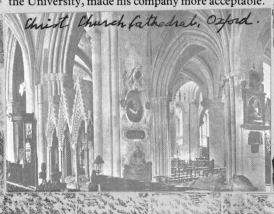

January 28th

King Henry VII

King Henry VIII

Sir Francis Drake

Sir Thomas Bodley

born: King Henry VII of England, 1457
died: King Henry VIII of England, 1547
Sir Francis Drake, circumnavigator, 1596
Sir Thomas Bodley, founder of the
Bodleian Library, Oxford, 1613

January 29th

King George III

The Bodleian Library. Oxford.

born: Thomas Paine, political
writer, 1737
died: King George III

January 30th

King Charles I

Execution of Charles I

born: Walter Savage Landor, author of "Imaginary Conversations", 1775

Charles Metcalfe, 1st Baron Metcalfe, provisional governor-general of India, 1785

died: William Chillingworth, theologian, 1644

King Charles I, executed 1649

Charles I was put to death upon a scaffold raised in front of the Banqueting House, Whitehall. There is reason to believe that he was conducted to this sad stage through a window, from which the frame had been taken out, at the north extremity of the building near the gate. It was not so much elevated above the street, but that he could hear people weeping and praying for him below.

The scaffold, as is well known, was graced that day by two executioners in masks; and as to the one who used the axe a question has arisen, who was he? The public seems to have been kept in ignorance on this point at the time; had it been otherwise, he could not have escaped the daggers of the royalists. The probability is that the King's head was in reality cut off by the ordinary executioner, Richard Brandon. When, after the Restoration, an attempt was made to fix the guilt on one William Hulett, the following evidence was given in his defence, and there is much reason to believe that it states the truth. 'When my Lord Capel, the Duke of Hamilton, and the Earl of Holland, were beheaded in the Palace Yard, Westminster, my Lord Capel asked the common hangman, "Did you cut off my master's head?" "Yes," saith he. "Where is the instrument that did it?" He then brought the axe. "Is this the same? are you sure?" said my Lord. "Yes, my Lord," saith the hangman; "I am very sure it is the same." My Lord Capel took the axe and kissed it, and gave him five pieces of gold. *I heard him say*, "Sirrah, wert thou not afraid?" Saith the hangman, "They made me cut it off, and I had thirty pounds for my pains." '

Charles Edward Stuart

The body of the unfortunate King was embalmed immediately after the execution, and taken to Windsor to be interred. A small group of his friends, including his relative the Duke of Richmond, was permitted by Parliament to conduct a funeral which should not cost above five hundred pounds. Disdaining an ordinary grave, which had been dug for the King in the floor of the chapel, they found a vault in the centre of the quire, containing two coffins, believed to be those of Henry VIII and his queen Jane Seymour; and there his coffin was placed, with no ceremony beyond the tears of the mourners, the Funeral Service being then under prohibition. The words 'King Charles, 1648', inscribed on the outside of the outer wooden coffin, alone marked the remains of the unfortunate monarch. These sad rites were paid at three in the afternoon of the 19th of February, three weeks after the execution.

died: Charles Edward Stuart, the Young Pretender, 1788

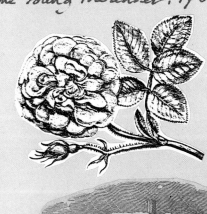

February was one of the two months (January being the other) introduced into the Roman Calendar by Numa Pompilius, when he extended the year to twelve of these periods. Its name arose from the practice of religious expiation and purification which took place among the Romans at the beginning of this month (*Februare*, to expiate, to purify). It has been on the whole an ill-used month, perhaps in consequence of its noted want (in the northern hemisphere) of what is pleasant and agreeable to the human senses. Numa let fall upon it the doom which was unavoidable for some one of the months, of having, three out of four times, a day less than even those which were to consist of thirty days. That is to say, he arranged that it should have only twenty-nine days, excepting in leap years; when, by the intercalation of a day between the 23rd and 24th, it was to have thirty. No great occasion here for complaint. But when Augustus chose to add a thirty-first day to August, that the month named from him might not lack in the dignity enjoyed by six other months of the year, he took it from February, which could least spare it, thus reducing it to twenty-eight in all ordinary years. In our own parliamentary arrangement for the reformation of the calendar, it being necessary to drop a day out of each century excepting those of which the original number could be divided by four, it again fell to the lot of February to be the sufferer. It was deprived of its 29th day for all such years, and so it befell the years 1800, 1900, and will in 2100, 2200, &c.

—— Then came old February, sitting
In an old wagon, for he could not ride,
Drawn of two fishes for the season fitting,
Which through the flood before did softly slide
And swim away; yet had he by his side
His plough and harness fit to till the ground,
And tools to prune the trees, before the pride
Of hasting prime did make them burgeon wide.

SPENSER

FEBRUARY

The tendency of this month to wet and its uncertain temperature, as hovering between Winter and Spring, are expressed proverbially:

> February fill the dyke [ditch]
> Either with black or white:

i.e. either with rain or snow. Popular wisdom, however, recognises an advantage, in its adhering to the wintry character, the above rhyme having occasionally added to it,

> If it be white, it's the better to like;

while other rhymes support the same view. Thus, in Ray's collection of English proverbs, we have:

> The Welshman would rather see his dam on her
>   bier,
> Than see a fair Februeer;

and from the Scotch collections:

> A' the months o' the year
> Curse a fair Februeer.

February 1st

Edward Coke *Charles Talbot*

John Philip Kemble *Mary Wollstonecraft Shelley*

born: Edward Coke., Lord Chief Justice, 1552,
John Philip Kemble, actor, 1757
died: Charles Talbot, Duke of Shrewsbury, 1718
Mary Wollstonecraft Shelley, novelist 1815

February 2nd

The Purification of the Virgin,
commonly called Candlemass Day.

Francis Hayman

died: John Sharp, Archbishop of York, 1714.
Francis Hayman, painter, 1776.
James "Athenian" Stuart, painter & Architect,
1793. Thomas Banks, sculptor, 1805.

Candlemass.

From a very early, indeed unknown date in the Christian history, the 2nd of February has been held as the Purification of the Virgin, and it is still a holiday of the Church of England. From the coincidence of the time with that of the *Februation* or purification of the people in pagan Rome, some consider this as a Christian festival engrafted upon a heathen one, in order to take advantage of the established habits of the people; but the idea is at least open to a good deal of doubt. The popular name Candlemass is derived from the ceremony which the Church of Rome dictates to be observed on this day; namely, a blessing of candles by the clergy, and a distribution of them amongst the people, by whom they are afterwards carried lighted in solemn procession. The more important observances were given up in England at the Reformation; but it was still, about the close of the eighteenth century, customary in some places to light up churches with candles on this day.

The festival, at whatever date it took its rise, has been designed to commemorate the churching or the purification of Mary; and the candle-bearing is understood to refer to what Simeon said when he took the infant Jesus in his arms, and declared that he was a *light to lighten the Gentiles*. Apparently, in consequence of the celebration of Mary's purification by candle-bearing, it became customary for women to carry candles with them, when, after recovery from child-birth, they went to be, as it was called, *churched*.

At the Reformation, the ceremonials of Candle-mass day were not reduced all at once. We find Herrick alluding to the customs of Candlemass eve: it appears that the plants put up in houses at Christmas were now removed.

> Down with the rosemary and bays,
> Down with the mistletoe;
> Instead of holly now upraise
> The greener box for show.
>
> The holly hitherto did sway,
> Let box now domineer,
> Until the dancing Easter day
> Or Easter's eve appear.

The same poet elsewhere recommends care in the thorough removal of the Christmas garnishings on this eve:

> That so the superstitious find
> No one least branch left there behind;
> For look, how many leaves there be
> Neglected there, maids, trust to me,
> So many goblins you shall see.

He also alludes to the reservation of part of the candles or torches to have the effect of protecting from mischief:

> Kindle the Christmas brand, and then
> Till sunset let it burn,
> Which quenched, then lay it up again,
> Till Christmas next return.
>
> Part must be kept, wherewith to tend
> The Christmas log next year;
> And where 'tis safely kept, the fiend
> Can do no mischief there.

February 3rd

died: John of Gaunt, 1399. Richard "Beau" Nash, "King of Bath", 1761.

February 4th

died: John Rogers, martyr, burnt at
Smithfield, 1555
John Hamilton Mortimer, painter,
1779

February 5th

born: Sir Robert Peel, statesman 1788
died: James Stanhope, 1st Earl Stanhope, 1721

February 6th

born: Queen Anne, 1665
died: King Charles II, 1685

A Royal Speech by Candlelight

The opening-day of the Session of Parliament in 1836 (February 4), was unusually gloomy, which, added to an imperfection in the sight of King William IV and the darkness of the House, rendered it impossible for his Majesty to read the royal speech with facility. On one occasion, he stuck altogether, and after two or three ineffectual efforts to make out the word, he was obliged to give it up; when, turning to Lord Melbourne, who stood on his right hand, and looking him most significantly in the face, he said in a tone sufficiently loud to be audible in all parts of the House, 'Eh! what is it?' Lord Melbourne having whispered the obstructing word, the King proceeded to toil through the speech; but by the time he got to about the middle, the librarian brought him two wax-lights, on which he suddenly paused; then raising his head, and looking at the Lords and Commons, he addressed them, on the spur of the moment, in a perfectly distinct voice, and without the least embarrassment or the mistake of a single word, in these terms:

'My Lords and Gentleman,—

'I have hitherto not been able, from want of light, to read this speech in the way its importance deserves; but as lights are now brought me, I will read it again from the commencement...'

Death of Charles the Second.

The winter of 1684–5 had been spent by the Court at Whitehall, amid the gaieties common to the season. Evelyn could never forget 'the inexpressible luxury and profaneness, and, as it were, a total forgetfulness of God (it being Sunday evening)' which he was witness of; 'the King sitting and toying with his concubines, Portsmouth, Cleveland, Mazarine, &c., a French boy singing love-songs in that glorious gallery, whilst about twenty of the great courtiers and other dissolute persons were at basset, round a large table, a bank of at least £2000 in gold before them; upon which two gentlemen who were with me made strange reflections. Six days after, all was in the dust.'

February 7th

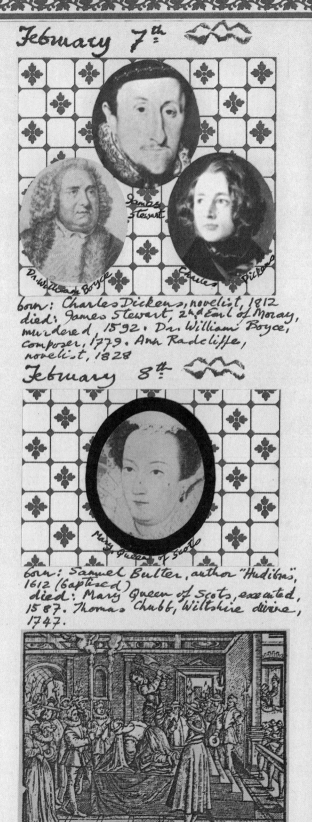

Dr. William Boyce

James Stewart

Charles Dickens

born: Charles Dickens, novelist, 1812
died: James Stewart, 2nd Earl of Moray,
murdered, 1592. Dr. William Boyce,
composer, 1779. Ann Radcliffe,
novelist, 1828

February 8th

Mary Queen of Scots

born: Samuel Butler, author "Hudibras",
1612 (baptised)
died: Mary Queen of Scots, executed,
1587. Thomas Chubb, Wiltshire divine,
1747.

Sedans

Evelyn, writing at Naples on the 8th of February 1645, describes the gay appearance of the city and its inhabitants, adding, 'The streets are full of gallants on horseback, in coaches and sedans', which last articles, he tells us, were 'from hence brought first into England by Sir Sanders Duncomb'. It would appear that Sir Sanders introduced this convenience into England in 1634, and, obtaining a patent for it from the king, prepared forty or fifty examples for public use. It is thus, in regard to its starting in England, very nearly contemporaneous with the hackney-coach, which dates from 1625.

It must have been a fine sight to see several gilt sedans passing along, with a set of ladies and gentlemen of one family, through the west-end streets of London, attended by link-boys, and being one by one ushered into some luxurious mansion, where company was received for the evening. When the whole party had been duly delivered, the link-boys thrust their flambeaux into the trumpet-like extinguishers which flourished at each aristocratic door-cheek in the metropolis, and withdrew till the appointed time when their services were required for returning home.

February 9th

John Hooper

John Gregory

Nevil Maskelyne

Benjamin Martin

died: John Hooper, Bishop of Gloucester
& Worcester, burnt, 1555.
Dr. John Gregory, author 'A Father's
Legacy to his Daughters', 1773
Benjamin Martin, philosophical
writer, 1782. Nevil Maskelyne,
astronomer-royal, 1811.

Shrove Tuesday

Throwing the Pancake in Westminster School

Shrove Tuesday derives its name from the ancient practice, in the Church of Rome, of confessing sins, and being *shrived* or *shrove*, i.e. obtaining absolution, on this day. Being the day prior to the beginning of Lent, it may occur on any one between the 2nd of February and the 8th of March. The pancake and Shrove Tuesday are inextricably associated in the popular mind in old literature. Before being eaten, there was always a great deal of contention among the eaters, to see which could most adroitly toss them in the pan.

Shakespeare makes his clown in *All's Well that Ends Well* speak of something being 'as fit as a pancake for Shrove Tuesday.' It will be recollected that the parishioners of the Vicar of Wakefield 'religiously ate pancakes at Shrovetide.' It was customary to present the first pancake to the greatest slut or lie-a-bed of the party, 'which commonly falls to the dog's share at last, for no one will own it their due.' Some allusion is probably made to the latter custom in a couplet placed opposite Shrove Tuesday in *Poor Robin's Almanack* for 1677:

> Pancakes are eat by greedy gut,
> And Hob and Madge *run for the slut*.

In the time of Elizabeth, it was a practice at Eton for the cook to fasten a pancake to a crow (the ancient equivalent of the knocker) upon the school door.

At Westminster School, the following custom is observed to this day: At 11 o' clock a.m. a verger of the Abbey, in his gown, bearing a silver baton, emerges from the college kitchen, followed by the cook of the school, in his white apron, jacket, and cap, and carrying a pancake. On arriving at the school-room door, he announces himself, 'The cook;' and having entered the school-room, he advances to the bar which separates the upper school from the lower one, twirls the pancake in the pan, and then tosses it over the bar into the upper school, among a crowd of boys, who scramble for the pancake; and he who gets it unbroken, and carries it to the deanery, demands the honorarium of a guinea (sometimes two guineas), from the Abbey funds, though the custom is not mentioned in the Abbey statutes; the cook also receives two guineas for his performance.

Among the revels which marked the day, football seems in most places to have been conspicuous. The London apprentices enjoyed it in Finsbury Fields. At Teddington, it was conducted with such animation that careful householders had to protect their windows with hurdles and bushes. The old plays make us aware of a licence which the London prentices took on this occasion to assail houses of dubious repute, and cart the unfortunate inmates through the city. This seems to have been done partly under favour of breaking down doors for sport, and of which we have perhaps some remains, in a practice which still exists in some remote districts, of throwing broken crockery and other rubbish at doors. In Dorsetshire and Wiltshire, the latter practice is called *Lent crocking*.

February 10th

Henry Lord Darnley

Sir William Dugdale

William Congreve

William Napier

Charles Lamb

Samuel Prout

Lent — Ash Wednesday.

It is an ancient custom of the Christian Church to hold as a period of fasting and solemnity the forty days preceding Easter, in commemoration of the miraculous abstinence of Jesus when under temptation. From *lengten-tide*, a Saxon term for spring (as being the time of lengthening of the day), came the familiar word, *Lent*. Originally, the period began on what is now the first Sunday in Lent; but, it being found that, when Sundays, as improper for fasting, were omitted, there remained only thirty-six days, the period was made by Pope Gregory to commence four days earlier; namely, on what has since been called Ash Wednesday. This name was derived from the notable ceremony of the day in the Romish Church. It being thought proper to remind the faithful, at the commencement of the great penitential season, that they were but dust and ashes, the priests took a quantity of ashes, blessed them, and sprinkled them with holy water. The worshipper then approaching in sackcloth, the priest took up some of the ashes on the end of his fingers, and made with them the mark of the cross on the worshipper's forehead, saying, '*Memento, homo, quia cinis es, et in pulverem reverteris*' (Remember, man, that you are of ashes, and into dust will return). The ashes used were commonly made of the palms consecrated on the Palm Sunday of the previous year. In England, soon after the Reformation, the use of ashes was discontinued, as 'a vain show,' and Ash Wednesday thence became only a day of marked solemnity, with a memorial of its original character in a reading of the curses denounced against impenitent sinners.

born: William Congreve, poet & dramatist (baptised) 1670. Benjamin Hoadley, bishop, 1706.
Charles Lamb, essayist, 1775. Rev. Dr. Henry
J. Millman, historian, 1791.
died: Henry, Lord Darnley, consort of Mary
Queen of Scots, murdered, 1567.
Sir William Dugdale, historian & antiquary
1686. Dr James Nares, composer, 1783.
Sir Geoffry Wyatville, architect, 1840.
Samuel Prout, painter 1852. Sir William
Napier, military historian, 1860.

February 11th

Elizabeth of York   William Shenstone

born: Elizabeth of York, Queen of England, 1465.

died: Elizabeth of York, Queen of England, 1503. William Shenstone, poet, 1763. Macvey Napier, editor of "Encyclopaedia Britannica" 1847.

February 12th

Edward Forbes   Sir Nicholas Throckmorton

Lady Jane Grey

born: William Mason, poet, 1724. Edward Forbes, naturalist, 1815.

died: Lady Jane Grey, executed 1555. Sir Nicholas Throckmorton, chief butler of England, 1571. George Heriot, founder of "Heriot's Hospital" 1623. Sir Astley Cooper, surgeon, 1841.

February 13th

Catherine Howard

Elizabeth of Bohemia

born: Alexander Wedderburn, Earl of Rosslyn 1733. George Rodney, 1st Baron Rodney, admiral, 1719. David Allan, Scottish painter, 1744.

died: Catherine Howard, Queen of England, executed, 1543. Elizabeth of Bohemia, 1662. Dr Samuel Croxall, fabulist 1752, Sharon Turner, historian, 1847.

February 14 a

Richard II

James Cook

Charles Talbot

died: Richard II, King of England, murdered 1400
Charles Talbot, Baron Talbot,
lord chancellor 1737.
Captain James Cook, explorer, 1779.

St Valentine's Day

The approach of St Valentine's Day is heralded by
the appearance in the printsellers' shop windows of
vast numbers of missives calculated for use on this
occasion, each generally consisting of a single sheet of
post paper, on the first page of which is seen some
ridiculous coloured caricature of the male or female
figure, with a few burlesque verses below. More
rarely, the print is of a sentimental kind, such as a
view of Hymen's altar, with a pair undergoing
initiation into wedded happiness before it, while
Cupid flutters above, and hearts transfixed with his
darts decorate the corners.

At some remote period it was very different.
Ridiculous letters were unknown; and, if letters of
any kind were sent, they contained only a courteous
profession of attachment from some young man to
some young maiden. The true proper ceremony of St
Valentine's Day was the drawing of a kind of lottery,
followed by ceremonies not much unlike what is
generally called the game of forfeits. Misson, a
learned traveller, of the early part of the last century,
gives apparently a correct account of the principal

ceremony of the day. 'On the eve of St Valentine's Day,' he says, 'the young folks in England and Scotland, by a very ancient custom, celebrate a little festival. An equal number of maids and bachelors get together; each writes their true or some feigned name upon separate billets, which they roll up, and draw by way of lots, the maids taking the men's billets, and the men the maids'; so that each of the young men lights upon a girl that he calls his *valentine*, and each of the girls upon a young man whom she calls hers. By this means each has two valentines; but the man sticks faster to the valentine that has fallen to him than to the valentine to whom he is fallen. Fortune having thus divided the company into so many couples, the valentines give balls and treats to their mistresses, wear their billets several days upon their bosoms or sleeves, and this little sport often ends in love.'

In that curious record of domestic life in England in the reign of Charles II, *Pepys's Diary*, we find some notable illustrations of this old custom. It appears that married and single were then alike liable to be chosen as a valentine, and that a present was invariably and necessarily given to the choosing party. Mr Pepys enters in his diary, on Valentine's Day, 1667: 'This morning came up to my wife's bedside (I being up dressing myself) little Will Mercer to be her valentine, and brought her name written upon blue paper in gold letters, done by himself, very pretty; and we were both well pleased with it. But I am also this year my wife's valentine, and it will cost me £5; but that I must have laid out if we had not been valentines.' Two days after, he adds: 'I find that Mrs Pierce's little girl is my valentine, she having drawn me: which I was not sorry for, it easing me of something more that I must have given to others. But here I do first observe the fashion of drawing mottoes as well as names, so that Pierce, who drew my wife, did draw also a motto, and this girl drew another for me. What mine was, I forget; but my wife's was "Most courteous and most fair", which, as it may be used, or an anagram upon each name, might be very pretty.' There was, it appears, a prevalent notion amongst the common people, that this was the day on which birds selected their mates. They seem to have imagined that an influence was inherent in the day, which rendered in some degree binding the lot or chance by which any youth or maid was now led to fix his attention on a person of the opposite sex. It was supposed, for instance, that the first unmarried person of the other sex whom one met on St Valentine's morning in walking abroad, was a destined wife or a destined husband. Thus Gay makes a rural dame remark:

Last Valentine, the day when birds of kind
Their paramours with mutual chirpings find,
I early rose just at the break of day,
Before the sun had chased the stars away:
A-field I went, amid the morning dew,
To milk my kine (for so should housewives do).
Thee first I spied—and the first swain we see,
In spite of Fortune shall our true love be.

Dr. Richard Mead

born: John Sharpe, Archbishop of York, 1645.
died: Dr Richard Mead, virtuoso, 1754.

John Philips

Anthony Ashley Cooper

John Martin

died: Henry Deane, Archbishop of Canterbury, 1503
John Philips, poet, 1709.
Anthony Ashley Cooper, 3rd Earl of Shaftesbury,
Moral philosopher, 1713.

born: John Pinkerton, historian & antiquarian, 1758.
died: John Martin, painter, 1854.
John Braham, singer & composer, 1856

February 18th

born: Mary I, Queen of England, 1516.
David Bogue, Independent divine, 1750.
died: George, Duke of Clarence, murdered
1478. Sir Richard Baker, chronicler, 1645.
Dr. Thomas Hyde, orientalist, 1703.

Funeral Garland   Matlock church.

Funeral Garlands,
Ashford-in-the-Water
church.

Funeral Garlands.

Among the many customs which have been handed down to us from early times, but which now, unfortunately, have become obsolete, one of the most beautiful, simple, and most poetically symbolic, was that of carrying garlands before the corpses of unmarried females on their way to the grave, and then hanging up the garland in the church as a memento of the departed one. This sweetly pretty custom was in former ages observed in most parts of the kingdom, but in Derbyshire its observance has, perhaps, been continued to a much later period than in any other district. Indeed, in some of the Peak villages the garland has been carried even within memory of their more aged inhabitants.

In early ages, doubtless, the funeral garlands were composed of real flowers, but this gradually gave way to those composed of hoops and paper intermixed with ribands, which were much more durable, and had a better appearance when suspended in the churches. The custom has been referred to by many of the old writers, and Shakespeare himself alludes to it when he says (Hamlet, Act V, scene i,) 'Yet here she is allowed her virgin *crants*'—'crants' signifying 'garlands'.

In a singular old book entitled the *Comical Pilgrim's Pilgrimage*, the author says: 'When a virgin dies, a garland made of all sorts of flowers and sweet herbs is carried by a young woman on her head, before the coffin, from which hang down two black ribands, signifying our mortal state, and two white, as an emblem of purity and innocence. The ends thereof are held by four young maids, before whom a basket full of herbs and flowers is supported by two other maids, who strew them along the streets to the place of burial; then, after the deceased, follow all her relations and acquaintance.'

In some districts the garlands were only allowed to remain suspended in the church for a twelvemonth after the burial of the young woman. In others, the garland was buried in the same grave with her. In Derbyshire, however, they appear to have remained hung up on the arches or on the beams of the roof, until they have either decayed away or been removed by order of some one whose love of change was greater than his veneration for these simple memorials of the dead.

Beautifully and touchingly has Anna Seward sung:

Now the low beams with paper garlands hung,
  In memory of some village youth or maid,
Draw the soft tear, from thrill'd remembrance
    sprung;
  How oft my childhood marked that tribute paid!
The gloves suspended by the garland's side,
White as its snowy flowers with ribands tied.
Dear village! long these wreaths funereal spread,
Simple memorial of the early dead!

Sir Henry Savile

Henry Frederick, Prince of Wales

Sir Nicholas Bacon

David Garrick   Sir Roderick I. Murchison   Dorothy Sidney   Joseph Hume

born: Henry Frederick, Prince of Wales, 1594
David Garrick, actor, 1717. Richard Cumberland,
dramatist, 1732. Sir Roderick I. Murchison,
geologist, 1792

died: Archbishop Arundel, 1414.
Sir Henry Savile, mathematician, 1622
Elizabeth Carter, classical scholar, 1806
Bernard Barton, poet, 1849

died: Sir Nicholas Bacon, Lord
Keeper, 1579. Dorothy Sidney,
Countess of Sunderland, 'Sacharissa',
1684. Mrs Elizabeth Rowe,
philanthropic - religious writer, 1737.
Richard Gough, antiquarian, 1809.
Joseph Hume, statesman, 1855

Pisces - the fishes of the Planet Jupiter, and his signification ♓

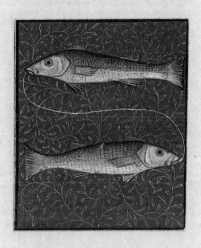

Manners and Actions when well placed

Then he is Magnanimous, Faithfull, Bashfull, Aspiring in an honourable way at high matters, in all his actions a Lover of faire Dealing, desiring to benefit all men, doing Glorious things, Honourable and Religious, of sweet and affable Conversation, wonderfully indulgent to his Wife and Children, reverencing Aged men, a great Reliever of the Poore, full of Charity and Godlinesse, Liberal, hating all Sordid actions, Just, Wise, Prudent, Thankfull, Vertuous : so that when you find ♃ the Significator of any man in a Question, or Lord of his Ascendant in a Nativity, and well dignified, you may judge him qualified as abovesaid.

When ill

When ♃ is unfortunate, then he wastes his Patrimony, suffers everyone to cozen him, is Hypocritically Religious, Tenacious, and stiffe in maintaining false Tenents in Religion; he is Ignorant, Carelesse, nothing Delightfull in the love of his Friends; of a grosse, dull Capacity, Schismaticall, abasing himselfe in all Companies, crooching and stooping where no necessity is.

February 21st ♓

John Thurloe

died: Robert Southwell, poet, executed Tyburn, 1595
John Thurloe, secretary of state, 1668

February 22nd ♓

Charles Lennox

James Barry

born: Charles Lennox, 3rd Duke of Richmond 1735
died: James Barry, painter, 1806.
Smithson Tennant, chemist, 1815.
Dr Adam Ferguson, historian, 1816
Rev. Sydney Smith, wit & literateur, 1845.

February 23rd ♓

Samuel Pepys

Sir Joseah Reynolds

John Keats

Sir William Allan

born: Samuel Pepys, diarist, 1633
died: Humphrey, Duke of Gloucester, 1447
Sir Josuah Reynolds, painter, 1792
John Keats, poet, 1821
Sir William Allan, painter, 1850

Scent-Balls & Pomanders

Among the minor objects of personal use which appear, from an inventory, to have belonged to Margaret de Bohun, daughter of Humphrey de Bohun, Earl of Hereford and Essex, slain at the battle of Boroughbridge, March 16, 1321, is a 'poume de aumbre,' or scent-ball, in the composition of which ambergris probably formed a principle ingredient. We here learn also that a nutmeg was occasionally used for the like purpose; it was set in silver, decorated with stones and pearls, and was evidently an object rare and highly prized. Amongst the valuable effects of Henry V, according to the inventory taken A.D. 1423, are enumerated a musk-ball of gold, weighing eleven ounces, and another of silver gilt. At a later period, the pomander was very commonly worn as the pendant of a lady's girdle.

The orange appears to have been used as a pomander soon after its introduction into England. Cavendish describes Cardinal Wolsey entering a crowded chamber 'holding in his hand a very fair orange, whereof the meat or substance within was taken out, and filled up again with the part of a sponge, wherein was vinegar and other confections against the pestilent airs; the which he most commonly smelt unto, passing among the press, or else he was pestered with many suitors.'

When the pomander was made of silver, it was perforated with holes, to let out the scent. Hence the origin of the *vinaigrette* of our day.

Pomanders

February 24th ♓

George Frederick Handel

James Quin

born: George Frederick Handel, composer, 1685.
James Quin, actor, 1693
Robert Gifford, 1st Baron Gifford, Master of
the rolls, 1779.
died: James Radcliffe, 3rd Earl of
Derwentwater, executed, 1716.
Thomas Coutts, banker, 1822

Fish and Fish Pies in Lent

The strictness with which our ancestors observed Lent and fast-days led to a prodigious consumption of fish by all classes; and great quantities are entered in ancient household accounts as having been bought for family use. In the 31st year of the reign of Edward III, the following sums were paid from the Exchequer for fish supplied to the royal household: fifty marks for five lasts (9,000) red herrings, twelve pounds for two lasts of white herrings, six pounds for two barrels of sturgeon, twenty-one pounds five shillings for 1300 stock-fish, thirteen shillings and ninepence for eighty-nine congers, and twenty marks for 320 mulwells.

The cooks had many ways of preparing fish. Herring-pies were considered as delicacies even by royalty. The town of Yarmouth, by ancient charter, was bound to send a hundred herrings, baked in twenty-four pies or pasties, annually to the king; and Eustace de Corson, Thomas de Berkedich and Robert de Withen, in the reign of Edward I, held thirty acres by tenure of supplying twenty-four pasties of fresh herrings, for the king's use, on their first coming into season.

Lampreys were the favourite dish of the mediæval epicures; they were always considered a great delicacy. So great was the demand for this fish in the reign of King John, as to have induced that monarch to issue a royal licence to one Sampson, to go to Nantes to purchase lampreys for the use of the Countess of Blois. The Corporation of Gloucester presented to the sovereign every Christmas, as a token of their loyalty, a lamprey-pie, which was sometimes a costly gift, as lampreys at that season could scarcely be procured at a guinea a piece. The Severn is noted for its lampreys, and Gloucester noted for its peculiar mode of stewing them; indeed, a Gloucester lamprey will almost excuse the royal excess of Henry I, who died at Rouen, of an illness brought on by eating too freely of this choice fish, after a day spent in hunting.

February 25th ♓

Robert Devereux

Sir Christopher Wren   Thomas Moore

died: Robert Devereux, 2ⁿᵈ Earl of
Essex, executed, 1601.
Sir Christopher Wren, architect, 1723.
Dr. William Buchan, author of
"Domestic Medicine", 1805.
Thomas Moore, poet, 1852.
George Don, naturalist, 1856.

February 26th ♓

born: Anthony Ashley Cooper, 3ʳᵈ Earl of
Shaftesbury, 1671.
died: Sir Nicholas Crisp, royalist, 1666

Tewkesbury Abbey.

Church Bells

Large bells in England are mentioned by Bede as early as A.D. 670. A complete peal, however, does not occur till nearly 200 years later, when Turketul, abbot of Croyland, in Lincolnshire, presented his abbey with a great bell, which was called Guthlac. At this early period, and for some centuries later, bell-founding, like other scientific crafts, was carried on by the monks. Dunstan, who was a skilful artificer, is recorded by Ingulph as having presented bells to the western churches. When in after times bell-founding became a regular trade, some founders were itinerant, travelling from place to place, and stopping where they found business; but the majority had settled works in large towns.

Bells were anciently consecrated, before they were raised to their places, each being dedicated to some divine personage, saint, or martyr. The ringing of such bells was considered efficacious in dispersing storms, and evil spirits were supposed to be unable to endure their sound. Hence the custom of ringing the 'passing bell' when any one was in articulo mortis, in order to scare away fiends who might otherwise molest the departing spirit, and also to secure the prayers of such pious folk as might chance to be within hearing.

The inscriptions on the oldest bells are in the Lombardic and black-letter characters, the former probably the more ancient; the black-letter was superseded by the ordinary Roman capitals, towards the close of the sixteenth century. The commonest black-letter inscription is a simple invocation, as 'Ave Maria,' or 'Sancte——ora pro nobis'. After the Reformation these invocations of course disappeared, and founders then more frequently placed their names on the bells, with usually some rhyme or sentiment, which, as some of the following specimens will prove, is often sad doggerel:

Of all the bells in Benet I am the best,
And yet for my casting the parish paid lest.

I value not who doth me see,
For Thomas Bilbie casted me;
All tho my voice it is but small
I will be heard among you all.

Ancient Bell Foundry Stamps

February 27th ♓

John Evelyn

Lord William Frederick Bentinck

The Abbey church ✠ Cirencester

born: Lord William Frederick Bentinck, statesman, 1802

died: John Evelyn, diarist, 1706

February 28th ♓

born: Henry Stubbs, physician and author, 1632.
died: Robert Fabyan, chronicler, 1513.
Dr Richard Grey, author of "Memoria Technica", 1771

February 29th ♓

John Whitgift

Fairford Church.

died: John Whitgift, Archbishop of Canterbury, 1604. John Landseer, printer and engraver, 1852

Ancient Bell Foundry stamps

The Bell Tower of Evesham Abbey

We derive the present name of this month from the Romans, among whom it was at an early period the first month of the year, as it continued to be in several countries to a comparatively late period, the legal year beginning even in England on the 25th of March, till the change of the style in 1752. For commencing the year with this month there seems a sufficient reason in the fact of its being the first season, after the *dead* of the year, in which decided symptoms of a renewal of growth take place. And for the Romans to dedicate their first month to Mars, and call it *Martius*, seems equally natural, considering the importance they attached to war, and the use they made of it.

Among our Saxon forefathers, the month bore the name of *Leneth-monat*—that is, length-month—in reference to the lengthening of the day at this season—the origin also of the term Lent.

'This month,' says Brady, 'is portrayed as a man of a tawny colour and fierce aspect, with a helmet on his head—so far typical of Mars—while, appropriate to the season, he is represented leaning on a spade, holding almond blossoms and scions in his left hand, with a basket of seeds on his arm, and in his right hand the sign Aries, or the Ram, which the sun enters on the 20th of this month, thereby denoting the augmented power of the sun's rays, which in ancient hieroglyphics were expressed by the horns of animals.

——Sturdy March, with brows full sternly bent,
And armed strongly, rode upon a ram,
The same which over Hellespontus swam,
Yet in his hand a spade he also bent
And in a bag all sorts of seeds, y same
Which on the earth he strewed as he went,
And filled her womb with fruitful hope of
    nourishment.

SPENSER

MARCH

March is noted as a dry month. Its dust is looked for, and becomes a subject of congratulation, on account of the importance of dry weather at this time for sowing and planting. The idea has been embodied in proverbs, as 'A peck of March dust is worth a king's ransom,' and 'A dry March never begs its bread.' Blustering winds usually prevail more or less throughout a considerable part of the month, but mostly in the earlier portion. Hence, the month appears to change its character as it goes on; the remark is, 'It comes in like a lion, and goes out like a lamb.'

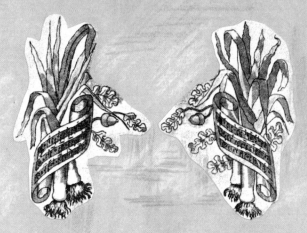

March 1ˢᵗ ♓
St. David, patron of Wales.

Queen Caroline

born: Dr John Pell, mathematician, 1611;
Caroline, Queen of England, 1683;
Sir Samuel Romilly, 1757;
died: Sir Thomas Herbert, traveller
& author, 1682; Edward Moore,
fabulist and dramatist 1757.

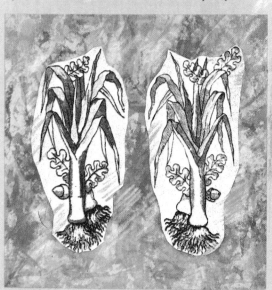

The Emblem of Wales.

Various reasons are assigned by the Welsh for wearing the leek on St David's Day. Some affirm it to be in memory of a great victory obtained over the Saxons. It is said that, during the conflict, the Welshmen, by order of St David, put leeks into their hats to distinguish themselves from their enemies.

Shakespeare makes the wearing of the leek to have originated at the battle of Cressy. In the play of *Henry V* Fluellen, addressing the monarch says:

Your grandfather, of famous memory, an't please your Majesty, and your great uncle, Edward the Black Prince of Wales, as I have read in the chronicles, fought a most prave pattle here in France.
King. They did, Fluellen!
Fluellen. Your Majesty says very true; if your Majesty is remembered of it, the Welshmen did goot service in a garden where leeks did grow; wearing leeks in their Monmouth caps, which your Majesty know to this hour is an honourable padge of the service; and do believe that your Majesty takes no scorn to wear leek upon St Tavy's Day.

The observance of St David's Day was long countenanced by royalty. Even sparing Henry VII could disburse two pounds among Welshmen on their saint's anniversary; and among the Household Expenses of the Princess Mary for 1544, is an entry of a gift of fifteen shillings to the Yeomen of the King's Guard for bringing a leek to Her Grace on St David's Day. Misson, alluding to the custom of wearing the leek, records that His Majesty William III was complaisant enough to bear his Welsh subjects company, and two years later we find the following paragraph in *The Flying Post* (1699): 'Yesterday, being St David's Day, the King, according to custom, wore a leek in honour of the Ancient Britons, the same being presented to him by the sergeant-porter, whose place it is, and for which he claims the clothes His Majesty wore that day; the courtiers in imitation of His Majesty wore leeks also.'

March 2nd ♓

Horace Walpole

born: William Murray, 1st Earl of Mansfield.
Lord Chief Justice, 1705.
died: Anne of Denmark, Queen of England, 1619;
John Wesley, founder of Methodism, 1719; Horace
Walpole, Earl of Orford, 1797; Francis, 5th Duke
of Bedford, 1802

Horace Walpole's great 'work' was *Strawberry Hill*. He had purchased this little mansion as a mere cottage in 1747, and for the remaining fifty years of his life he was constantly adding to it, decorating it, and increasing the number of the pictures, old china, and other objects of *virtu* which he had assembled in it. The glories of Strawberry Hill came to an end in 1842 when the whole of the pictures and curiosities which it contained were dispersed by a twenty-four days' sale. The mansion was found to contain a Great Staircase, highly decorated, an Armoury, a room called the Star-chamber, a Gallery, and some other apartments. All were as full as they could hold of pictures, armour, articles of bijouterie, china, and other curiosities. One room was devoted to portraits by Holbein. In another was the hat of Cardinal Wolsey, together with a clock which had been presented by King Henry VIII as a morning gift to Anne Boleyn. The general style of Strawberry Hill was what passed in Walpole's days as Gothic.

March 3rd ♓

Edmund Waller   William Stukeley

born: Edmund Waller, poet, 1606;
William charles Macready, actor, 1793
died: Sir Nicholas Carew, Master of the
Horse to Henry VIII, executed, 1539;
George Herbert, poet, 1633. Dr William
Stukeley, antiquary, 1765; Robert
Adam, architect, 1792; Francis, 3rd
Duke of Bridgewater, canal builder 1803

March 4th ♓

John Anstis

Sir John Somers Lord

born: John, Lord Somers, Lord chancellor
of England 1651.
died: John Anstis, Garter King of Arms
1744

March 5th ♓

John Holt   Thomas Arne

born: John Collins, F.R.S. mathematician, 1625;
George Stanhope, Dean of Canterbury, 1660.
died: Francis Beaumont, dramatist, 1616;
Sir John Holt, Judge, 1710; Dr Thomas
Arne, composer, 1778.

March 6th ♓

Henry Benedict Cardinal York

born: Henry Benedict, Cardinal of York, 1725
Sir Charles Napier, admiral, 1786.
died: Dr Samuel Parr, pedagogue, 1825;
George Meikle Kemp, architect, 1844.

Midlent, or Mothering Sunday.

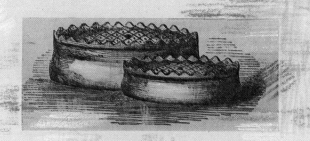

The harshness and general painfulness of life in old times must have been much relieved by certain simple and affectionate customs which modern people have learned to dispense with. Amongst these was a practice of going to see parents, and especially the female one, on the mid Sunday of Lent, taking them some little present, such as a cake or a trinket. A youth engaged in this amiable act of duty was said to go *a-mothering*, and thence the day itself came to be called Mothering Sunday. One can readily imagine how, after a stripling or maiden had gone to service, or launched in independent housekeeping, the old bonds of filial love would be brightened by this pleasant annual visit, signalised, as custom demanded it should be, by the excitement attending some novel and perhaps surprising gift. There was also a cheering and peculiar festivity appropriate to the day, the prominent dish being *furmety*—which we have to interpret as wheat grains boiled in sweet milk, sugared and spiced. In the northern parts of England, and in Scotland, there seems to have been a greater leaning to steeped pease fried in butter, with pepper and salt. Pancakes so composed passed by the name of *carlings*; and so conspicuous was this article, that from it Carling Sunday became a local name for the day.

> Tid, Mid, and Misera,
> *Carling*, Palm, Pase-egg day,

remains in the north of England as an enumeration of the Sundays of Lent, the first three terms being probably taken from words in obsolete services for the respective days, and the fourth being the name of Midlent Sunday from the cakes by which it was distinguished.

Herrick, in a canzonet addressed to Dianeme, says—

> I'll to thee a *simnel* bring,
> 'Gainst thou go a-mothering;
> So that, when she blesses thee,
> Half that blessing thou'lt give me.

He here obviously alludes to the sweet cake which the young person brought to the female parent as a gift; but it would appear that the term 'simnel' was in reality applicable to cakes which were in use all through the time of Lent.

Simnel Cakes.

It is an old custom in Shropshire and Herefordshire, and especially at Shrewsbury, to make during Lent and Easter, and also at Christmas, a sort of rich and expensive cakes, which are called *Simnel Cakes*. They are raised cakes, the crust of which is made of fine flour and water, with sufficient saffron to give it a deep yellow colour, and the interior is filled with the materials of a very rich plum cake, with plenty of candied lemon peel, and other good things. They are made up very stiff, tied up in a cloth, and boiled for several hours, after which they are brushed over with egg, and then baked. When ready for sale the crust is as hard as if made of wood, a circumstance which has given rise to various stories of the manner in which they have at times been treated by persons to whom they were sent as presents, and who had never seen one before, one ordering his simnel to be boiled to soften it, and a lady taking hers for a footstool.

March 7th ♓

Lord Collingwood.

died: William Longespée, 3rd Earl of Sailsbury, 1226; Thomas Wilson, Bishop of Sodor and Man, 1755; Vice-Admiral Lord Collingwood, 1810.

March 8th ♓

William III

John Hough

born: Dr John Campbell, miscellaneous writer, 1708; Dr John Fothergill, physician, 1712; William Roscoe, historian, 1753.
died: William III, King of England 1702; John Hough, Bishop of Worcester, 1743; Thomas Blackwell, classical scholar 1757

March 9th ♓

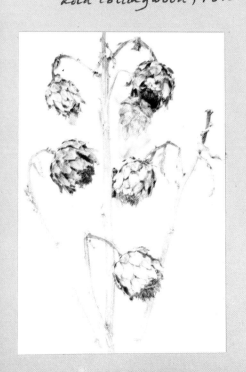

James, Duke of Hamilton

Henry, Earl of Holland

born: William Cobbett, essayist and agriculturist, died: James, 1st Duke of Hamilton, executed 1649, Arthur, Lord Capel, executed 1649, Henry, 1st Earl of Holland, executed 1649.

March 10th ♓

William Paulet
William Etty
John, Earl of Bute
E. H. Baily

born: Brian Duppa, Bishop of Worcester, 1588; John Playfair, mathematician and geologist, 1748; William Etty, painter, 1787; E.H. Baily, sculptor, 1788.
died: William Paulet, 1st Marquis of Winchester, 1572; John, 3rd Earl of Bute, Prime Minister, 1792; Henry Cavendish, natural philosopher, 1810

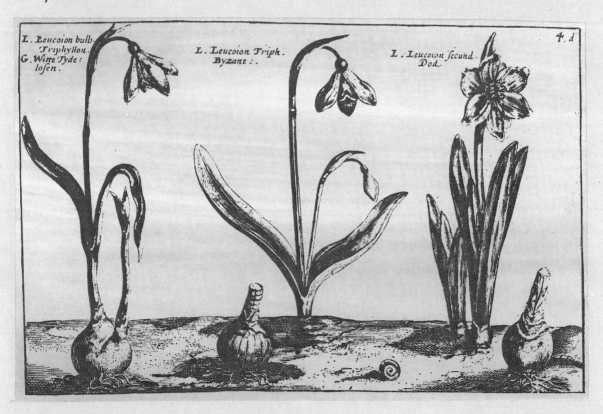

L. Leucoion bulb.
Triphyllon.
G. Witte Tyde:
losen.

L. Leucoion Triph.
Byzant:.

L. Leucoion secund.
Dod.

4. d

March 11th ♓

born: William Huskisson, statesman, 1770.
died: John Toland, deist, 1722;
Hannah Cowley, dramatist and poet, 1809;
Benjamin West, painter, 1820.

The Butchers' Serenade

Hogarth, in his delineation of the Marriage of the Industrious Apprentice to his master's daughter, takes occasion to introduce a set of butchers coming forward with marrowbones and cleavers, and roughly pushing aside those who doubtless considered themselves as the legitimate musicians. We are thus favoured with a memorial of what might be called one of the old institutions of the London vulgar—one just about to expire, and which has, in reality, become obsolete in the greater part of the metropolis. The custom in question was one essentially connected with marriage. The performers were the butchers' men—'the bonny boys that wear the sleeves of blue.' A set of these lads, having duly accomplished themselves for the purpose, made a point of attending in front of a house containing a marriage party, with their cleavers, and each provided with a marrowbone, wherewith to perform a sort of rude serenade, of course with the expectation of a fee in requital of their music. Sometimes, the group would consist of four, the cleaver of each ground to the production of a certain note; but a full band—one entitled to the highest grade of reward—would be not less than eight, producing a complete octave; and, where there was a fair skill, this series of notes would have all the fine effect of a peal of bells. When this serenade happened in the evening, the men would be dressed neatly in clean blue aprons, each with a portentous wedding favour of white paper in his breast or hat. It was wonderful with what quickness and certainty, under the enticing presentiment of beer, the serenaders got wind of a coming marriage, and with what tenacity of purpose they would go on with their performance until the expected crown or half-crown was forthcoming.

March 12th ♓

George Berkeley

born: George Berkeley, Bishop of
Cloyne, 1685
died: Dr George Gregory, divine; and man
of letters, 1808; Rev. R. Polwhele,
miscellaneous writer, 1838

March 13th ♓

Richard Burbage — *Thomas Herring*

born: Charles, 2nd Earl Grey, statesman 1764
died: Richard Burbage, actor, 1619;
John Gregory, orientalist, 1646; Thomas Herring,
Archbishop of Canterbury, 1757.

March 14th ♓

James, 2nd Earl Waldegrave — *Lodowick Muggleton*

died: John, 1st Earl of Bedford, 1555; Lodowicke
Muggleton, heresiarch, 1698; James, 2nd Earl
Waldegrave, 1715; George Wade, Field Marshal,
1748; Admiral John Byng, shot at Portsmouth, 1757;
Daines Barrington, lawyer, antiquary & naturalist,
1800.

The Greybeard, or Bellarmine.

The manufacture of a coarse strong pottery, known as 'stoneware,' from its power of withstanding fracture and endurance of heat, originated in the Low Countries in the early part of the sixteenth century. The people of Holland particularly excelled in the trade, and the productions of the town of Delft were known all over Christendom. During the religious feuds which raged so horribly in Holland, the Protestant party originated a design for a drinking jug, in ridicule of their great opponent, the famed Cardinal Bellarmine, who had been sent into the Low Countries to oppose in person, and by his pen, the progress of the Reformed religion. He is described as 'short and hard-featured,' and thus he was typified in the corpulent beer-jug here delineated. To make the resemblance greater, the Cardinal's face, with the great square-cut beard then peculiar to ecclesiastics, and termed 'the cathedral beard,' was placed in front of the jug, which was as often called a 'greybeard' as it was a 'Bellarmine.' It was so popular as to be manufactured by thousands, in all sizes and qualities of cheapness; sometimes the face was delineated in the rudest and fiercest style. It met with a large sale in England, and many fragments of these jugs of the reign of Elizabeth and James I have been exhumed in London.

March 15th ♓

Sir Thomas Egerton

Earl St. Vincent

died: Sir Thomas Egerton, Baron Ellesmere and Viscount Brackley, 1617; John 1st Earl of Loudon, chancellor of Scotland, 1663; Admiral John Jervis, Earl St. Vincent 1823; Sebastian Pether, landscape painter, 1844; Sir Samuel Brown, engineer, 1852

Last Words of Remarkable Persons.

It may amuse the reader to glance over a small collection of the final expressions of remarkable persons, as these are communicated by biographers and historians.

DR JOHN DONNE. 'Thy will be done.'

GEORGE HERBERT. 'And now, Lord—Lord, now receive my soul!'

SIR WALTER RALEIGH. (To the executioner, who was pausing:) 'Why dost thou not strike? Strike, man!'

ROBERT CECIL, IST EARL OF SALISBURY. 'Ease and pleasure quake to hear of death; but my life, full of cares and miseries, desireth to be dissolved.'

GEORGE VILLIERS, IST DUKE OF BUCKINGHAM. (To the assassin Felton.) 'Traitor, thou hast killed me!'

CHARLES I. (To Bishop Juxon, on the scaffold.) 'Remember!'

OLIVER CROMWELL. 'It is not my design to drink or sleep, but my design is to make what haste I can to be gone.'

CHARLES II. (Referring to his mistress, Nell Gwynn.) 'Don't let poor Nelly starve.'

WILLIAM III. (To his physician.) 'Can this last long?'

JOHN LOCKE. (To Lady Marsham, who had been reading the Psalms to him.) 'Cease now.'

ALEXANDER POPE. 'There is nothing that is meritorious but virtue and friendship, and, indeed, friendship itself is but a part of virtue.'

GENERAL WOLFE. (Alluding to the intelligence given him as he lay wounded on the field, that the French were beaten.) 'What, do they run already? then I die happy.'

DR FRANKLIN. (To his daughter, who had advised him to change his position in bed.) 'A dying man can do nothing easy.'

DR WILLIAM HUNTER. 'If I had strength enough to hold a pen, I would write how easy and pleasant a thing it is to die.'

DR SAMUEL JOHNSON. (To Miss Morris, a friend's daughter.) 'God bless you, my dear.'

THOMAS GAINSBOROUGH. 'We are all going to heaven, and Van Dyck is of the company.'

HORATIO NELSON. 'I thank God I have done my duty.'

WILLIAM PITT. 'Oh my country! how I leave my country!'

SIR JOHN MOORE (To the Hon Captain Stanhope.) 'Stanhope, remember me to your sister.'

GEORGE, LORD BYRON. 'I must sleep now.'

GEORGE IV. 'Watty, what is this? It is death, my boy —they have deceived me.'

SIR WALTER SCOTT. (To his family.) 'God bless you all!'

PRINCESS CHARLOTTE. (To her medical attendants.) 'You have made me drunk. Pray leave me quiet. I find it affects my head.'

March 16th ♓

Lord Berners.

Born: Caroline Lucretia Herschel, astronomer, 1750
died: Sir John Hawkwood, general, 1394; John, 2nd Lord Berners, statesman and author, 1533.

March 17th ♓

born: Dr Thomas Chalmers, theologian, preacher and philanthropist, 1780.
Ebenezer Elliott, the corn-law rhymer, 1781.
died: William Herbert, 1st Earl of Pembroke, 1570; Thomas Randolph, poet and dramatist (buried), 1635; Gilbert Burnet, Bishop of Salisbury, 1715; George, 2nd Earl of Macclesfield, 1764; Mrs Anna Brownwell Jameson, 1860.

March 18th ♓

died: George Stanhope, Dean of Canterbury, 1728; Robert Walpole, Earl of Oxford, statesman, 1745; Rev. Laurence Sterne, author, 1768; John Tooke, politician and statesman, 1812

Introduction of Inoculation

March 18th, 1718, Lady Mary Wortley Montague, at Belgrade, caused her infant son to be inoculated with the virus of small-pox, as a means of warding off the ordinary attack of that disease. As a preliminary to the introduction of the practice into England, the fact was one of importance; and great credit will always be due to this lady for the heroism which guided her on the occasion.

It was in the course of her residence in Turkey, with her husband Mr Edward Wortley Montague, the British ambassador there, that Lady Mary made her famous experiment in inoculation. Her own experience of small-pox had made her observe the Turkish practice of inoculation with peculiar interest. On Sunday the 23rd of March 1718, a note addressed to her husband at Pera contained the following passage: 'The boy was ingrafted on Tuesday, and is at this time singing and playing, very impatient for his supper.'

Lady Mary Wortley Montague, after her return from the East, effectively, though gradually and slowly, accomplished her benevolent intention of rendering harmless the malignant disease in her own country as she had found it to be in Turkey.

March 19th

Thomas Ken

died: Spencer Compton, 2nd Earl of Northampton, 1643; Thomas Ken, Bishop of Bath and Wells, 1711; Sir Hugh Palliser, admiral, 1796; Stephen Storace, composer, 1796; Thomas Daniell, landscape painter, 1840.

March 20th

King Henry IV

Isaac Newton

died: Henry IV, King of England, 1413; Sir Thomas Elyot, diplomatist and author, 1546; Thomas, Lord Seymour of Sudeley, executed, 1549; Sir Isaac Newton, natural philosopher, 1727; Frederick, Prince of Wales, 1715; William Murray, 1st Earl of Mansfield, judge, 1793.

Palm Sunday

The brief popularity which Jesus experienced on his last entry into Jerusalem, when the people 'took branches of palm trees, and went forth to meet Him, crying Hosanna, &c,' has been commemorated from an early period in the history of the Church on the Sunday preceding Easter, which day was consequently called PALM SUNDAY. Throughout the greater part of Europe, in defect of the palm tree, branches of some other tree such as box, yew, or willow, were blessed by the priests after mass, and distributed among the people.

Before the change of religion, the Palm Sunday customs of England were of the usual elaborate character. The flowers and branches designed to be used by the clergy were laid upon the high altar; those to be used by the laity upon the south step of the altar. The priest, arrayed in a red cope, proceeded to consecrate them by a prayer, beginning, 'I conjure thee thou creature of flowers and branches, in the name of God the Father,' &c. The flowers and branches being then distributed, the procession commenced in which the most conspicuous figures were two priests bearing a crucifix. When the procession had moved through the town, it returned to church, where mass was performed, the communion taken by the priests, and the branches and flowers offered at the altar.

Another custom of the day was to cast cakes from the steeple of the parish church, the boys scrambling for them below, to the great amusement of the bystanders. Latterly, an angel appears to have been introduced as a figure in the procession: in the accounts of St Andrew Hubbard's parish in London, under 1520, there is an item of eightpence for the hire of an angel to serve on this occasion. Angels, however, could fall in more ways than one, for, in 1537, the hire was only fourpence. Crosses of palm were made and blessed by the priests, and sold to the people as safeguards against disease. In Cornwall, the peasantry carried these crosses to 'Our Lady of Nantswell,' where, after a gift to the priest, they were allowed to throw the crosses into the well, when, if they floated, it was argued that the thrower would outlive the year; if they sunk, that he would not. It was a saying that he who had not a palm in his hand on Palm Sunday, would have his hand cut off.

After the Reformation, 1536, Henry VIII declared the carrying of palms on this day to be one of those ceremonies not to be contemned or dropped. The custom was kept up by the clergy till the reign of Edward VI, when it was left to the voluntary observance of the people. Fuller, who wrote in the ensuing age, speaks of it, respectfully, as 'in memory of the receiving of Christ into Hierusalem a little before his death, and that we may have the same desire to receive him into our hearts.' It has continued down to a recent period, to be customary in many parts of England to go *a-palming* on the Saturday before Palm Sunday; that is, young persons go to the woods for slips of willow, which seems to be the tree chiefly employed in England as a substitute for the palm, on which account it often receives the latter name. They return with slips in their hats or button-holes, or a sprig in their mouths, bearing the branches in their hands. Not many years ago, one stall-woman in Covent-Garden market supplied the article to a few customers, many of whom, perhaps, scarcely knew what it meant. Slips of willow, with its velvety buds, are still stuck up on this day in some rural parish churches in England.

March 21st

Thomas Cranmer

Charlotte de la Tremouille

Humphrey Wanley

Robert Southey

born; Humphrey Wanley, antiquary, 1672.
died; Thomas Cranmer, Archbishop of Canterbury, burnt, 1556; Charlotte de la Tremouille, Countess of Derby, defender of Lathom House, 1664; Robert Southey, poet & historian, 1843.

Aries - the ram ♈
of the planet Mars, and his
severall significations

March 21 to April 20

Manners when well dignified

In feats of Warre and Courage invincible, scorning any should exceed him, subject to no Reason, Bold Confident immoveable, Contentious, challenging all Honour to themselves, Valiant, lovers of Warre and things pertaining thereto, hazarding himselfe to all Perils, willingly will obey no body, or submit to any; a large Reporter of his owne Acts, one that slights all things in comparison of Victory, and yet of prudent behaviour in his owne affaires.

When ill placed

Then he is a Pratler without modesty or honesty, a lover of Slaughter and Quarrels, Murder, Theevery, a promoter of Sedition, Frayes and Commotions, an Highway-Theefe, as wavering as the Wind, a Traytor, of turbulent Spirit, Perjured, Obscene, Rash, Inhumane, neither fearing God or caring for man, Unthankful, Trecherous, Oppressors, Ravenous, Cheaters, Furious, Violent.

March 22nd V

Thomas Turquet de Mayerne — Anthony van Dyck

born: Sir Anthony van Dyck, painter 1599; Edward Moore, dramatist, 1782.
died: Sir Theodore Turquet de Mayerne, physician, 1655; Anne Clifford, Countess of Dorset, Pembroke and Montgomery, 1676; John Canton, electrician 1772; John Liston, actor, 1846

March 23rd V

died: Henry Cromwell, 4th son of Oliver Cromwell, 1674; Thomas Holcroft, dramatist, novelist and translator, 1809

Campden House, Kensington

On the morning of Sunday, March 23, 1862, at about four o'clock, the mansion known as Campden House, built upon the high ground of Kensington, was almost entirely destroyed by fire. It was built for Sir Baptist Hicks, about the year 1612; and his arms, with that date, and those of his son-in-law, Edward Lord Noel, and Sir Charles Morison, were emblazoned upon a large bay-window of the house. Baptist Hicks was the youngest son of a wealthy silk-mercer, at the sign of the White Bear, at Soper Lane end, in Cheapside. He was brought up to his father's business, in which he amassed a considerable fortune. In 1603, he was knighted by James I. Sir Baptist was created a baronet July 1st 1620; and was further advanced to the peerage as Baron Hicks, of Ilmington, in the county of Warwick; and Viscount Campden, in Gloucestershire, May 5th, 1628.

The Campden House estate was purchased by Sir Baptist Hicks from Sir Walter Cope. Bowack, in his *Antiquities of Middlesex*, describes it as 'a very noble pile, and finished with all the art the architects of that time were masters of; the situation being upon a hill, makes it extreme healthful and pleasant.' Sir Baptist Hicks had two daughters, co-heiresses, who are reputed to have had £100,000 each for their fortune; the eldest, Juliana, married Lord Noel, to whom the title devolved at the first Viscount Campden's decease.

In 1691, Anne, Princess of Denmark, hired Campden House from the Noel family, and resided there for about five years with her son, William, Duke of Gloucester, then heir-presumptive to the throne. The young Duke's amusements were chiefly of a military cast; and at a very early age he formed a regiment of boys, chiefly from Kensington, who were on constant duty there. He was placed under the care of the Earl of Marlborough and of Bishop Burnet. When King William gave him into the hands of the former, 'Teach him to be what you are,' said the King, 'and my nephew cannot want accomplishments.' He was, however, of weak constitution. His birthday was on the 24th of July 1700, and he was then eleven years old: 'he complained the next day,' writes the Bishop, 'but we imputed that to the fatigue of a birthday, so that he was too much neglected; the day after, he grew much worse, and it proved to be a malignant fever. He died (at Windsor) on the fourth day of his illness: he was the only remaining child of seventeen that the Princess had borne.'

March 24th

Elizabeth I

Elizabeth I   Philip Stanhope

died: Elizabeth I, Queen of England, 1603; Daniel Whitby, polemical divine, 1726; Philip Stanhope, 4th Earl of Chesterfield, politician, letter-writer and wit, 1773; John Harrison, horologist 1776; Mrs Mary Tighe, poet, 1810.

Maundy Thursday.

The day before Good Friday has been marked from an early age of the church by acts of humility, in imitation of that of Christ in washing the feet of his disciples on the eve of his passion. Ecclesiastics small and great, laymen of eminence, not excepting sovereign princes, have thought it fitting, in the spirit of their religion, to lay by personal dignity on this occasion, and condescend to the menial act of washing the feet of paupers. It is in consequence of an associated act of charity, the distribution of food in baskets, or *maunds*, that the day has come to be distinguished in England as Maundy Thursday. Another popular old name of the day in England is *Shere* Thursday, from the custom of shearing the hair which the priesthood used to observe.

The King of England was formerly accustomed on Maundy Thursday to have brought before him as many poor men as he was years old, whose feet he washed with his own hands, after which his majesty's maunds, consisting of meat, clothes, and money, were distributed amongst them. Queen Elizabeth, when in her thirty-ninth year, performed this ceremony at her palace of Greenwich, on which occasion she was attended by thirty-nine ladies and gentlewomen. Thirty-nine poor persons being assembled, their feet were first washed by the yeomen of the laundry with warm water and sweet herbs, afterwards by the sub-almoner, and finally by the queen herself, kneeling; these various persons, the yeomen, the sub-almoner, and the queen, after washing each foot, marked it with the sign of the cross above the toes, and then kissed it. Clothes, victuals, and money were then distributed. This strange ceremonial, in which the highest was for a moment brought beneath the lowest, was last performed in its full extent by James II.

An Elizabethan Maundy

King William left the washing to his almoner; and such was the arrangement for many years afterwards. 'Thursday, April 15 [1731], being Maundy Thursday, there was distributed at the Banqueting House, Whitehall, to forty-eight poor women (the King [George II]'s age being forty-eight), boiled beef and shoulders of mutton, and small bowls of ale, which is called dinner; after that large wooden platters of fish and loaves, viz. undressed, one large old ling, and one large dried cod; twelve red herrings and twelve white herrings, and four half-quarter loaves. Each person had one platter of this provision; after which were distributed to them shoes, stockings, linen and woollen cloth, and leather bags, with one penny, twopenny, threepenny, and fourpenny pieces of silver and shillings; to each about four pounds in value. His Grace the Lord Archbishop of York, Lord High Almoner, performed the annual ceremony of washing the feet of a certain number of poor in the Royal Chapel, Whitehall, which was formerly done by the kings themselves, in imitation of Our Saviour's pattern of humility.' For a considerable number of years, the washing of the feet has been entirely given up; and since the beginning of the reign of Queen Victoria, an additional sum of money has been given in lieu of provisions.

Death of Queen Elizabeth

From the diary of the barrister, John Manningham:

'March 24. This morning about three at clocke, her majestie departed this lyfe, mildly like a lambe, easely like a ripe apple from the tree; *cum levi quadam febre, absque gemitu.* Dr Parry told me that he was present, and sent his prayers before hir soule; and I doubt not but shee is amongst the royall saints in heaven in eternall joyes.'

The Funeral of Queen Elizabeth I

March 25th

John Williams   Nicholas Hawksmoor

born: John Williams, Archbishop of York, 1582; George Bull, Bishop of St David's, 1634; Sir Richard Cox, Lord Chancellor of Ireland, 1650. died: John Williams, Archbishop of York, 1650; Nehemiah Grew, vegetable physiologist, 1712; Nicholas Hawksmoor, architect, 1736.

Queen Mary I hallowing cramp rings on Good Friday

Good Friday

The day of the Passion has been held as a festival by the Church from the earliest times. In England the day is one of two (Christmas being the other) on which all business is suspended. In the churches, which are generally well attended, the service is marked by an unusual solemnity.

The king went through the ceremony of blessing certain rings, to be distributed among the people, who accepted them as infallible cures for cramp. Coming in state into his chapel, he found a crucifix laid upon a cushion, and a carpet spread on the ground before it. The monarch crept along the carpet to the crucifix, as a token of his humility, and there blessed the rings in a silver basin, kneeling all the time, with his almoner kneeling likewise by his side. After this was done, the queen and her ladies came in, and likewise crept to the cross. The blessing of the cramp-rings is believed to have taken its rise in the efficacy for that disease supposed to reside in a ring of Edward the Confessor, which used to be kept in Westminster Abbey. There can be no doubt that a belief in the medical power of the cramp-ring was once as faithfully held as any medical maxim whatever. Lord Berners, the accomplished trans-lator of Froissart, while ambassador in Spain, wrote to Cardinal Wolsey, June 21, 1518, entreating him to reserve a few cramp-rings for him, adding that he hoped, with God's grace, to bestow them well.

A superstition regarding bread baked on Good Friday appears to have existed from an early period. Bread so baked was kept by a family all through the ensuing year, under a belief that a few gratings of it in water would prove a specific for any ailment, but particularly for diarrhoea. We see a memorial of this ancient superstition in the use of what are called hot-cross buns, which may now be said to be the most prominent popular observance connected with the day.

In London, and all over England (not, however, in Scotland), the morning of Good Friday is ushered in with a universal cry of 'Hot cross-buns!' A parcel of them appears on every breakfast table. It is a rather small bun, more than usually spiced, and having a brown sugary face marked with a cross. Thousands of poor children and old frail people take up for this day the business of disseminating these quasi-religious cakes, only intermitting the duty during church hours; and if the eagerness with which young and old eat them could be held as expressive of an appropriate sentiment within their hearts, the English might be deemed a pious people. The ear of every person who has ever dwelt in England is familiar with the cry of the street bun-vendors:

One a penny, buns,
Two a penny, buns,
One a penny, two a penny,
Hot cross-buns!

Hot cross-bun   Seller.

March 26th Y

John Vanbrugh

born: William Wollaston, moral philosopher 1650.
died: Sir John Vanbrugh, architect & dramatist
1726.

March 27th Y

James I *King of England*

born: John Keill, physician, 1673;
died: James I, King of England, 1625;
Edward Stillingfleet, Bishop of Worcester, 1699.

Easter

Easter, the anniversary of Our Lord's resurrection from the dead, is one of the three great festivals of the Christian year—the other two being Christmas and Whitsuntide. From the earliest period of Christianity down to the present day, it has always been celebrated by believers with the greatest joy, and accounted the Queen of Festivals.

Though there has never been any difference in the Christian Church as to *why* Easter is kept, there has been a good deal as to *when* it ought to be kept. It is one of the movable feasts; that is, it is not fixed to one particular day—like Christmas Day, *e.g.*, which is always kept on the 25th of December—but moves backwards or forwards according as the full moon next after the vernal equinox falls nearer or further from the equinox. The rule given at the beginning of the Prayer-book to find Easter is this: 'Easter-day is always the first *Sunday* after the full moon which happens upon or next after the twenty-first day of *March*; and if the full moon happens upon a *Sunday*, Easter-day is the *Sunday* after.'

The preaching cross.   St Paul's.

A Zealous Friend of St Paul's Cathedral.

On the 26th of March 1620, being Midlent Sunday, a remarkable assemblage took place around St Paul's Cross, London.

St Paul's Cathedral had lain in a dilapidated state for above fifty years, having never quite recovered the effects of a fire which took place in 1561. At length, about 1612, an odd busy being, called Henry Farley, took up the call of the fine old church, resolved never to rest till he had procured its thorough restoration. He issued a variety of printed appeals on the subject, beset state officers to get bills introduced into Parliament, and in 1616 had three pictures painted on panel; one representing a procession of grand personages, another the said personages seated at a sermon at St Paul's Cross. The picture represents that curious antique structure, the Preaching Cross, which for centuries existed in the vacant space at the north-east corner of St Paul's churchyard, till it was demolished by a Puritan lord mayor at the beginning of the Civil War. A gallery placed against the choir of the church contains, in several compartments, the King, Queen, and Prince of Wales, the Lord Mayor, &., while a goodly corps of citizens sit in the area in front of the Cross. Most probably, when the King came in state with his family and court, to hear the sermon that was actually preached here on Midlent Sunday, 1620, the scene was very nearly what is here presented.

Easter Customs

The old Easter customs which still linger among us vary considerably in form in different parts of the kingdom. The custom of distributing the 'pace' or 'pasche ege,' which was once almost universal among Christians, is still observed by children, and by the peasantry in Lancashire. Even in Scotland, where the great festivals have for centuries been suppressed, the young people still get their hard-boiled dyed eggs, which they roll about, or throw, and finally eat. In Lancashire, and in Cheshire, Staffordshire, and Warwickshire, and perhaps in other counties, the ridiculous custom of 'lifting' or 'heaving' is practised. On Easter Monday the men lift the women, and on Easter Tuesday the women lift or heave the men. The process is performed by two lusty men or women joining their hands across each other's wrists; then, making the person to be heaved sit down in their arms, they lift him up aloft two or three times, and often carry him several yards along a street.

In Durham, on Easter Monday, the men claim the privilege to take off the women's shoes, and the next day the women retaliate. Anciently, both ecclesiastics and laics used to play at ball in the churches for tansy-cakes on Eastertide; and, though the profane part of this custom is happily everywhere discontinued, tansy-cakes and tansy-puddings are still favourite dishes at Easter in many parts. In some parishes in the counties of Dorset and Devon, the clerk carries round to every house a few white cakes as an Easter offering; these cakes, which are about the eighth of an inch thick, and of two sizes—the larger being seven or eight inches, the smaller about five in diameter—have a mingled bitter and sweet taste. In return for these cakes, which are always distributed after Divine Service on Good Friday, the clerk receives a gratuity according to the circumstances or generosity of the householder.

March 28th

George I, King of England

Peg Woffington

born: George I, King of England, 1660, Dr Andrew Kippis, nonconformist divine and biographer, 1725.
died: Patrick Forbes, Bishop of Caithness, 1635, Peg Woffington, actress, 1760; James Tunstall, divine and classical scholar, 176 Sir Ralph Abercromby, general, 1801.

March 29th

Tobias Matthew

Thomas Coram

born: Edward, 14th Earl of Derby, statesman 1799.
died: Tobias Matthew, Archbishop of York 1628; William Courten, naturalist, 1702 Captain Thomas Coram, philanthropist, 1751; Sir William Drummond, scholar and diplomatist, 1828; Charles Dignum singer, 1827.

March 30th ♈

born: Field Marshal Henry, 1st
Viscount Hardinge, 1785.
born: Dr William Hunter,
anatomist, 1783.

March 31st ♈

born: Dr Joseph Towers, biographer, 1757;
Richard D. Guyon, general in the
Hungarian army, 1803.
died: Dr John Donne, poet, 1631;
John Constable, painter, 1837;
Edward Riddle, mathematician, and
astronomer, 1854; Charlotte Brontë,
novelist, 1855; Lady Charlotte Bury,
novelist, 1861.

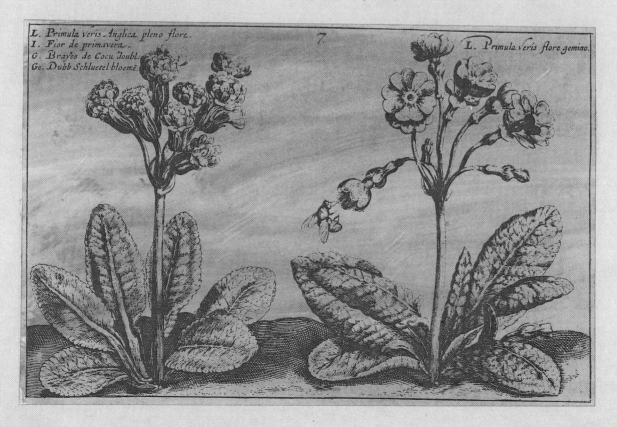

L. Primula veris Anglica pleno flore.
I. Fior de primavera.
G. Brayes de Cocu doubl.
Ge. Dubb Schluetel-bloeme.

7.

L. Primula veris flore gemino.

Sweet month! thy pleasures bid thee be
  The fairest child of spring;
And every hour, that comes with thee,
  Comes some raw joy to bring:
The trees still deepen in their bloom,
  Grass greens the meadow lands,
And flowers with every morning come,
  As dropt by fairy hands.

The field and garden's lovely hours
  Begin and end with thee;
For what's so sweet, as peeping flowers
  And bursting buds to see,
What time the dew's unsullied drops,
  In burnish'd gold, distil
On crocus flowers' unclosing tops,
  And drooping daffodil?

To see thee come all hearts rejoice;
  And, warm with feelings strong,
With thee all nature finds a voice,
  And hums a waking song.
The lover views thy welcome hours,
  And thinks of summer come,
And takes the maid the early flowers,
  To tempt her steps from home.

JOHN CLARE

Next came fresh April, full of lustyhed,
And wanton as a kid whose horne new buds;
Upon a bull he rode, the same which led
Europa floating through th'Argolick fluds:
His horns were gilden all with golden studs,
And garnished with garlands goodly sight,
Of all the fairest flowers and freshest buds,
Which th'earth brings forth; and wet he seemed in
  sight
With waves through which he waded for his love's
  delight.

SPENSER

In the ancient Alban calendar, in which the year was
represented as consisting of ten months of irregular
length, April stood first, with thirty-six days to its
credit. In the calendar of Romulus, it had the second
place, and was composed of thirty days. Numa's
twelve-month calendar assigned it the fourth place,
with twenty-nine days; and so it remained till the
reformation of the year by Julius Caesar, when it
recovered its former thirty days, which it has since
retained.

It is commonly supposed that the name was
derived from the Latin, *aperio*, I open, as marking the
time when the buds of the trees and flowers open. If
this were the case it would make April singular
amongst the months, for the names of none of the
rest, as designated in Latin, have any reference to
natural conditions or circumstances. There is not the
least probability in the idea. April was considered
amongst the Romans as Venus's month, obviously
because of the reproductive powers of nature now set
agoing in several of her departments. The first day
was specially set aside as *Festum Veneris et Fortunae
Virilis*. The probability, therefore, is that *Aprilis* was
Aphrilis, founded on the Greek name of Venus
(*Aphrodite*).

Our Anglo-Saxon forefathers called the month
Oster-monath; and for this appellation the most
plausible origin assigned is—that it was the month
during which east winds prevailed. The term Easter
may have come from the same origin.

APRIL

It is eminently a spring month, and in England some of the finest weather of the year occasionally takes place in April. Generally, however, it is a month composed of shower and sunshine rapidly chasing each other; and often a chill is communicated by the east winds. The sun enters Taurus on the 20th of the month, and thus commences the second month past the equinox.

Proverbial wisdom takes, on the whole, a kindly view of this flower-producing month. It even asserts that—

> A cold April
> The barn will fill.

The rain is welcomed:

> In April flood
> Carries away the frog and his brood.

And

> April showers
> Make May flowers.

Nor is there any harm in wind:

> When April blows his horn,
> It's good for both hay and corn.

April 1st ♈

William Harvey · Thomas Fowell Buxton

born: William Harvey, physician
and discoverer of the circulation
of the blood, 1578; Sir Thomas
Fowell Buxton, philanthropist,
1786.
died: Dr Isaac Milner, Dean of
Carlisle, mathematician and
divine, 1820.

April Fools.

The 1st of April, of all days in the year, enjoys a character of its own, in as far as it, and it alone, is consecrated to practical joking. On this day it becomes the business of a vast number of people, especially the younger sort, to practise innocent impostures upon their unsuspicious neighbours, by way of making them what in France are called *poissons d'Avril*, and with us April fools. The great object is to catch some person off his guard, to pass off upon him, as a simple fact, something barely possible, and which has no truth in it; to impose upon him, so as to induce him to go into positions of absurdity, in the eye of a laughing circle of bystanders.

The literature of the last century, from the *Spectator* downwards, has many allusions to April fooling; no references to it in our earlier literature have as yet been pointed out. English antiquaries appear unable to trace the origin of the custom, or to say how long it has existed among us.

April 2nd V

Arthur, Prince of Wales

born: Arthur, Prince of Wales, 1502;
Thomas Carte, historian, 1754;
Dr. James Gregory, professor of
medecine at Edinburgh, 1821

April 3rd V

Edward Somerset

Reginald Heber

born: Rev. George Herbert, poet, 1593;
Rev. Dionysius Lardner, scientific
writer, 1793;
died: Edward Somerset, 2nd Marquis of
Worcester, 1667; John Berkenhout,
physician, naturalist, 1791;
Reginald Heber, Bishop of Calcutta,
1826.

April 4th V

Oliver Goldsmith

born: John Jackson, theological
writer, 1686.
died: John Napier, 8th laird of
Merchiston, inventor of logarithms, 1617;
Robert Ainsworth, lexicographer, 1743;
Oliver Goldsmith, poet, 1774; Lloyd Kenyon,
1st Baron Kenyon, master of the rolls,
1802; Rev. John Campbell, philanthropist,
and traveller, 1840.

April 5th ♈

born: Thomas Hobbes, philosopher, 1588;
Dr. Edmund Calamy, biographical
historian of nonconformity, 1671.
died: William, 2nd Viscount
Brouncker, first President of the
Royal Society, 1684; Rev. William
Derham, divine, 1735; Edward
Young, poet, 1765; Rev. William
Silvin, miscellaneous writer, 1804;
Robert Raikes, promoter of Sunday
Schools, 1811.

Wiltshire Shepherds.

John Aubrey was a native of Wiltshire, and therefore proud of its downs, which, in his odd, quaint way, he tells us, 'are the most spacious plaines in Europe, and the greatest remaines that I can hear of the smooth primitive world when it lay all under water. The turfe is of a short sweet grasse, good for the sheep. About Wilton and Chalke, the downes are intermixt with boscages, that nothing can be more pleasant, and in the summer time doe excell Arcadia in verdant and rich turfe.'

It is curious to find that the shepherds and other villagers, in Aubrey's time, took part in welcoming any distinguished visitors to their country by rustic music and pastoral singing. We read of the minister of Bishop's Cannings, an ingenious and excellent musician, making several of his parishioners good musicians; and they sung psalms in concert with the organ in the parish church. When King James I visited Sir Edward Baynton at Bromham, the minister entertained his Majesty, at the Bush, in Cotefield, with bucolics of his own making and composing, of four parts; which were sung by his parishioners, who wore frocks and whips like carters. Whilst his Majesty was thus diverted, the eight bells rang merrily, and the organ was played. The minister afterwards entertained the king with a football match of his own parishioners; who, Aubrey tells us, 'would, in those days, have challenged all England for musique, football, and ringing.' For the above loyal reception King James made the minister of Bishop's Cannings one of his chaplains.

April 6th ♈

born: James Mill, utilitarian
philosopher, 1773.
died: Sir Francis Walsingham, statesman
1590; John Stow, chronicler and
antiquarian, 1606; Dr. Richard
Busby, headmaster of Westminster
School, 1695; William Melmouth,
religious writer and lawyer 1743;
Sir William Hamilton, diplomatist
and archaeologist, 1803.

April 7th

born: William Wordsworth, poet, 1770;
Sir Francis Chantrey, sculptor, 1781.
died: Sir William Davenant, poet and
dramatist, 1668; William Godwin,
author of "Political Justice", 1836;
James Scarlett, 1st Baron Abinger,
lord chief baron of the exchequer,
1844.

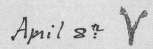

April 8th

born: John C. Loudon, landscape-
gardener and horticultural writer, 1783.
died: Sir Simonds D'Ewes, antiquarian
writer, 1650; Thomas Gale, Dean of
York, 1702.

Edward IV   *Francis Bacon*

Simon Fraser   *William Craven*

born: George Peacock, mathematician
and Dean of Ely, 1791.
died: Edward IV, King of England,
1483; Francis Bacon, Lord Chancellor,
1626; William Craven, Earl of Craven,
1697; Simon Fraser, 12th Lord Lovat,
Jacobite, executed 1747; Dr William
Prout, physician, 1850

William, Earl of Craven.

William Craven, the wealthy grandson of a Yorkshire
peasant, at an early age took service in the army of
Henry, Prince of Orange, and acquitted himself with
honour and distinction. Afterwards, being one of the
English volunteers who joined Gustavus Adolphus,
he led the forlorn hope at the storming of
Creutznach. One of the avowed objects of Gustavus
was the reinstatement of the Count-Palatine
Frederick in the Palatinate. The character of
Frederick was not of a description to excite the
respect or admiration of bold and politic men; but his
wife, the Princess Elizabeth, daughter of James I,
was endowed with all the romantic qualities of a true
heroine, as certainly as she was the heroine of a sad
but true romance. The days of chivalry had not then
quite passed away. The ferocious Christian, Duke of
Brunswick, was her most tractable slave; so was
young Thurm, and so was Sir William Craven. But
the death of Gustavus destroyed the last hope of
recovering the Palatinate, and Sir William Craven
entered the service of the States of Holland, and
continued in their army till the Restoration.

Though Sir William took no part in the civil war of
England, yet from his great wealth, combined with
his exceedingly simple, soldier-like habits of life, he
was enabled to afford the exiled royal family very
considerable pecuniary supplies. On this account
Parliament confiscated his estates, and though the
States-General interferred through their ambassador, no effect ensued from the mediation. At the
Restoration he regained his estates, and Charles
conferred upon him the title of Earl.

When the Princess arrived in England, Earl
Craven began to build a magnificent palace for her,
on his estate of Hampstead Marshall, in Berkshire;
but Elizabeth scarcely lived a year after her return
from the continent, and this house was burned to the
ground ere its completion. On the death of Monk he
received the colonecy of the Coldstream Guards, and
during the latter part of the seventeenth century, the
stout old Earl was one of the most conspicuous
characters in London. His city birth, warlike fame,
and romantic connexion with a queen—for Elizabeth
was always styled in England by her fatal title of
Queen of Bohemia—rendered him the most popular
man in London. He died in 1696, at the advanced age
of eighty-eight years.

Elizabeth,
Queen of Bohemia
painted by Peter Oliver
c. 1594 - 1647.

April 10th ♈

William Hazlitt

born: Sir John Pringle, physician, 1707; William Hazlitt, essayist, 1778.
died: William Cheselden, surgeon and anatomist, 1752; Vice-Admiral John Byron, 1786; Alexander Nasmyth, portrait and landscape painter, 1840.

April 11th ♈

George Canning

born: Christopher Smart, poet, 1722; George Canning, statesman, 1770.
died: Cardinal Beaufort 1447; John Galt, novelist, 1839.

Hock-Tide.

A fortnight after Easter our forefathers celebrated a popular anniversary, the origin and meaning of which has been the subject of some dispute. It was called Hock-tide, and occupied two days, the Monday and Tuesday following the second Sunday after Easter, though the Tuesday was considered the principal day. On this day it was the custom for the women to go out into the streets and roads with cords, and stop and bind all those of the other sex they met, holding them till they purchased their release by a small contribution of money. The meaning of the word *hoke*, or *hock*, seems to be totally unknown, and none of the derivations yet proposed seem to be deserving of our consideration. The custom may be traced, by its name at least, as far back as the thirteenth century, and appears to have prevailed in all parts of England, but it became obsolete early in the last century. At Coventry, which was a great place for pageantry, there was a play or pageant attached to the ceremony, which, under the title of 'The old Coventry play of Hock Tuesday,' was performed before Queen Elizabeth during her visit to Kenilworth, in July 1575. It represented a series of combats between the English and the Danish forces, in which twice the Danes had the better, but at last, by the arrival of the Saxon women to assist their countrymen, the Danes were overcome, and many of them were led captive in triumph by the women. Queen Elizabeth 'laughed well' at this play, and is said to have been so much pleased with it, that she gave the actors two bucks and five marks in money.

Kenilworth Castle

April 12th Y

William Kent

John George Lambton

Charles Burney

born: Dr Charles Burney, musician
and author, 1726; Edward Bird,
painter, 1772; John George Lambton,
1st Earl of Durham, 1792.
died: William Kent, painter,
sculptor and architect, 1748.

April 13th Y

Charles Burney

Thomas Wentworth

born: Thomas Wentworth, Earl of Stafford,
statesman, 1593; Frederick North,
2nd Earl of Guildford, 1732; Dr.
Thomas Beddoes, physician, 1760.
died: Dr George Cheyne, physician, 1743;
Dr. Charles Burney, musician and author,
1814.

Rushes and Rush-Bearing

In ages long before the luxury of carpets was known in England, the floors of houses were covered with a much more homely material. When William the Conqueror invested his favourites with some of the Aylesbury lands, it was under the tenure of providing 'straw for his bed-chamber; three eels for his use in winter, and in summer straw, rushes, and two green geese thrice every year.'

In the *Herball to the Bible*, 1587, mention is made of 'sedge and rushes, the whiche manie in the countrie doe use in sommer-time to strewe their parlors or churches, as well for coolness as for pleasant smell.' The species preferred was the *Calamus aromaticus*, which, when bruised, gives forth an odour resembling that of the myrtle; in the absence of this, inferior kinds were used. Provision was made for strewing the earthen or paved floors of churches with straw or rushes, according to the season of the year.

The Rev G. Miles Cooper, in his paper on the Abbey of Bayhem, in the *Sussex Archaeological Collections*, vol ix, 1857, observes:

'Though few are ignorant of this ancient custom, it may not perhaps be so generally known, that the strewing of churches grew into a religious festival, dressed up in all that picturesque circumstance wherewith the old church well knew how to array its ritual. Remains of it linger to this day in remote parts of England. In Westmoreland, Lancashire, and districts of Yorkshire, there is still celebrated between hay-making and harvest a village fête called the Rush-bearing. Young women dressed in white, and carrying garlands of flowers and rushes, walk in procession to the parish church, accompanied by a crowd of rustics, with flags flying and music playing. There they suspend their floral chaplets on the chancel rails, and the day is concluded with a simple feast.'

In Cheshire, at Runcorn, and Warburton, the annual rush-bearing wake is carried out in grand style. A large quantity of rushes—sometimes a cartload—is collected, and being bound on the cart, are cut evenly at each end, and on Saturday evening a number of men sit on the top of the rushes, holding garlands of artificial flowers, tinsel, &c. The cart is drawn round the parish by three or four spirited horses, decked with ribbons, the collars being surrounded with small bells. It is attended by morris-dancers fantastically dressed; there are men in women's clothes, one of whom, with his face blackened, has a belt with a large bell attached, round his waist, and carries a ladle to collect money from the spectators. The party stop and dance at the public-house in their way to the parish church, where the rushes are deposited, and the garlands are hung up, to remain till the next year.

April 14th

Sydney Lady Morgan   George Frederick Handel

born: William Henry Cavendish, 3rd
Duke of Portland, prime minister, 1738.
died: Richard Nevill, Earl of Warwick 1471;
James Hepburn, 4th Earl of Bothwell,
husband of Mary Queen of Scots, 1578;
Thomas Otway, dramatist, 1685;
George Frederick Handel, composer, 1759;
Sydney, Lady Morgan, novelist, 1859.

April 15th

William Augustus   James Clark Ross

born: William Augustus, Duke of
Cumberland, 1721; Sir James Clark
Ross, rear-admiral, 1800.
died: George Calvert, 1st Lord
Baltimore, statesman, 1632;
Rev. James Granger, collector
and biographer, 1776

The Nightingale

The nightingale is pre-eminently the bird of April. Arriving in England about the middle of the month, it at once breaks forth into full song, which gradually decreases in compass and volume, as the more serious labours of life, nest-building, incubating, and rearing the young, have to be performed. In an exquisite sonnet by Sir Philip Sidney, set to music by Bateson in 1604, we read:

> The nightingale, as soon as April bringeth
> Unto her rested sense a perfect waking,
> While late bare earth, proud of her clothing
>   springeth,
> Sings out her woes, a thorn her song-book
>   making;
> And mournfully bewailing,
> Her throat in time expresseth,
> While grief her heart oppresseth,
> For Tereus o'er her chaste will prevailing.

The earliest notice of this myth by an English poet is, probably, that in the *Passionate Pilgrim* of Shakespeare.

> Everything did banish moan,
> Save the nightingale alone;
> She, poor bird, as all forlorn,
> Leaned her breast up till a thorn,
> And there sung the dolefull'st ditty,
> That to hear it was great pity.

April 16th ✓

Hans Sloane | George Villiers
Madame Tussaud | Henry Fuseli

born : Sir Hans Sloane, physician,
1660 ;
died : George Villiers, 2nd Duke of
Buckingham, 1687; Aphra Behn,
dramatist and novelist, 1689;
Henry Fuseli, painter and author,
1825 ; Madame Tussaud, founder
of the waxworks, 1850.

April 17th ✓

Benjamin Hoadly

born ; John Ford, dramatist (baptized)
1586 ; Edward Stillingfleet,
Bishop, 1635.
died : Benjamin Hoadly, bishop, 1761

April 18th ✓

John Ford | George Jeffreys

born : Sir Francis Baring, bt., founder
of Baring Bros., 1740.
died : John Leland, antiquary, 1587;
George, 1st Lord Jeffreys, judge, 1689;
Charles Pratt, 1st Earl of Camden,
Lord Chancellor, 1794 ; Dr. Erasmus
Darwin, physician, 1802.

April 19th ✓

Thomas Sackville | Lord Byron

born : Edward Pellew, 1st Viscount
Exmouth, admiral, 1757.
died : Thomas Sackville, 1st Earl of
Dorset, 1608; George, 6th Lord Byron,
poet, 1824.

The Cuckoo

The 20th of April is the fair-day of Tenbury, in Worcestershire, and there is a belief in that county that you never hear the cuckoo till Tenbury fair-day, or after Pershore fair-day which is the 26th of June.

The following is a very common rhyme in England, regarding the period of the cuckoo:

> In April
> The cuckoo shows his bill;
> In May
> He is singing all day;
> In June
> He changes his tune;
> In July
> He prepares to fly;
> In August
> Fly he must.

It is a popular belief in Norfolk that whatever you are doing the first time you hear the cuckoo, that you will do most frequently all the year. Another is that an unmarried person will remain single as many years as the cuckoo, when first heard, utters its call.

There are, or have been not long ago, in different parts of England, remnants of other old customs, marking the position which the cuckoo held in the superstitions of the Middle Ages. In Shropshire, till very recently, when the first cuckoo was heard, the labourers were in the habit of leaving their work, making holiday of the rest of the day, and carousing in what they called the cuckoo ale. Among the peasantry in some parts of the kingdom, it is considered to be very unlucky to have no money in your pocket when you hear the cuckoo's note for the first time in the season. It was also a common article of belief, that if a maiden ran into the fields early in the morning, to hear the first note of the cuckoo, and when she heard it took off her left shoe, and looked into it, she would there find a man's hair of the same colour as that of her future husband.

April 20th Y

died: Elizabeth Barton, the Nun of Kent, executed, 1534; Arthur Young, agriculturalist and author "Travels in France, 1820.

COOCOU.

April 21ˢᵗ ♉

Reginald Heber

born: James Harris, Earl of Malmesbury, diplomatist, 1746; Samuel Hibbert Ware, antiquary and geologist, 1782; Reginald Heber, Bishop of Calcutta, 1783.
died: David Mallet, poet and miscellaneous writer, 1765.

April 22ⁿᵈ ♉

Henry VII

born: Henry Fielding, novelist, 1707; James Grahame, Scotch poet, 1765.
died: Henry VII, King of England, 1509.

Taurus - the bull ♉
of the Planet Venus and her
severall significations and nature

April 21 to May 20

Manners and qualities when well placed

Shee signifies a quiet man, not given to Law, Quarrel or Wrangling; not Vitious, Pleasant, Neat and Spruce, Loving Mirth in his words and actions, cleanly in Apparel, rather Drinking much than Gluttonous, prone to Venery, oft entangled in love-matters, Zealous in their affections, Musicall, delighting in Baths, and all honest merry Meetings, or Maskes and Stage-plays, easie of Beliefe, and not given to Labour, or take any Pains, a Company keeper, Cheerful, nothing Mistrustful, a right vertuous Man or Woman, oft had in some Jealousie, yet no cause for it.

When ill

Then he is Riotous, Expensive, wholly given to Loosenesse and Lewd companies of Women, nothing regarding his Reputation, coveting unlawful Beds, Incestuous, an Adulterer, Fantastical, a meer Skip-jack, of no Faith, no Repute, no Credit; spending his Meanes in Ale Houses, Taverns, and amongst Scandalous, Loose people; a meer Lazy companion, nothing careful of the things of this Life, or any thing Religious; a meer Atheist and natural man.

April 23rd ♉

St. George.

George, Prince of Denmark. George, Lord Anson.

Joseph Nollekens. William Wordsworth.

born: George, Prince of Denmark,
husband of Queen Anne, 1653;
George, Lord Anson, admiral of
the Fleet, 1697; Gilbert Elliot,
1st Earl of Minto, Governor-general
of India, 1751.
died: William Shakespeare,
dramatist and poet, 1616;
Joseph Nollekens, sculptor, 1823;
Aaron Arrowsmith, geographer, 1823
William Wordsworth, poet, 1850.

Whatever the real character of St George might have been, he was held in great honour in England from a very early period. While in the calendars of the Greek and Latin churches he shared the twenty-third of April with other saints, a Saxon Martyrology declares the day dedicated to him alone; and after the Conquest his festival was celebrated after the approved fashion of Englishmen. In 1344, this feast was made memorable by the creation of the noble Order of St George, or the Blue Garter, the institution being inaugurated by a grand joust, in which forty of England's best and bravest knights held the lists against the foreign chivalry attracted by the proclamation of the challenge through France, Burgundy, Hainault, Brabant, Flanders and Germany. In the first year of the reign of Henry V, a council held at London decreed, at the instance of the king himself, that henceforth the feast of St George should be observed by a double service; and for many years the festival was kept with great splendour at Windsor and other towns. Shakespeare, in *Henry VI*, makes the Regent Bedford say, on receiving the news of disasters in France:

> Bonfires in France I am forthwith to make
> To keep our great St George's feast withal!

In olden times, the standard of St George was borne before our English kings in battle, and his name was the rallying cry of English warriors. According to Shakespeare, Henry V led the attack on Harfleur to the battle-cry of 'God for Harry! England! and St George!' and 'God and St George' was Talbot's slogan on the fatal field of Patay. Edward of Wales exhorts his peace-loving parents to

> Cheer these noble lords,
> And hearten those that fight in your defence;
> Unsheath your sword, good father, cry St George!

The fiery Richard invokes the same saint, and his rival can think of no better name to excite the ardour of his adherents:

> Advance our standards, set upon our foes,
> Our ancient word of courage, fair St George,
> Inspire us with the spleen of fiery dragons.

Shakespeare.

One of the few certainties about Shakespeare is the date of his baptism, for it is inserted in the baptismal register of his native town of Stratford in the following clear, though ungrammatical fashion: '1564, April 26, Gulielmus, filius Joannes Shakspere.' We know, then, that he was baptized on the 26th of April 1564. When was he born? A fond prepossession in favour of St George's Day has led to an assumption that the 23rd of April might be his natal morn, thus allowing him to be three days old at the time of his baptism; and accordingly it has long been customary to hold festivals in his honour on that day.

Dragon Legends

The festival of the Rogations, anciently held on the three days preceding Ascension Day, were the prime source of dragon legends. During these days the clergy, accompanied by the church officers and people, walked round the boundaries of their respective parishes; and at certain prescribed spots offered up prayers, beseeching blessings on the fruits of the earth, and protection from the malevolent spirit of all evil. To a certain extent, the custom is still observed in many English parishes. In the ancient processions, there was always carried the image of a dragon, the emblem of the infernal spirit, whose overthrow was solicited from heaven, and whose final defeat was attributed to the saint more particularly revered by the people of the diocese or parish. On the third day of the processions, the dragon was stoned, kicked, buffeted, and treated in a very ignominious, if not indecent manner. Thus every parish had its dragon as well as its saint, with a number of dragon localities—the dragon's rock, the dragon's well, &c., so named from being the spots where the dragon was deposited, when the processions stopped for refreshment or prayer.

The collar and great George

April 24th ♉

born: Edmund Cartwright,
reputed inventor of the power-
loom, 1743.
died: William Seward, man
of letters, 1799

The Bell Tower of Evesham Abbey

The Passing Bell

There are many practices and ceremonies in use amongst us at the present day for the existence of which we are at a loss to account. Of such is the ceremony of tolling the bell at the time of death, formerly called the passing-bell, or the soul-bell, which seems to be as ancient as the first introduction of bells themselves, about the seventh century. Venerable Bede is the first who makes mention of bells, where he tells us that, at the death of St Thilda, one of the sisters of a distant monastery, as she was sleeping, thought she heard the bell which called to prayers when any of them departed this life. The custom was therefore as ancient as his days, and the reason for the institution was not, as some imagine, for no other end than to acquaint the neighbourhood that such a person was dead, but chiefly that whoever heard the bell should put up their prayers for the soul that was departing, or *passing*.

There are also some regulations belonging to the parish of Wolchurch for the fines of the ringing and tolling of bells, amongst which one item is: 'The clerke to have for tollynge of the passynge belle, for manne, womanne, or childes, if it be in the day, four-pence; it it be in the night, eight-pence for the same.'

Of the reason for calling it the soul-bell, Bishop Hall says: 'We call them soul-bells because they signify the departure of the soul, not because they help the passage of the soul.' Whatever its origin and meaning, as it remains to us at present, it is a ceremony which accords well with our feelings upon the loss of a friend, and when we hear the tolling of the bell, whether at the hour of death or at the hour of burial, the sound is to us like the solemn expression of our grief.

MONTGOMERY

April 25th ♉

Oliver Cromwell   William Cowper

Edward II

born: Edward II, King of England, 1284;
Oliver Cromwell, 1599; Sir Mark
Isambard Brunel, civil engineer,
1769.
died: Dr Henry Hammond, divine,
1660; Dr John Woodward, geologist
and physician, 1728; Dr Patrick
Colquhoun, metropolitan police
magistrate, 1820; Samuel Wesley,
divine and poet, 1735; Thomas
Duncan, painter, 1845; William
Cowper, poet, 1800.

St Mark's Eve

In the northern parts of England, it is still believed that if a person, on the eve of St Mark's Day, watch in the church porch from eleven at night till one in the morning, he will see the apparitions of all those who are to be buried in the churchyard during the ensuing year. Of a similar tendency was a custom indulged in among cottage families on St Mark's Eve, of riddling out all the ashes on the hearth-stone over night, in the expectation of seeing impressed upon them, in the morning, the footstep of any one of the party who was to die during the ensuing year.

St Peter's church, Tiverton

April 26th ♉

John Somers — Henry Cockburn

born: Thomas Reid, philosopher, 1710;
David Hume, philosopher and
historian, 1711.
died: John Somers, Lord Somers, 1716;
Daniel Defoe, journalist and novelist,
1731; Sir Eyre Coote, general, 1783;
Henry Cockburn, Lord Cockburn,
Scotch judge, 1854.

April 28th ♉

Edward Codrington — Anthony Ashley-Cooper

born: Charles Cotton, poet, 1630;
Anthony Ashley-Cooper, 7th Earl of
Shaftesbury, philanthropist, 1801.
died: Thomas Betterton, actor and
dramatist 1710; Sir Charles Bell,
discoverer of the distinct functions
of the nerves, 1842; Sir Edward
Codrington, admiral, 1851.

April 29th ♉

Edward IV — John Cleveland

born: Edward IV, King of England, 1442;
Nicholas Vansittart, Lord Bexley,
chancellor of the exchequer, 1766.
Died: John Cleveland, the cavalier
poet, 1658.

April 27th ♉

Edward Gibbon

born: Edward Gibbon, historian, 1737.
died: Sir William Jones, oriental scholar,
1794; Thomas Stothard painter &
illustrator, 1834.

April 30th ♉

Mary II — William Lilly

born: William Lilly, astrologer, 1602;
Mary II, Queen of England, 1662.
died: Dr Robert Plot, antiquarian, 1696;
James Montgomery, poet, 1854.

Come, Queen of Months! in company
With all thy merry minstrelsy:
The restless cuckoo, absent long,
And twittering swallows' chimney-song;
With hedgerow crickets' notes, that run
From every bank that fronts the sun;
And swarthy bees, about the grass,
That stop with every bloom they pass,
And every minute, every hour,
Keep teasing weeds that wear a flower . . .

How lovely now are lanes and balks,
For lovers in their Sunday walks!
The daisy and the buttercup—
For which the laughing children stoop
A hundred times throughout the day,
In their rude romping summer play—
So thickly now the pasture crowd,
In a gold and silver sheeted cloud,
As if the drops of April showers
Had woo'd the sun, and changed to flowers.
The brook resumes her summer dresses,
Purling 'neath grass and water-cresses,
And mint and flagleaf, swording high
Their blooms to the unheeding eye,
And taper, bow-bent, hanging rushes,
And horsetail, children's bottle-brushes;
The summer tracks about its brink
Are fresh again where cattle drink;
And on its sunny bank the swain
Stretches his idle length again;
While all that lives enjoys the birth
Of frolic summer's laughing mirth.

JOHN CLARE

Then came fair MAY, the fayrest mayd on ground,
Deckt all with dainties of her season's pryde,
And throwing flowres out of her lap around:
Upon two brethren's shoulders she did ride,
The twinnes Leda; which on either side
Supported her, like to their soveraine queene.
Lord! how all creatures laught, when her they
        spide,
And leapt and daunc't as they had ravisht beene!
And Cupid selfe about her fluttered all in greene.
SPENSER

May was the second month in the old Alban calendar,
the third in that of Romulus, and the fifth in the one
instituted by Numa Pompilius—a station it has held
from that distant date to the present period. It
consisted of twenty-two days in the Alban, and of
thirty-one in Romulus's calendar; Numa deprived it
of the odd day, which Julius Caesar restored, since
which it has remained undisturbed. The most
receivable account of the origin of the name of the
month is that which represents it as being assigned in
honour of the *Majores*, or *Maiores*, the senate in the
original constitution of Rome, June being in like
manner a compliment to the *Juniores*, or inferior
branch of the Roman legislature. The notion that it
was in honour of Maia, the mother by Jupiter of the
god Hermes, or Mercury, seems entirely gratuitous,
and merely surmised in consequence of the resemblance of the word. Amongst our Saxon forefathers the month was called *Tri-Milchi*, with an
understood reference to the improved condition of
the cattle under benefit of the spring herbage, the cow
being now able to give milk thrice a-day.

It is an idea as ancient as early Roman times, stated
by Ovid in his *Fasti*, and still prevalent in Europe,
that May is an unlucky month in which to be married.

MAY

While there is a natural eagerness to hail May as a summer month—and from its position in the year it ought to be one—it is after all very much a spring month. The cold winds of spring still more or less prevail; the east wind has generally a great hold; and sometimes there are even falls of snow within the first ten or fifteen days. On this account proverbial wisdom warns us against being too eager to regard it as a time for light clothing:

> Change not a clout
> Till May be out.

Other proverbs regarding May are as follows:

> Be it weal or be it woe,
> Beans blow before May doth go.

> Come it early or come it late,
> In May comes the cow-quake.

> A swarm of bees in May
> Is worth a load of hay.

> The haddocks are good,
> When dipped in May flood.

> Mist in May, and heat in June,
> Make the harvest right soon.

May 1st

Arthur Wellesley

John Dryden

Joseph Addison

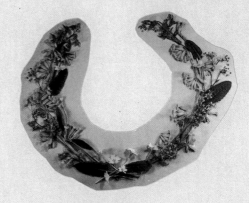

born: Dr John Woodward, geologist and physician, 1665; Joseph Addison, essayist, poet and statesman 1672; Arthur Wellesley, 1st Duke of Wellington, field-Marshal, 1769

died: John Dryden, poet, 1700; Richmall Mangnall, schoolmistress, 1820.

May Day

In England we have to go back several generations to find the observances of May-day. In the sixteenth century it was still customary for the middle and humbler classes to go forth at an early hour of the morning, in order to gather flowers and hawthorn branches, which they brought home about sunrise, with accompaniments of horn and tabor, and all possible signs of joy and merriment. With these spoils they would decorate every door and window in the village. By natural transition of ideas, they gave to the hawthorn bloom the name of the May; they called this ceremony 'the bringing home the May'; they spoke of the expedition to the woods as 'going a-Maying.' The fairest maid of the village was crowned with flowers, as the 'Queen of the May;' the lads and lasses met, danced and sang together.

Not content with a garlanding of their brows, of their doors and windows, these merry people of the old days had in every town, or considerable district of a town, and in every village, a fixed pole, as high as the mast of a vessel of a hundred tons, on which each May morning they suspended wreaths of flowers, and round which they danced in rings pretty nearly the whole day. The May-pole, as it was called, had its place equally with the parish church or the parish stocks; or, if anywhere one was wanting, the people selected a suitable tree, fashioned it, brought it triumphantly, and erected it in the proper place, there from year to year to remain. The Puritans caused May-poles to be uprooted, and a stop put to all their jollities; but after the Restoration they were everywhere re-erected, and the appropriate rites recommenced. Now, alas! in the course of the mere gradual change of manners, the May-pole has again vanished.

The only relic of the custom now surviving is to be found among the children of a few out-lying places, who, on May-day, go about with a finely-dressed doll, which they call *the Lady of the May*, and with a few small semblances of May-poles, modestly presenting these objects to the gentlefolks they meet, as a claim for a halfpence, to be employed in the purchasing of sweetmeats.

Milk Maids Dancing on May-day.

Carrying the Garland

The Chimney Sweepers Garland

In London there are, and have long been, a few forms of May-day festivity in a great measure peculiar. The day is still marked by a celebration, well known to every resident in the metropolis, in which the chimney-sweeps play the sole part. What we usually see is a small band, composed of two or three men in fantastic dresses, one smartly dressed female glittering with spangles, and a strange figure called Jack-in-the-green, being a man concealed within a tall frame of herbs and flowers, decorated with a flag at the top. All of these figures or persons stop here and there in the course of their rounds, and dance to the music of a drum and fife, expecting of course to be renumerated by halfpence from the onlookers. How this black profession should have been the last sustainers of the old rites of May-day in the metropolis does not appear.

There was a somewhat similar demonstration from the milk-maids. In the course of the morning the eyes of the householders would be greeted with the sight of a milch-cow, all garlanded with flowers, led along by a small group of dairy-women, who, in light and fantastic dresses, and with heads wreathed in flowers, would dance around the animal to the sound of a violin or clarinet. At an earlier time, there was a curious addition to this choral troop, in the form of a man bearing a frame which covered the whole upper half of his person, on which were hung a cluster of silver flagons and dishes, each set in a bed of flowers. With this extraordinary burden, the legs, which alone were seen, would join in the dance—rather clumsily, as might be expected, but much to the mirth of the spectators—while the strange pile above floated and flaunted about with an air of heavy decorum, that added not a little to the general amusement. We are introduced to the prose of this old custom, when we are informed that the silver articles were regularly lent out for the purpose at so much an hour by pawn-brokers, and that one set would serve for a succession of groups of milk-maids during the day.

May 2nd ♉

John Salt · William Beckford · William Camden

born: William Camden, antiquary and historian, 1551; John Salt, novelist, 1764.
died: William Beckford, author of "Vathek", 1844

Gange Days.

The Gange Days are the same as the three Rogation Days, and were so called from the ancient custom of perambulating the boundaries of the parish on those days, the name being derived from the Saxon word *gangen*, to go. In Roman Catholic times, this perambulation was a matter of great ceremony, attended with feastings and various superstitious practices. Banners, which the parish was bound to provide, hand-bells, and lights enlivened the procession. At one place the perambulators would stop to feast; and at another assemble round a cross to be edified with some godly admonition, or the legend of some saint or martyr, and so complete the circuit of the parish. When processions were forbidden, the useful part of these perambulations was retained. By the injunctions of Queen Elizabeth it was required that, in order to retain the perambulation of the circuits of parishes, the people should once in the year, at the time accustomed, with the curate and substantial men of the parish, walk about the parishes, as they were accustomed, and at their return to the church make their common prayers. And the curate in these perambulations was at certain convenient places to admonish the people to give thanks to God, as they beheld his benefits, and for the increase and abundance of the fruits upon the face of the earth. The 104th Psalm was appointed to be said on these occasions, and the minister was to inculcate such sentence as '*Cursed be he which translateth the bounds and doles of his neighbour.*'

May 3rd ♉

Thomas Hood · William Windham

born: Humphrey Prideaux, orientalist, 1648; William Windham, statesman, 1750.
died: James Morison, self-styled "the Hygeist", 1840; Thomas Hood, poet, 1845.

May 4th ♉

Isaac Barrow

born: John Dunton, bookseller, 1659; Dr Francis Peck, antiquarian, 1692.
died: Dr Isaac Barrow, master of Trinity College, Cambridge, 1677; Eustace Budgell, miscellaneous writer, 1737.

May 5th

Samuel Cooper
Charles Robert Leslie
Robert Harry Inglis

died: Samuel Cooper, miniaturist, 1672;
Thomas Davies, bookseller, 1785;
Robert Mylne, architect and engineer,
1811; Sir Robert Harry Inglis, Bt.,
politician, 1855; Charles Robert Leslie,
painter 1859

Ascension Day

Ascension Day, or Holy Thursday, is a festival
observed by the Church of England in commemoration of the glorious ascension of the Messiah
into heaven. It occurs forty days after Easter Sunday,
such being the number of days which the Saviour
passed on earth after his resurrection. The observance is thought to be one of the very earliest in the
Church—so early, it has been said, as the year 68.

May 6th

Robert Bruce Cotton

died: Sir Robert Bruce Cotton,
antiquarian, 1631; Andrew Michael
Ramsay, chevalier de Ramsay, 1743;
Patrick Delany, divine, 1768.

May 7th

William Petty

died: William Petty, Lord Shelburne
and 1st Marquis of Lansdowne, 1805;
William Cumberland, dramatist, 1811;
W.H. Bunbury, caricaturist, 1811;
Thomas Barnes, editor of the "Times",
1841.

May 8th

Beilby Porteus

born: Dr Beilby Porteus, bishop of
London, 1731; William Jay, dissenting
minister, 1769.
died: Dr Peter Heylyn, theologian and
historian, 1662.

May 9th

Francis Russell

died: Francis Russell, 4th Duke of
Bedford, 1641; Bonnel Thornton,
miscellaneous writer, 1768.

May 10th ♉

died: Barton Booth, actor, 1733;
George Clint, painter and
engraver, 1854.

May 11th ♉

William Pitt, Earl of Chatham

Spencer Perceval

born: David Hamilton, architect,
1722.
died: Catherine Cockburn, dramatist
and philosophical writer, 1749;
William Pitt, Earl of Chatham, 1778;
Spencer Perceval, statesman, 1812.

May 12th ♉

Thomas Wentworth

born: John Bell, surgeon, 1763;
Sir George Cathcart, general, 1794.
died: Thomas Wentworth, Earl
of Stafford, executed, 1641;
John Rushworth, historian, 1690;
Francis Grose, antiquarian, 1791.

Francis Grose on the
Country Squire.

Another character, now worn out and gone, was the
little independent gentleman, of £300 per annum,
who commonly appeared in a plain drab or plush
coat, large silver buttons, a jockey cap, and rarely
without boots. His travels never exceeded the
distance of the county town, and that only at assize
and session time, or to attend an election. Once a
week he commonly dined at the next market town
with the attorneys and justices. This man went to
church regularly, read the weekly journal, settled the
parochial disputes between the parish officers at the
vestry, and afterwards adjourned to the neighbouring ale-house, where he usually got drunk for the
good of his country. He never played cards but at
Christmas, when a family pack was produced from
the mantel-piece. He was commonly followed by a
couple of greyhounds and a pointer, and announced
his arrival by smacking his whip, or giving the view-
halloo. . . .

The best parlour, which was never opened but on particular occasions, was furnished with Turk-worked chain, and hung round with portraits of his ancestors; the men in the character of shepherds, with their crooks, dressed in full suits and huge full-bottomed perukes . . . The females likewise as shepherdesses, with the lamb and crook, all habited in high heads and flowing robes.

The mansion of one of these squires was of plaster striped with timber, not unaptly called calamanco work, or of red brick, large casemented bow windows, a porch with seats in it, and over it a study; the eaves of the house well inhabited by swallows, and the court set round with holly-hocks. Near the gate a horse-block for the convenience of mounting.

The hall was furnished with flitches of bacon, and the mantel-piece with guns and fishing-rods of various dimensions, accompanied by the broad-sword, partisan, and dagger, borne by his ancestors in the civil wars. . . .

In the corner, by the fire-side, stood a large wooden two-armed chair, with a cushion; and within the chimney-corner were a couple of seats. Here, at Christmas, he entertained his tenants assembled round a glowing fire made of the roots of trees, and other great logs, and told and heard the traditionary tales of the village respecting ghosts and witches, till fear made them afraid to move.

Alas! these men and these houses are no more; the luxury of the times has obliged them to quit the country, and become the humble dependants on great men, to solicit a place or commission to live in London. The venerable mansion, in the mean time, is suffered to tumble down, or is partly upheld as a farm-house; till, after a few years, the estate is conveyed to the steward of the neighbouring lord, or else to some nabob, contractor, or limb of the law.

May 13th ♉

Charles Watson-Wentworth   James Thornhill

born: Charles Watson-Wentworth,
2nd Marquis of Rockingham, 1730.
died: Sir James Thornhill,
painter, 1734

May 14th ♉

born: Robert Owen, socialist,
1771.

May 15th ♉

Daniel O'Connell   Edmund Kean

born: Constantine Henry Phipps,
Marquis of Normanby, 1797.
died: Ephraim Chambers, encyclopaedist,
1740; Edmund Kean, actor, 1833;
Daniel O'Connell, politician, 1847

Whit Sunday

Whit Sunday is a festival of the Church of England, in commemoration of the descent of the Holy Ghost on the Apostles, when 'they were all with one accord in one place,' after the ascension of Our Lord; on which occasion they received the gift of many tongues, that they might impart the gospel to foreign nations. This event having occurred on the day of Pentecost, Whit Sunday is of course intimately associated with that great Jewish festival.

In mediaeval Western Europe, Pentecost was a period of great festivity. It was one of the great festivals of the kings and great chieftains in the mediaeval romances. It was that especially on which King Arthur is represented as holding his most splendid court. More substantial monarchs than Arthur held Pentecost as one of the grand festivals of the year; and it was always looked upon as the special season of chivalrous adventure of tilt and tournament.

Whitsuntide still is, and always has been, one of the most popularly festive periods of the year. It was commonly celebrated in all parts of the country by what was termed the Whitsun-ale, and it was the great time for the morris-dancers. Sixty or seventy years ago, a Whitsun-ale was conducted in the following manner: 'Two persons are chosen, previously to the meeting, to be lord and lady of the ale, who dress as suitably as they can to the characters they assume. A large empty barn, or some such building, is provided for the lord's hall, and fitted up with seats to accommodate the company. Here they assemble to dance in the best manner their circumstances and the place will afford; and each young fellow treats his girl with a riband or favour. The lord and lady honour the hall with their presence, attended by the steward, sword-bearer, purse-bearer, and mace-bearer, with their several badges and ensigns of office. They have likewise a train-bearer or page, and a fool or jester, drest in a party-coloured jacket, whose ribaldry and gesticulation contribute not a little to the entertainment of some part of the company. The lord's music, consisting of a pipe and tabor, is employed to conduct the dance.'

The Morris Dance

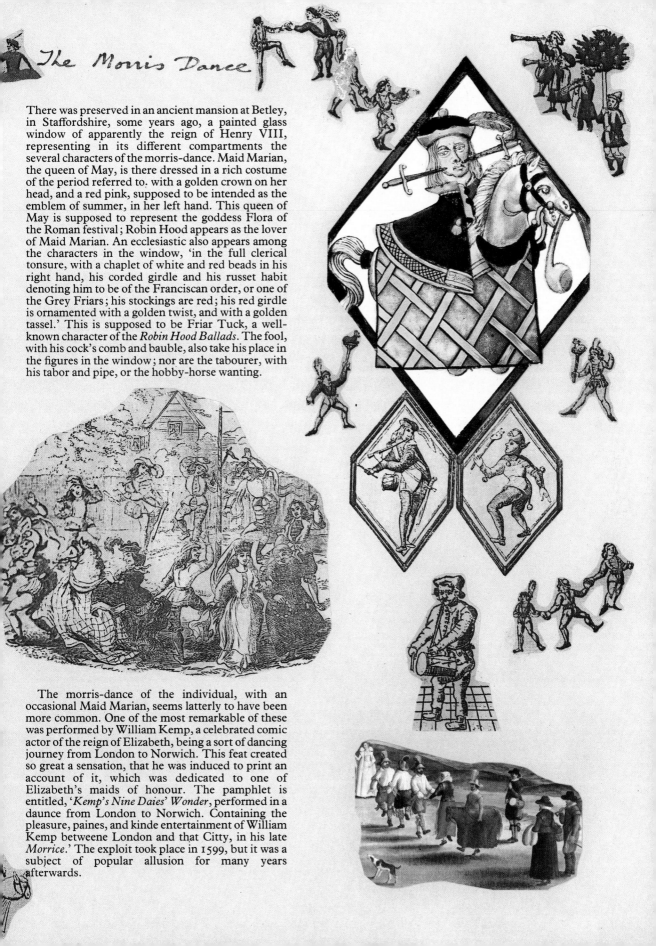

There was preserved in an ancient mansion at Betley, in Staffordshire, some years ago, a painted glass window of apparently the reign of Henry VIII, representing in its different compartments the several characters of the morris-dance. Maid Marian, the queen of May, is there dressed in a rich costume of the period referred to. with a golden crown on her head, and a red pink, supposed to be intended as the emblem of summer, in her left hand. This queen of May is supposed to represent the goddess Flora of the Roman festival; Robin Hood appears as the lover of Maid Marian. An ecclesiastic also appears among the characters in the window, 'in the full clerical tonsure, with a chaplet of white and red beads in his right hand, his corded girdle and his russet habit denoting him to be of the Franciscan order, or one of the Grey Friars; his stockings are red; his red girdle is ornamented with a golden twist, and with a golden tassel.' This is supposed to be Friar Tuck, a well-known character of the *Robin Hood Ballads*. The fool, with his cock's comb and bauble, also take his place in the figures in the window; nor are the tabourer, with his tabor and pipe, or the hobby-horse wanting.

The morris-dance of the individual, with an occasional Maid Marian, seems latterly to have been more common. One of the most remarkable of these was performed by William Kemp, a celebrated comic actor of the reign of Elizabeth, being a sort of dancing journey from London to Norwich. This feat created so great a sensation, that he was induced to print an account of it, which was dedicated to one of Elizabeth's maids of honour. The pamphlet is entitled, '*Kemp's Nine Daies' Wonder*, performed in a daunce from London to Norwich. Containing the pleasure, paines, and kinde entertainment of William Kemp betweene London and that Citty, in his late *Morrice*.' The exploit took place in 1599, but it was a subject of popular allusion for many years afterwards.

May 16th ♉

Born: Sir Dudley North, financier and economist, 1641.

died: Dr. Daniel Solander, botanist, 1782; Sir William Congreve, bt., inventor of Congreve's rocket, 1828; James Stevens Henslow, botanist, 1861.

May 17th ♉

Matthew PARKER   Edward Jenner

born: Dr Edward Jenner, discoverer of vaccination, 1749; Henry Paget, 1st Marquess of Anglesey, 1768.
died: Matthew Parker, Archbishop of Canterbury, 1575; Dr Samuel Clarke, divine, 1729; Samuel Boyse, poet, 1749; Dr William Heberden, physician, 1801.

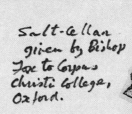

Salt-Cellar given by Bishop Fox to Corpus Christi College, Oxford.

Sitting Below the Salt.

One of the customs of great houses, in former times, was to place a large ornamental *salt-vat* (commonly but erroneously called salt-foot) upon the table, about the centre, to mark the part below which it was proper for tenants and dependants to sit. We find in an old English ballad the following sufficiently pointed allusion:

Thou art a carle of mean degree,
The salt it doth stand between me and thee;
But, an' thou hadst been of gentle strain,
I would have bitten my gant again.

Archbishop Parker's Salt-Vat.

May 18th ♉

died: Herbert Croft, bishop of Hereford, 1691; Elias Ashmole, herald and Antiquarian, 1692; John Douglas, bishop of Salisbury, 1807.

May 19th ♉

died: Anne Boleyn, Queen of England, executed, 1536; John Hales, the "ever memorable", 1656; Charles Montagu, 1st Earl of Halifax, 1719; Thomas Gent, printer, 1779; James Boswell, biographer of Dr Johnson, 1795.

May 20th ♉

Thomas Sprat William Petty

born: Elijah Fenton, poet 1683;
William Petty, Earl of Shelburne,
1st Marquess of Lansdowne, 1737.
died: Thomas Spratt, bishop of
Rochester, 1713; Nicholas Brady,
divine and poet, 1726; Thomas
Boston, Scottish divine, 1732;
Rev. J. Blanco White, theological
writer, 1841.

Gemini - the twins of Mercury, and his signification, nature and property

♊ May 21 to June 21

Manners when well placed

Being well dignified, he represents a man of a subtill and politick braine, intellect, and cogitation; an excellent disputant or Logician, arguing with learning and discretion, and using much eloquence in his speech, a searcher into all kinds of Mysteries and Learning, sharp and witty, learning almost any thing without a Teacher; ambitious of being exquisite in every Science, desirous naturally of travell and seeing foraign parts: a man of an unwearied fancie, curious in the search of any occult knowledge; able by his owne *Genius* to produce wonders; given to Divination and the more secret knowledge; if he turne Merchant no man exceeds him in way of Trade or invention of new ways whereby to obtain wealth.

Manners, when ill placed or dignified

A troublesome wit, a kinde of Phrenetick man, his tongue and Pen against every man, wholly bent to foole his estate and time in prating and trying nice conclusions to no purpose; a great lyar, boaster, pratler, busybody, false, a tale-carrier, given to wicked Arts, as Necromancy, and such like ungodly knowledges; easie of beleefe, an asse or very ideot, constant in no place or opinion, cheating and theeving every where; a newes-monger, pretending all manner of knowledge, but guilty of no true or solid learning; a trifler; a meere frantick fellow; if he prove a Divine, then a meer verball fellow, frothy, of no judgement, easily perverted, constant in nothing but idle words and bragging.

May 21st ♊

Robert Harley

James Graham   Thomas Warton

born: Bryan Edwards, West India merchant, 1743; John Singleton Copley, Lord Lyndhurst, 1772.
died: James Graham, 1st Marquis of Montrose, executed, 1660; Robert Harley, 1st Earl of Oxford, 1724; Christopher Smart, poet, 1771; Dr Thomas Warton, historian of English Poetry, 1790

May 22nd ♊

Henry VI

Alexander Pope   Maria Edgeworth

born: Alexander Pope, poet, 1688.
died: Henry VI, King of England, 1471; Maria Edgeworth, novelist, 1849

Trinity Sunday

The mystery of the Holy Trinity has been from an early date commemorated by a festival, the observance of which is said to have been established in England by Thomas à Becket near the close of the twelfth century. In the fact of three hundred and ten churches in England being dedicated to the holy and undivided Trinity, we read the reverence paid to the mystery in mediaeval times. Architects and other artists in early times racked their brains for devices expressive of the Three in One, and many very curious ones are preserved.

May 23rd ♊

Elias Ashmole

born: Elias Ashmole, herald and antiquarian, 1617; Dr William Hunter, anatomist, 1718; James Boaden, biographer, dramatist and journalist, 1762.
died: William Woolett, draughtsman and engraver, 1785; George Brydges Rodney, 1st Lord Rodney, admiral, 1792

May 24th ♊

Queen Victoria

John Jewel

Robert Cecil

born: John Jewel, bishop of Salisbury, 1522; Sir Robert Adair, friend of Charles James Fox, 1763; Albert Smith, author and lecturer, 1816; John Henry Foley, sculptor, 1818; Queen Victoria, 1819.
died: Robert Cecil, 1st Earl of Salisbury, statesman, 1612; Jane Porter, novelist, 1850

May 25th ♊

born: Dr. John Mason Good, physician, 1764; John Pye Smith, nonconformist divine, 1774.
died: Dr. George Fordyce, physician, 1802; Dr William Paley, archdeacon of Carlisle, 1805.

May 26th ♊

William Petty

Samuel Pepys

Shute Barrington

born: Sir William Petty, political economist, 1623; Shute Barrington, bishop of Durham, 1734.
died: Samuel Pepys, naval administrator and diarist, 1703; Capel Lofft, miscellaneous writer, 1812.

May 27th ♊

born: Rev. Thomas Dudley Fosbroke, antiquarian, 1770.
died: Archibald Campbell, Marquis of Argyll, executed, 1661.

May 28th ♊

William Eden   William Pitt

Thomas Moore   Richard Hurd

born: William Pitt, statesman,
1759; Thomas Moore, poet, 1780.
died: Thomas Howard, 1st Earl
of Suffolk, 1626; Richard Hurd,
bishop of Worcester, 1808; Henry
Dundas, 1st Viscount Melville,
1811; William Eden, 1st Lord
Auckland 1814

May 29th ♊

Charles II

born: Charles II, King of England.
died: Dr Andrew Ducarel, antiquarian,
1785; William Pyne, painter and author
1843.

Charles II and the Royal Oak.

Among the acts passed by parliament immediately
after the Restoration was one enacting 'That in all
succeeding ages the 29th of May be celebrated in
every parish church and chapel in England, and the
dominions thereof, by rendering thanks to God for
the king's (Charles II's) restoration to actual
possession and exercise of his legal authority over his
subjects,' &c. The service for the Restoration, like
that for the preservation from the Gunpowder
Treason, and the death of Charles I, was kept up till
the year 1859.

The restoration of the king, after a twelve years'
interregnum from the death of his father, naturally
brought into public view some of the remarkable
events of his intermediate life. None took a more
prominent place than what had happened in
September 1651, immediately after his Scottish army
had been overthrown by Cromwell at Worcester. It
was heretofore obscurely, but now became clearly
known, that the royal person had for a day been
concealed in a bushy oak in a Shropshire forest, while
the commonwealth's troopers were ranging about in
search of the fugitives from the late battle. The
incident was romantic and striking in itself, and, in

proportion to the joy in having the king once in his legal place, was the interest felt in the tree by which he had been to all appearance providentially preserved. The ROYAL OAK accordingly became one of the familiar domestic ideas of the English people. A spray of oak in the hat was a badge of a loyalist on the recurrence of the Restoration-day. A picture of an oak tree, with a crowned figure sitting amidst the branches, and a few dragoons scouring about the neighbouring ground, was assumed as a sign upon many a tavern in town and country. And 'Oak Apple-day' became a convertible term for the Restoration-day among the rustic population.

There are still a few dreamy old towns and villages in rural England, where almost every ruin that Time has unroofed, and every mouldering wall his silent teeth have gnawed through, are attributed to the cannon of Cromwell and his grim Ironsides; though, in many instances, history has left no record that either the stern Protector or his dreaded troopers were ever near the spot. In many of these old-fashioned and out-of-the-way places, the 29th of May is still celebrated, in memory of King Charles's preservation in the oak of Boscobel, and his Restoration.

Charles II

Boscobel House

John Charles Spencer   Alexander Pope

born: John Charles Spencer,
3ʳᵈ Earl Spencer, 1782; Samuel
Spalding, writer and moral
philosopher, 1807.
died: Alexander Pope, poet, 1744.

Pope's Garden.

That part of Pope's garden which has always excited the greatest curiosity was the grotto and subterraneous passage which he made. Pope himself describes them thus fully in 1725: 'I have put my last hand to my works of this kind, in happily finishing the subterraneous way and grotto. I there formed a spring of the clearest water, which falls in a perpetual rill that echoes through the cavern day and night. From the River Thames you see through my arch up a walk of the wilderness to a kind of open temple, wholly composed of shells in a rustic manner, and from that distance under the temple you look down through a sloping arcade of trees, and see the sails on the river passing suddenly and vanishing, as through a perspective glass. When you shut the doors of this grotto, it becomes on the instant, from a

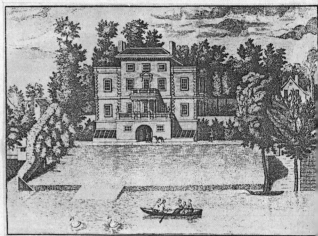

Pope's Villa

If we could always discover the personal tastes and pleasurable pursuits of authors, we should find these the best comments on their literary productions. And apropos of this ought to be noted how much time and skill Pope expended on his garden. He altered and trimmed it like a favourite poem, and was never satisfied he had done enough to adorn it.

The Shell Temple in Pope's Garden.
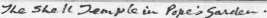

Pope in his Grotto. By William Kent

luminous room, a camera obscura; on the walls of which all objects of the river—hills, woods, and boats—are forming a moving picture in their visible radiations; and when you have a mind to light it up, it affords you a very different scene. It is finished with shells, interspersed with pieces of looking-glass in angular forms; and in the ceiling is a star of the same material, at which, when a lamp (of an orbicular figure of thin alabaster) is hung in the middle, a thousand pointed rays glitter, and are reflected over the place.

'There are connected to this grotto by a narrower passage two porches, one towards the river, of smooth stones, full of light, and open; the other towards the gardens, shadowed with trees, rough with shell, flints, and iron ore. The bottom is paved with simple pebble, as is also the adjoining walk up the wilderness to the temple, in the natural taste agreeing not ill with the little dripping murmur and the aquatic idea of the whole place. It wants nothing to complete it but a good statue with an inscription, like the beautiful antique one which you know I am so fond of:

Nymph of the grot, these sacred springs I keep,
And to the murmur of these waters sleep;
Ah! spare my slumbers, gently tread the cave,
And drink in silence, or in silence lave.

You'll think I have been very poetical in this description, but it is pretty near the truth. I wish you were here to bear testimony how little it owes to art, either the place itself or the image I give of it.'

May 31st Ⅱ

Simon Patrick

born: Dr James Currie, physician, 1756.
died: Simon Patrick, bishop of Ely, 1707;
Joseph Grimaldi, actor 1837.

Ⅱ June ♋

Now summer is in flower, and Nature's hum
Is never silent round her bounteous bloom;
Insects, as small as dust, have never done
With glitt'ring dance, and reeling in the sun;
And green wood-fly, and blossom-haunting bee,
Are never weary of their melody.
Round field and hedge, flowers in full glory
    twine,
Large bindweed bells, wild hop, and streak'd
    woodbine,
That lift athirst their slender-throated flowers,
Agape for dew-falls, and for honey showers;
These o'er each bush in sweet disorder run,
And spread their wild hues to the sultry sun.
The mottled spider, at eve's leisure, weaves
His webs of silken lace on twigs and leaves,
Which every morning meet the poet's eye,
Like fairies' dew-wet dresses hung to dry.
The wheat swells into ear, and hides below
The May-month wild flowers and their gaudy
    show,
Leaving a schoolboy's height, in snugger rest,
The Leveret's seat, and lark and partridge nest.

            . . . The timid maid,
Pleased to be praised, and yet of praise afraid,
Seeks the best flowers; not those of woods and
    fields,
But such as every farmer's garden yields—
Fine cabbage-roses, painted like her face,
The shining pansy, trimm'd with golden lace,
The tall-lopp'd larkheels, feather'd thick with
    flowers,
The woodbine, climbing o'er the door in bowers,
The London tufts, of many a mottled hue,
The pale pink pea, and monkshood darkly blue,

The white and purple gillyflowers, that stay
Ling'ring, in blossom, summer half away,
The single blood-walls, of a luscious smell,
Old-fashion'd flowers which housewives love so
    well . . .
With marjoram knots, sweetbrier, and ribbon-
    grass,
And lavender, the choice of ev'ry lass,
And sprigs of lad's love—all familiar names,
Which every garden through the village claims.

                JOHN CLARE

    . . . After her came jolly JUNE arrayed
All in green leaves, as he a player were;
    Yet in his time he wrought as well as played,
That by his plough-irons mote right well appear.
    Upon a crab he rode, that did him bear,
With crooked crawling steps, an uncouth pace,
    And backward rode, as bargemen wont to fare,
Bending their force contrary to their face;
Like that ungracious crew which feigns demurest
    grace.

                SPENSER

Ovid, in his *Fasti*, makes Juno claim the honour of
giving a name to this month; but there had been
ample time before his day for an obscurity to invest
the origin of the term. Standing as the fourth month
in the Roman calendar, it was in reality dedicated *à
Junioribus*—that is, to the junior or inferior branch of
the original legislature of Rome, as May was *à
Majoribus*, or to the superior branch.

JVNE

Though the summer solstice takes place on the 21st day, June is only the third month of the year in respect of temperature, being preceded in this respect by July and August. The mornings, in the early part of this month especially, are liable to be even frosty, to the extensive damage of the buds of the fruit-trees. Nevertheless, June is the month of the greatest summer beauty. 'The leafy month of June', Coleridge well calls it, the month when the flowers are at the richest in hue and profusion.

The sun, formally speaking, reaches the most northerly point in the zodiac, and enters the constellation of Cancer, on the 21st of June.

June was the month which the Romans considered the most propitious season of the year for contracting matrimonial engagements, especially if the day chosen were that of the full moon or the conjunction of the sun and moon; the month of May was especially to be avoided, as under the influence of spirits adverse to happy households.

June 1st ♊   The "Glorious First of June."

David Wilkie

In April 1794, Lord Howe, as Admiral-in-Chief of the Channel fleet, went out to look after the French fleet at Brest, and a great French convoy known to be expected from America and the West Indies. He had with him twenty-six sail of the line, and five frigates. For some weeks the fleet was in the Atlantic, baffled by foggy weather in the attempt to discover the enemy; but towards the close of May the two fleets sighted each other, and a great naval battle became imminent. The French admirals had often before avoided when possible a close contest with the English; but on this occasion Admiral Villaret Joyeuse, knowing that a convoy of enormous value was at stake, determined to meet his formidable opponent. The two fleets were about equal in the number of ships; but the French had the advantage in number of guns, weight of metal, and number of men. On the 1st of June, Howe achieved a great victory over Villaret Joyeuse, the details of which are given in all the histories of the period.

It was not until the 10th that the admiral's despatches reached the Government. On the evening of that day the Earl of Chatham made known the news at the opera; and the audience, roused with excitement, called loudly for 'God save the King' and 'Rule Britannia'.

died: Christopher Marlowe, dramatist, 1593; James Gillray, caricaturist, 1815; Sir David Wilkie, painter, 1841.

June 2nd ♊

Thomas Howard

James Douglas

died: Thomas Howard,
4th Duke of Norfolk, executed,
1572 ; James Douglas, 4th Earl
of Morton, Regent of Scotland,
executed, 1581.

June 3rd ♊

William Harvey

born: Dr John Gregory, Professor of
medecine, 1724; Sir William Ross,
miniaturist, 1794.
died: John Aylmer, Bishop of London,
1594; Dr William Harvey, discoverer
of the circulation of the blood, 1657.

June 4th ♊

William Juxon

George III

John Scott

Marguerite, Countess of Blessington

born: George III, King of Great
Britain, 1738 ; John Scott, 1st
Earl of Eldon, lord chancellor,
1751.
died: William Juxon, Archbishop
of Canterbury, 1636; Henry Grattan,
statesman, 1820; Marguerite,
Countess of Blessington, authoress,
1849.

June 5th ♊

Adam Smith

born: Adam Smith, political economist, 1723.
died: Henry Sacheverell, political preacher, 1724; T.H. Lister, novelist and dramatist, 1842.

June 6th ♊

Jeremy Bentham   George Anson

born: Dr Nathaniel Lardner, nonconformist divine, 1684.
died: George Anson, Lord Anson, Admiral, 1762; Jeremy Bentham, writer, 1832.

June 7th ♊

John Aubrey   John Rennie
William Warburton   Robert Jenkinson

born: John Rennie, engineer, 1761; Robert Jenkinson, 2nd Earl of Liverpool, prime minister, 1770.
died: John Aubrey, antiquary, (buried) 1697; William Warburton Bishop of Gloucester, 1779; Sir John Graham Dalyell, antiquary and naturalist, 1851.

The Dunmow Flitch of Bacon.

Far back in the grey dimness of the Middle Ages, while as yet men were making crusades, and the English commons had not a voice in the state, we see a joke arise among the flats of Essex. What makes it the more remarkable is, it arose in connection with a religious house—the priory of Dunmow—showing that men who then devoted themselves to prayers could occasionally make play out of the comicalities of human nature. Taking upon themselves to assume that perfect harmony between married persons for any considerable length of time was a thing of the greatest rarity—so much so as to be scarce possible—they ordered, and made their order known, that if any pair could, after a twelvemonth of matrimony, come forward and make oath at Dunmow that, during the whole time, they had never had a quarrel, never regretted their marriage, and, if again open to an engagement, would make exactly that they had made, they should be rewarded with a flitch of bacon.

And immediately thereupon, the said William Parsley and Jane his wife claiming the said gammon of bacon, the court pronounced the sentence for the same, in these words, or to the effect following:

Since to these conditions, without any fear,
Of your own accord you do freely swear,
A whole gammon of bacon you do receive,
And bear it away with love and good leave:
For this is the custom of Dunmow well known;
Tho' the pleasure be ours, the bacon's your own.

And accordingly a gammon was delivered unto the said William Parsley and Jane his wife, with the usual solemnity.

And that the joke was not altogether an ill-based one certainly appears on an *a facie* view of the history of the custom, as far as it has been preserved, for between the time of King John and the Reformation—in which upwards of three centuries slid away—there are shown but three instances of an application for the flitch by properly qualified parties. The first was made in 1455 by one Richard Wright, of Bradbury, in the county of Norfolk, a labouring man; his claim was allowed, and the flitch rendered to him. The second was made in 1467 by one Stephen Samuel, of Ayston-parva, in Essex, a husbandman. Having made the proper oaths before Roger Bulcott, prior, in the presence of the convent and a number of neighbours, he, too, obtained the bacon. The third application on record came from Thomas le Fuller, of Cogshall, in Essex, before John Tils, prior, in the presence of the convent and neighbours. This person also made good his claim, and carried off a gammon of bacon.

The priory of Dunmow was of course amongst the religious establishments suppressed by the Defender of the Faith. The old religion of the place was gone; but the bacon was saved. Doubtless, the records of many applications during the sixteenth and seventeenth centuries are lost to us; but at length, in 1701, we are apprized of one which seems to have been conducted with all due state and ceremony. The record of it in the court roll of Dunmow is as follows:

Be it remembered, that at this court, in full and open court, it is found and presented by the homage aforesaid, that William Parsley, of Much Easton, in the county of Essex, butcher, and Jane his wife, have been married for the space of three years last past, and upward; and it is likewise found, presented, and adjudged by the homage aforesaid, that the said William Parsley and Jane his wife, by means of their quiet, peaceable, tender, and loving cohabitation for the space of time aforesaid (as appears by the said homage), are fit and qualified persons to be admitted by the court to receive the ancient and accustomed oath, whereby to entitle themselves to have the bacon of Dunmow, delivered unto them, according to the custom of the Manor . . .

The bacon was again presented in 1763; but the name of the recipient has escaped record. After this the custom was discountenanced by the lord of the manor, the swearing stones were removed from the churchyard, and the old oaken chair remained undisturbed in the priory. One John Gilder and his wife claimed the flitch in 1772; but when he and his sympathizers arrived at the priory, they found the gates fast; the expectant couple were compelled to go away empty-handed, and the Dunmow festival henceforth was consigned to the limbo of extinct customs.

June 8th

Rosa alba ple: flo:

L. Rosa rubra prænestina.

born: John Smeaton, engineer, 1724; Rev. Thomas Dunham Whitaker, topographer, 1759; Robert Stevenson, engineer, 1772.
died: Thomas Randolph, ambassador, 1590; Douglas William Jerrold, man of letters, 1857

born: James Stuart, the Old Pretender, 1688; John Dolland, politician, 1706; James Short, optician, 1710.
died: Thomas Hearne, antiquary, 1735; William Kenrick, writer, 1779; James Smith, agricultural engineer, 1850; Dr. Robert Brown, botanist, 1858.

June 9th

died: William Maitland, secretary, 1573; William Lilly, astrologer, 1681; Dr. Abraham Rees, cyclopaedist, 1825.

June 11th ♊

June 12th ♊

George I

Kenelm Digby

Harriet Martineau

born: George Wither, poet, 1588.
died: Sir Kenelm Digby, author,
1665; William Robertson, historian,
1793; Douglas Stewart, philosopher,
1828

St. Barnaby's Day.

Before the change of style, the 11th of June was the day of the summer solstice. This was expressed proverbially in England—

> Barnaby bright
> The longest day and the shortest night.

It appears to have been customary on St Barnaby's day for the priests and clerks in English churches to wear garlands of rose and woodroff. A miraculous walnut-tree in the abbey churchyard of Glastonbury was supposed to bud invariably on St Barnaby's day.

born: Harriet Martineau, writer,
1802; Charles Kingsley, author,
1819.
died: George I, King of Great
Britain, 1727; William Collins,
poet, 1759. Edward Troughton,
instrument maker, 1835.

June 13th ♊

Frances Burney

born: Frances Burney, Mme. D'Arblay,
novelist, 1752; Dr Thomas Young, physician
and physicist, 1773; Dr Thomas Arnold,
head master of Rugby, 1795.
died: Richard Lovell Edgeworth,
author, 1817.

June 14th ♊

born: Thomas Pennant, traveller and naturalist, 1726.
died: Dr Ralph Bathurst, Dean of Wells, 1704; Colin Maclaurin, mathematician and natural philosopher, 1746.

June 16th ♊

born: Sir John Cheke, tutor to Edward VI, 1514; Henrietta Stuart, Duchess of Orleans, 1644.
died: John Churchill, Duke of Marlborough, 1722; Joseph Butler, Bishop of Durham, 1752.

June 15th ♊

born: Edward, the Black Prince, 1330; Thomas Randolph, poet and dramatist (baptized) 1605.
died: Thomas Campbell, poet, 1844.

June 17th ♊

born: John Wesley, leader of Methodism, 1703; Andrew Crosse, electrician, 1784.
died: Joseph Addison, essayist, 1719; Selina Hastings, Countess of Huntingdon; Lord William Cavendish Bentinck, governor general of India, 1839; Richard Harris Barham, author, 1845.

June 18th ♊

born: Robert Stewart, 2nd Marquess
of Londonderry, Viscount
Castlereagh, 1769.
died: Thomas Bilson, Bishop of
Worcester, 1616; Ambrose Philips,
poet, 1749.

The Battle of Waterloo.

When William IV was lying on his death-bed at Windsor, the firing for the anniversary of Waterloo took place, and on his inquiring and learning the cause, he breathed out faintly, 'It was a great day for England.' We may say it was so, in no spirit of vainglorious boasting on account of a well-won victory, but as viewed in the light of a liberation for England, and the civilized world generally.

When Napoleon recovered his throne at Paris, in March 1815, he could only wring from an exhausted and but partially loyal country about two hundred thousand men to oppose to a million of troops which the allied sovereigns were ready to muster against him. His first business was to sustain the attack of the united British and Prussians, posted in the Netherlands, and it was his obvious policy to make an attack on these himself before any others could come up to their assistance. His rapid advance at the beginning of June, before the English and Prussian commanders were aware of his having left Paris; his quick and brilliant assaults on the separate bodies of Prussians and British at Ligny and Quatre Bras on the 16th, were movements marked by all his brilliant military genius. And even when, on the 18th, he commenced the greater battle of Waterloo with both, the advantage still remained to him in the divided positions of his double enemy, giving him the power of bringing his whole host concentratedly upon one of theirs; thus neutralizing to some extent their largely superior forces. And, beyond a doubt, through the superior skill and daring which he thus showed, as well as the wonderful gallantry of his soldiery, the victory at Waterloo ought to have been his. There was just one obstacle, and it was decisive—the British infantry stood in their squares immovable upon the plain till the afternoon, when the arrival of the Prussians gave their side the superiority. It is unnecessary to repeat details which have been told in a hundred chronicles. Enough that that evening saw the noble and in large part veteran army of Napoleon retreating and dispersing never to re-assemble, and that within a month his sovereignty in France had definitely closed. An heroic, but essentially rash and ill-omened adventure, had ended in consigning him to those six years of miserable imprisonment which form such an anti-climax to the twenty of conquest and empire that went before.

If we must consider it a discredit to Wellington that he was unaware on the evening of the 15th that the action was so near—even attending a ball that evening in Brussels—it was amply redeemed by the marvellous coolness and sagacity with which he made all his subsequent arrangements, and the patience with which he sustained the shock of the enemy, both at Quatre Bras on the 16th, and on the 18th in the more terrible fight of Waterloo. Thrown on that occasion into the central position among the opponents of Bonaparte, he was naturally and justly hailed as the saviour of Europe. Though at the same time nothing can be more clear than the important part which the equal force of Prussians bore in meeting the French battalions. Thenceforth the name of Wellington was venerated above that of any living Englishman.

June 19th ♊

James I   Joseph Banks

born: James VI of Scotland and
I of England, 1566.
died: Dr William Sherlock,
Dean of St Paul's, 1707;
Sir Joseph Banks, President
of the Royal Society, 1820.

Magna Carta.

Effigy of King John
on his tomb in
Worcester Cathedral

The 19th of June remains an ever-memorable day to Englishmen, and to all nations descended from Englishmen, as that on which the Magna Carta was signed. The mean wickedness and tyranny of King John had raised nearly the whole body of his subjects in rebellion against him, and it at length appeared that he had scarcely any support but that which he derived from a band of foreign mercenaries. Appalled at the position in which he found himself, he agreed to meet the army of the barons under their elected general, Fitz-Walter, on Runnymede, by the Thames, near Windsor, in order to come to a pacification with them. They prepared a charter, assuring the rights and privileges of the various sections of the community, and this he felt himself compelled to sign, though not without a secret resolution to disregard it, if possible, afterwards.

It was a stage, and a great one, in the establishment of English freedom. The barons secured that there should be no liability to irregular taxation, and it was conceded that the freemen, merchants, and villeins (bond labourers) should be safe from all but legally imposed penalties. As far as practicable, guarantees were exacted from the king for the fulfilment of the conditions. Viewed in contrast with the general conditions of Europe at that time, the making good of such claims for the subjects seems to imply a remarkable peculiarity of character inherent in English society. With such a fact possible in the thirteenth century, we are prepared for the greater struggles of the seventeenth century, and for the happy union of law and liberty which now makes England the admiration of continental nations.

The Great Charter

June 20th ♊

William IV

born: Dr George Hickes, non-
juror, 1642; Dr Adam Ferguson,
professor of philosophy, 1723;
Anna Letitia Aiken, Mrs Barbauld,
poet, 1743.
died: William Cavendish, 2nd Duke
of Devonshire, 1628; Karl Friedrich
Abel, player of the viol-di-gamba, 1787;
William IV, King of Great Britain, 1837.

June 21st ♊

Edward III
Silbert Elliot
Inigo Jones
Mary Anne Clarke

born: Anthony Collins, deist, 1676.
died: Edward III, King of England,
1377; Inigo Jones, architect,
1652; William Beckford, lord
mayor of London, 1770;
Silbert Elliot, 1st Earl of Minto,
governor-general of India, 1814;
Mary Anne Clarke, mistress of
Frederick, Duke of York, 1852.

June 22nd ♋

John Fisher
Benjamin Haydon
John Campbell

born: Thomas Day, author, 1748.
died: John Fisher, bishop of Rochester,
executed, 1535; Benjamin Robert
Haydon, painter, 1846; John
Campbell, 1st Lord Campbell, legal
biographer, 1861.

June 23rd ♋

John Fell
Hester Stanhope

born: John Fell, Bishop of Oxford,
1625.
died: James Mill, utilitarian
philosopher, 1836; Lady
Hester Stanhope, eccentric, 1839.

Cancer - the crab of Moon her properties and significations

June 22 to July 23

Manners or actions when well placed or dignified.

When ill

She signifieth one of composed Manners, a soft, tender creature, a Lover of all honest and ingenuous Sciences, a Searcher of, and Delighter in Novelties, naturally propense to flit and shift his Habitation, unstedfast wholly caring for the present Times, Timorous, Prodigal, and easily Frighted, however loving Peace, and to live free from the cares of this Life; if a Mechannick, the man learnes many Occupations, and frequently will be tampering with many wayes to trade in.

A meer Vagabond, idle Person, hating Labour, a Drunkard, a Sot, one of no Spirit or Forecast, delighting to live beggarly and carelessly, one content in no condition of Life, either good or ill.

June 24th ☿

Mary Tudor

John Ross

born: Sir John Ross, Arctic
navigator, 1777.
died: Mary Tudor, Duchess of
Suffolk, 1533; John Hampden,
statesman, 1643; Dr. Thomas
Amory, dissenting tutor, 1774.
Midsummer Day.

Considering the part borne by the Baptist in the transactions on which Christianity is founded, it is not wonderful that the day set apart for the observance of his nativity should be, in all ages and most parts of Europe, one of the most popular of religious festivals. It enjoys the greater distinction that it is considered as Midsummer Day, and therefore has inherited a number of observances from heathen times.

The observances connected with the Nativity of St John commenced on the previous evening, called, as usual, the eve or vigil of the festival, or Midsummer's eve. On that evening the people were accustomed to go into the woods and break down branches of trees, which they brought to their homes, and planted over their doors, amidst great demonstrations of joy, to make good the Scripture prophecy respecting the Baptist, that many should rejoice in his birth. This custom was universal in England till the recent change in manners.

Towards night, materials for a fire were collected in a public place and kindled. To this the name of bonfire was given, a term of which the most rational explanation seems to be, that it was composed of contributions collected as *boons*, or gifts of social and charitable feeling. Around this fire the people danced with almost frantic mirth, the men and boys occasionally jumping through it, not to show their agility, but as a compliance with ancient custom. There can be no doubt that this leaping through the fire is one of the most ancient of all known superstitions, and is identified with that followed by Manasseh.

It was customary in town to keep a watch walking about during the Midsummer Night, although no such practice might prevail at the place from motives of precaution. They paraded the town in parties during the night, every person wearing a garland of flowers upon his head, additionally embellished in some instances with ribbons and jewels. In London, during the Middle Ages, this watch, consisting of not less than two thousand men, paraded both on this night and on the eves of St Paul's and Peter's days. The watchmen were provided with cressets, or torches, carried in barred pots on the tops of long poles, which, added to the bonfires on the streets, must have given the town a striking appearance in an age when there was no regular street-lighting. The great came to give their countenance to this marching watch, and made it quite a pageant. A London poet, looking back from 1616, thus alludes to the scene:

The goodly buildings that till then did hide
Their rich array, open'd their windows wide,
Where kings, great peers, and many a noble dame,
Whose bright pearl-fluttering robes did mock the
  flame
Of the night's burning lights, did sit to see
How every senator in his degree,
Adorn'd with shining gold and purple weeds,
And stately mounted on rich-trapped steeds,
Their guard attending, through the streets did
  ride,
Before their foot-bands, graced with glittering
  pride
Of rich-gilt arms, whose glory did present
A sunshine to the eye, as if it meant,
Among the cresset lights shot up on high,
To chase dark night for ever from the sky;
While in the streets the sticklers to and fro,
To keep decorum, still did come and go,
Where tables set were plentifully spread,
And at each door neighbour with neighbour fed.

King Henry VIII, hearing of the marching watch, came privately, in 1510, to see it; and was so much pleased with what he saw, that he came with Queen Catherine and a noble train to attend openly that of St Peter's Eve, a few nights after. But this king, in the latter part of his reign, thought proper to abolish the ancient custom.

The observance of St John's Day seems to have been, by a practical bull, confined mainly to the previous evening. On the day itself, we only find that the people kept their doors and beds embowered in the branches set up the night before, upon the understanding that these had a virtue in averting thunder, tempest, and all kinds of noxious physical agencies.

June 25th

born: John Horne Tooke, politician
and philologist, 1736.
died: John Marston, dramatist
and divine, 1634; Robert Leighton,
Archbishop of Glasgow, 1684; Roger
Gale, antiquary, 1744; Thomas
Sandby, draughtsman and architect,
1798; George IV, King of Great
Britain, 1830.

June 26th

born: George Morland, painter, 1763.
died: Sir Richard Fanshawe,
diplomatist and author, 1666;
Ralph Cudworth, divine, 1688;
Rev. Gilbert White, naturalist, 1793;
Samuel Crompton, inventor of the
Spinning mule, 1827.

Richard Fanshawe

George Morland

June 27th

died: Nicholas Tindal, historical
writer, 1774; William Dodd, forger,
1777; John Murray, publisher,
1843.

June 28th

born: Henry VIII, King of England,
1491; Charles Mathews, actor, 1776.
died: Francis Wheatley, painter, 1801;
Charles Mathews, actor, 1835.

Henry VIII

Charles Mathews

June 29th ℞

Margaret Beaufort.

born: Sir Henry Yelverton, judge, 1566.

died: Margaret Beaufort, Countess of Richmond, 1509; Rev. David Williams, founder of the Royal Literary Fund, 1816; Rev. Edward Smedley, miscellaneous writer, 1836.

St Peter the Apostle.

The 29th of June is a festival of the Anglican Church in honour of St Peter the Apostle. St Peter has in England 830 churches dedicated in his sole honour, and thirty jointly with St Paul, and 10 in connection with some other saint, making 1070 in all.

June 30th

Henrietta Stuart

Elizabeth Barrett Browning

died: Alexander Brome, poet,
1666 ; Henrietta Stuart, Duchess
of Orleans, 1670; Archibald
Campbell, 9th Earl of Argyll,
executed, 1685 ; Richard
Parker, mutineer, executed, 1797;
Henry Kett, miscellaneous writer,
1825 ; James Silk Buckingham,
author and traveller, 1855;
Elizabeth Barrett Browning,
poet, 1861.

July

July, the month of summer's prime,
Again resumes his busy time;
Scythes tinkle in each grassy dell;
And meadows, they are mad with noise
Of laughing maids and shouting boys,
Making up the withering hay
With merry hearts as light as play.
The very insects on the ground
So nimbly bustle all around,
Among the grass, or dusty soil,
They seem partakers in the toil.
The landscape even reels with life,
While mid the busy stir and strife
Of industry, the shepherd still
Enjoys his summer dreams at will,
Bent o'er his hook, or listless laid
Beneath the pasture's willow shade,
Whose foliage shines so cool and grey
Amid the sultry hues of day,
As if the morning's misty veil
Yet linger'd in its shadows pale . . .

Loud is the summer's busy song;
The smallest breeze can find a tongue;
While insects of each tiny size
Grow teasing with their melodies,
Till noon burns with its blistering breath
Around, and day dies still as death.
The busy noise of man and brute
Is on a sudden lost and mute;
Even the brook that leaps along
Seems weary of its bubbling song,
And, so soft its waters creep,
Tired silence sinks in sounder sleep . . .

Now to the pleasant pasture dells,
Where hay from closes sweetly smells,
Adown the pathway's narrow lane
The milking maiden hies again,
With scraps of ballads never dumb,

And rosy cheeks of happy bloom,
Tann'd brown by summer's rude embrace,
Which adds new beauties to her face,
And red lips never pale with sighs,
And flowing hair, and laughing eyes
That o'er full many a heart prevailed,
And swelling bosom loosely veiled,
White as the love it harbours there,
Unsullied with the taunts of care.

JOHN CLARE

Then came hot JULY, boiling like to fire,
    That all his garments he had cast away;
Upon a lion raging yet with ire
    He boldly rode, and made him to obey:
(It was the beast that whilom did foray
    The Nemaean forest, till the Amphitrionide
Him slew, and with his hide did him array:)
    Behind his back a scythe, and by his side
Under his belt he bore a sickle circling wide.

SPENSER

July was originally the fifth month of the Roman year, and thence denominated *Quintilis*. In the Alban Calendar, it had a complement of thirty-six days. Romulus reduced it to thirty-one, and Numa to thirty days, and it stood thus for many centuries. At length, it was restored to thirty-one days by Julius Caesar, who felt a personal interest in it as his natal month. After the death of this great reformer of the calendar, Mark Antony changed the name to July, in honour of the family name of Caesar.

Our Saxon ancestors called July *Hey monath*, 'because therein they usually mowed and made their hay-harvest; and also *Maed monath*, from the meads being then in their bloom.'

IVLY

July is allowed all over the northern hemisphere to be the warmest month of the year, notwithstanding that the sun has then commenced his course of recession from the tropic of Cancer. The great heat of the month led to a superstition among the Romans: they conceived that this pre-eminent warmth, and the diseases and other calamities flowing from it, were somehow connected with the rising and setting of the star Canicula—the Little Dog—in coincidence with the sun. They accordingly conferred the name of DOG-DAYS upon the period between the 3rd of July and the 11th of August.

July 1st ♋

Joseph Hall

July 2nd ♋

Thomas Cranmer

Henry Petty-Fitzmaurice

Robert Peel

born: Joseph Hall, Bishop of
Norwich, 1574.
died: Frederick, Duke of
Schomberg, soldier, 1690; Henry
Fox, 1st Lord Holland, politician,
1774; William Huntington,
eccentric preacher, 1813.

born: Thomas Cranmer, Archbishop of
Canterbury, 1489; Henry Petty-
Fitzmaurice, 3rd Marquess of Lansdowne
statesman, 1780.
died: Sir Robert Peel, bt., statesman
1850; William Berry, geologist, 1851

Holy Wells

On the 1st of July 1652, the eccentric John Taylor, commonly called the Water Poet, from his having been a waterman on the Thames, paid a visit to St Winifred's Well, at Holywell, in Flintshire. This was a place held in no small veneration even in Taylor's days; but in Catholic times, it filled a great space indeed.

Some wells were held specially efficacious for certain diseases. St Tegla's Well was patronised by sufferers from 'the falling sickness'; St John's, Balmanno, Kincardineshire, by mothers whose children were troubled with rickets or sore eyes. The Tobirnimbuadh, or spring of many virtues, in St Kilda's Isle, was pre-eminent in deafness and nervous disorders; while the waters of Trinity Gask Well, Perthshire, enabled every one baptized therein to face the plague without fear. Others, again, possessed peculiar properties. Thus, St Loy's Well, Tottenham, was said to be always full but never overflowing; the waters of St Non's ebbed and flowed with the sea; and those of the Toberi-clerich, St Kilda, although covered twice in the day by the sea, never became brackish.

Wells were also used as divining-pools. By taking a shirt or a shift off a sick person, and throwing it into the well of St Oswald (near Newton), the end of the illness could easily be known—if the garment floated, all would be well; if it sank, it was useless to hope. The same result was arrived at by placing a wooden bowl softly on the surface of St Andrew's Well (Isle of Lewis), and watching if it turned from or towards the sun; the latter being the favourable omen. A foreknowledge of the future, too, was to be gained by shaking the ground round St Madern's Spring, and reading fate in the rising bubbles.

St Winifred's Well, Flintshire.

July 3rd

Henry Grattan

born: Henry Grattan, statesman, (baptised) 1750.

July 5th

Sarah Siddons

born: Sarah Siddons, actress 1755; C. A. Stothard, antiquarian draughtsman, 1786.
died: Sir Richard Strange, engraver, 1792.

July 4th

Samuel Richardson

died: William Byrd, composer, 1623; Samuel Richardson, novelist, 1761; Dorothea Jordan, actress, 1816; Richard Watson, Bishop of Llandaff, 1816; Rev. William Kirby, entomologist, 1850; Richard Grainger, architect, 1861.

July 6th

*born: John Flaxman, sculptor, 1755;
Sir Stamford Raffles, colonial
governor 1781.
died: Henry II, King of England, 1189;
Sir Thomas More, lord chancellor,
executed, 1535; Edward VI, King
of England, 1553; George Augustus
Elliot, Lord Heathfield, defender
of Gibraltar 1790; Sir Francis
Palgrave, historian, 1861.*

Sir Thomas More's Head.

The body of Sir Thomas More was first interred in St Peter's Church, in the Tower, and afterwards in Chelsea Church; but his head was stuck on a pole, and placed on London Bridge, where it remained fourteen days. His eldest and favourite daughter, Margaret Roper, much grieved and shocked at this exposure of her father's head, determined, if possible, to gain possession of it. She succeeded; and, according to Aubrey, in a very remarkable manner. 'One day,' says he, 'as she was passing under the bridge, looking on her father's head, she exclaimed: "That head has lain many a time in my lap, would to God it would fall into my lap as I pass under!" She had her wish, and it did fall into her lap!' Improbable as this incident may appear, it is not unlikely that it really occurred. For having tried in vain to gain possession of the head by open and direct means, she bribed or persuaded one of the bridge-keepers to throw it over the bridge, as if to make room for another, just when he should see her passing in a boat beneath. And she doubtless made the above exclamation to her boatmen, to prevent the suspicion of a

concerted scheme between her and the bridge-keeper. However some of these particulars may be questioned, it appears certain that Margaret Roper gained possession of her father's head by some such means, for when summoned before the council for having it in her custody, she boldly declared that 'her father's head should not be food for fishes!' For this she was imprisoned, but was soon liberated, and allowed to retain her father's head, which she had enclosed in a leaden box, and preserved it with the tenderest devotion.

July 7th

*died: Edward I, King of England, 1307;
Henry Compton, Bishop of London, 1713;
Richard Brinsley Sheridan, statesman
and dramatist, 1816.*

Convent garden

Somerset h.　Arundel house　Efsex house

Thomas Howard, Earl of Arundel and the Arundel Marbles

There is such a singularity in the idea of an English nobleman of the early part of the seventeenth century interesting himself in art and its treasures, that this peer stands out in a prominence much beyond what either his rank or personal qualities would have otherwise entitled him to. It does not seem to have been from any high conception of the value of beautiful things, that he busied himself so much in collecting relics of ancient sculpture in Italy. He was travelling there—the objects struck his fancy, and he thought of getting them brought home to England. Clarendon speaks of him as a rather illiterate man. More certainly, he was a man of great formality and stateliness—unbending—even a little austere—all of them qualities that one does not naturally associate with a lover of the fine arts for their own sake.

The Arundelian Marbles, as they came to be called, were all stored in and about a mansion which the earl possessed in the Strand, on the river side, between Essex House and Somerset House. His lordship's descendants acceding to the dukedom of Norfolk, the curiosities and their mansion became in time the property of that family. There is something melancholy, and a good deal that is surprising, in the ultimate history of the marbles.

'Arundel House,' says Mr Theobald, 'being now about to be pulled down, great part of the furniture was removed to Stafford House, with the museum, &c. And as there were many fine statues, bas-relieves, and marbles, they were received into the lower part of the gardens, and many of them placed under a colonnade there ... When the workmen began to build next the Strand, in order to prevent encroachments, a cross-wall was built to separate the ground let to builders from that reserved for the family mansion; and many of the workmen, to save the

expense of carrying away the rubbish, threw it over this cross-wall, where it fell upon the colonnade; and at last, by its weight, broke it down, and falling on the statues placed there, broke several of them. A great part of these in that sad condition, was purchased by Sir William Fermor, from whom the present Earl of Pomfret is descended. He removed these down to his seat at Easton Neston, in Northamptonshire, where he employed some statuary to repair such as were not too much demolished.

'Here these continued till the year 1755, when the countess made a present of them to the university of Oxford, for which she received their thanks in due state; and in the year following, the university celebrated a public act, where, in a set oration, and a full theatre, the countess was again complimented.'

Some other of the broken statues, not thought worth replacing, were begged by Boyder Cuper, who had been gardener to the Arundel family, and were removed by him to decorate a piece of garden-ground, which he had taken opposite Somerset House water-gate, in the parish of Lambeth. However, these 'broken statues' must have been of great merit; for Mr Freeman, of Fawley Court, near Henley, and Mr Edmund Waller, of Beaconsfield, happening to see the marbles, were struck with their beauty, and commissioned Mr Theobald to treat with Cuper for their purchase, leaving in his hands a bank-note of £100; eventually they were bought by Mr Theobald for £75, and were sent, part to Fawley Court, and part to Beaconsfield.

The remaining statues and fragments in Arundel gardens were removed, by permission of the Crown, to a piece of waste-ground in the manor of Kennington, belonging to the Principality of Wales; of which piece of ground a grant was obtained, at a small rent, for a term of years, which was renewed. Such fragments as were thought not worth removing, were buried in the foundations of the buildings in the lower parts of Norfolk Street, and in the gardens.

The ground at Kennington, whither some of the marbles had been removed, was subsequently let for a timber-yard, and a wharf built thereon; and when the ground was cleared for rebuilding St Paul's Cathedral, great quantities of the rubbish were taken there, to raise the ground, which used to be overflowed every spring-tide; so that, by degrees, the statues and fragments were buried under the rubbish, and there lay almost forgotten for many years. About the year 1712, this piece of ground was rented by Mr Theobald's father, who, in digging foundations for buildings, frequently met with some of the fragments; of which the Earl of Burlington hearing, his lordship went to Kennington, to inspect the remains, and prevailed upon Mr Theobald to permit him to take his choice of a few specimens; these were conveyed to Chiswick House, where one piece of bas-relief was placed in the pedestal of an obelisk which he erected in his grounds. Mr Theobald next allowed Lord Petre to dig for fragments at Kennington, when six statues, some colossal, without heads or arms, were found lying close to each other, and were soon after sent to Worksop, the seat of the Duke of Norfolk, in Nottinghamshire.

Mr Theobald also found several blocks of grayish-veined marble, out of which he cut chimney-pieces and slabs for his house, the Belvedere, in Lambeth. He also found the fragment of a column, which he had conveyed to his seat, Waltham Place, in Berkshire, and there converted this fragment of precious art into a roller for his bowling-green!

July 8th

Henry Raeburn

born: Sir Henry Raeburn, painter, 1823.

July 10th

John Fell

born: Frederick Marryatt, naval captain and novelist, 1792.
died: John Fell, Bishop of Oxford, 1686; Dr Alexander Monro, physician, 1767

July 9th

Henry Hallam   Edmund Burke

born: Ann Radcliffe, novelist, 1764; Henry Hallam, historian, 1777;
died: Edmund Burke, statesman, 1797.

July 11th

Charles Macklin

died: Charles Macklin, actor, 1797

July 12th ♌

Titus Oates

died: Isaac Casaubon,
classical scholar, 1614;
Titus Oates, perjurer, 1705;
Dr. John Jamieson, antiquary, 1838;
Horace Smith, poet and author,
1849; Robert Stevenson, engineer,
1850.

If a grave is open on Sunday, there will be another dug in the week.

If a corpse does not stiffen after death, or if the *rigor mortis* disappears before burial, it is a sign that there will be a death in the family before the end of the year.

In the case of a child of my own, every joint of the corpse was as flexible as in life. I was perplexed at this, thinking that perhaps the little fellow might, after all, be in a trance. While I was considering the matter, I perceived a bystander looking very grave, and evidently having something on her mind. On asking her what she wished to say, I received for answer that, though she did not put any faith in it herself, yet people *did* say that such a thing was the sign of another death in the family within the twelve month.

Fires and candles also afford presages of death. Coffins flying out of the former, and winding-sheets guttering down from the latter. A winding-sheet is produced from a candle, if, after it has guttered, the strip, which has run down, instead of being absorbed into the general tallow, remains unmelted: if, under these circumstances, it curls over away from the flame, it is a presage of death to the person in whose direction it points.

The howling of a dog at night under the window of a sick-room, is looked upon as a warning of death's being near.

July 13th ♌

July 14th ♌

John Dee   *John Conybeare*

born: Dr. John Dee, mathematician
and astrologer, 1527;
died: Sir William Berkley
Governor of Virginia (buried) 1677;
Richard Cromwell, Lord Protector,
1712; John Conybeare, Bishop of
Bristol, 1755; Dr. James Bradley,
astronomer-royal, 1762.

born: Sir Robert Strange, engraver,
1727; Aaron Arrowsmith, geographer,
1750.
died: Dr. William Bates, divine,
1699; Richard Bentley, scholar
and critic, 1742; Colin Maclaurin,
mathematician, 1746.

July 15th

James, Duke of Monmouth
Richard Cumberland
William Mackworth Praed

born: Richard Cumberland, Bishop
of Peterborough, 1632; Gerard
Langbaine, biographer and critic
1656.
died: James Duke of Monmouth,
executed, 1685; John Wilson,
botanist, 1751; Bryan Edwards,
West India merchant, 1800;
William Mackworth Praed, poet
1839.

St Swithin's Day.

The common adage regarding St Swithin, as every one knows, is to the effect that, as it rains or is fair on St Swithin's Day, the 15th of July, there will be a continuous track of wet or dry weather for the forty days ensuing.

> St Swithin's Day, if thou dost rain,
> For forty days it will remain:
> St Swithin's Day, if thou be fair,
> For forty days 'twill rain nae mair.

How did the popular notion about St Swithin's Day arise? Most probably, it was derived from some primeval pagan belief regarding the meteorologically prophetic character of some day about the same period of the year as St Swithin's. Such adaptations, it is well known, were very frequent on the supplanting throughout Europe of heathenism by Christianity.

The belief in the peculiar characteristics of St Swithin's Day is thus alluded to in *Poor Robin's Almanac* for 1697:

> In this month is St Swithin's Day,
> On which, if that it rain, they say,
> Full forty days after it will,
> Or more or less, some rain distil.

In the next century, Gay remarks in his *Trivia*—

> Now if on Swithin's feast the welkin lours,
> And every penthouse streams with hasty showers,
> Twice twenty days shall clouds their fleeces drain,
> And wash the pavement with incessant rain.
> Let not such vulgar tales debase thy mind;
> Nor Paul nor Swithin rule the clouds and wind!

July 16th

John Pearson
Joshua Reynolds
Anne of Cleves

born: Joseph Wilton, sculptor, 1722;
Sir Joshua Reynolds, painter, 1723.
died: Anne of Cleves, fourth wife
of Henry VIII, 1557; John Pearson,
Bishop of Chester, 1686; Dr Thomas
Yalden, poet, 1736.

July 17th

July 19th

Isaac Watts

Charles Grey

Gilbert Sheldon

John Martin

born: Dr Isaac Watts, hymn-
writer 1674
died: Sir William Wyndham,
politician, 1740; William
Somerville, poet, 1742; Dr John
Roebuck, inventor, 1794; Charles
Grey, 2nd Earl of Grey, statesman,
1845; Rev. John Lingard, Cambridge
Historian, 1851.

born: Gilbert Sheldon, Archbishop
of Canterbury 1598; John Martin,
painter, 1789.
died: Nathaniel Hooke, author,
1763.

July 18th

July 20th

Thomas Sherlock

Jane Austen

born: Robert Hooke, experimental
philosopher, 1635; Gilbert White,
naturalist 1720;
died: Abraham Sharp, mathematician,
1742; Thomas Sherlock, Bishop of
London, 1761; Jane Austen,
novelist, 1817.

born: Sir James Phillips Kay-
Shuttleworth, educationalist 1804;
John Sterling, author, 1806.
died: John Playfair, mathematician
and geologist, 1819; William Scrope,
artist and sportsman, 1852;
Caroline Anne Southey, poet, 1854.

July 21st

William Russell   Matthew Prior

Robert Burns

born: Matthew Prior, poet, 1664.
died: William Russell, Lord Russell,
"the patriot; executed, 1683;
James Butler, 1st Duke of Ormond,
1688; Robert Burns, poet, 1796;
Peter Thellusson, merchant, 1797.

July 22nd

Anthony Ashley Cooper

born: Anthony Ashley Cooper, 1st Earl
of Shaftesbury, 1621.
died: Francis Garden, Lord Gardenstone,
judge, 1793; George Shaw, naturalist,
1813.

July 23rd

Henry Carey   Richard Gibson

died: Henry Carey, Lord Hunsdon,
chamberlain of the household, 1596;
Richard Gibson, miniature painter
and dwarf, 1690; Elizabeth Hamilton,
miscellaneous writer, 1816.

Richard Gibson

On the 23rd of July 1690, died Richard Gibson, aged seventy-five; and nineteen years afterwards, his widow died at the advanced age of eighty-nine. Nature thus, by length of years, compensated this compendious couple, as Evelyn terms them, for shortness of stature—the united heights of the two amounting to no more than seven feet. Gibson was miniature-painter, in every sense of the phrase, as well as court-dwarf, to Charles I; his wife, Ann Shepherd, was court-dwarf to Queen Henrietta Maria. Her majesty encouraged a marriage between these two clever but diminutive persons; the king giving away the bride, the queen presenting her with a diamond ring; while Waller, the court-poet, celebrated the nuptials in one of his prettiest poems.

> Design or chance make others wive,
> But nature did this match contrive;
> Eve might as well have Adam fled,
> As she denied her little bed
> To him, for whom Heaven seemed to frame
> And measure out this little dame.

The conclusion of the poem is very elegant.

> Ah Chloris! that kind nature, thus,
> From all the world had severed us;
> Creating for ourselves, us two,
> As Love has me, for only you.

July 24th

George Vertue

born: Roger Dodsworth, antiquary, 1585;
Rev. John Newton, divine, 1725;
John Philpot Curran, Irish judge, 17.
died: George Vertue, antiquary,
1756.

Leo — the Lion of the Sun, and his generall and particular significations

July 24 to August 23

Manners when well dignified

Very faithfull, keeping their Promises with all punctuality, a kind of itching desire to Rule and Sway where he comes: Prudent, and of incomparable Judgment; of great Majesty and Statelinesse, Industrious to acquire Honour and a large Patrimony, yet as willingly departing therewith againe: the Solar man usually speaks with gravity, but not many word, and those with great confidence and command of his owne affection; full of Thought, Secret, Trusty, speaks deliberately, and notwithstanding his great Heart, yet he is Affable, Tractable, and very humane to all people, one loving Sumptuousnesse and Magnificence, and whatsoever is honorable; no sordid thoughts can enter his heart, &c.

When ill dignified

Then the Solar man is Arrogant and Proud, disdaining all men, cracking of his Pedegree, he is Pur-blind in Sight and Judgment, restlesse, troublesome, domineering, a meer vapour, expensive, foolish, endued with no gravity in words or sobernesse in Actions, a Spend-thrift, wasting his Patrimony and hanging on other mens charity, yet thinks all men are bound to him, because a Gentleman borne.

Charles Dibdin

born: Rev. William Burkitt, divine,
1650.
died: Robert Fleming, divine, 1694;
Charles Dibdin, dramatist and
song writer, 1814; John Emery,
actor, 1822; William Sharp,
engraver, 1824; James
Kenney, dramatist, 1849.

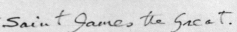

Saint James the Great.

The 25th of July is dedicated to St James the Great, the patron saint of Spain. According to legendary lore, James preached the gospel in Spain, and afterwards returning to Palestine, was made the first bishop of Jerusalem.

The shrine of St James, at Compostella, was a great resort of pilgrims, from all parts of Christendom, during the medieval period; and the distinguishing badge of pilgrims to this shrine, was a scallop shell worn on the cloak or hat. In the old ballad of the *Friar of Orders Gray*, the lady describes her lover as clad, like herself, in 'a pilgrim's weedes:'

> And how should I know your true love
> From many an other one?
> O by his scallop shell and hat,
> And by his sandal shoon.

There is some folk lore connected with St James's Day. They say in Herefordshire:

> Till St James's Day is past and gone,
> There may be hops or they may be none;

implying the noted uncertainty of that local crop. Another proverb more general is 'Whoever eats oysters on St James's Day, will never want money.' In point of fact, it is customary in London to begin eating oysters on St James's Day, when they are necessarily somewhat dearer than afterwards; so we may presume that the saying is only meant as a jocular encouragement to a little piece of extravagance and self-indulgence. In this connection of oysters with St James's Day, we trace the ancient association of the apostle with pilgrims' shells. There is a custom in London which makes this relation more evident. In the course of the few days following upon the introduction of oysters for the season, the children of the humbler class employ themselves diligently in collecting the shells which have been cast out from taverns and fish-shops, and of these they make piles in various rude forms. By the time that old St James's Day (the 5th of August) has come about, they have these little fabrics in nice order, with a candle stuck in the top, to be lighted at night. As you thread your way through some of the denser parts of the metropolis, you are apt to find a cone of shells, with its votive light, in the nook of some retired court, with a group of youngsters around it, some of whom will be sure to assail the stranger with a whining claim 'Mind the grotto!' by which is meant a demand for a penny wherewith professedly to keep up the candle. It cannot be doubted that we have here, at the distance of upwards of three hundred years from the Reformation, a relic of the habits of our Catholic ancestors.

July 26th

died: John Wilmot, 2nd Earl of
Rochester, poet and libertine, 1680;
Thomas Osborne, Duke of Leeds, 1712;
William Romaine, divine, 1795;
Dr John Friend, physician & politician,
1728.

July 27th

born: Isaac Maddox, Bishop of
Worcester, 1697; Thomas Campbell,
poet, 1777; Dr John Dalton,
chemist and natural philosopher, 1844.

July 28th

died: Thomas Cromwell, Earl of Essex,
executed, 1540; John Speed, historian
and cartographer, 1629; Abraham
Cowley, poet, 1667; John George
Lambton, 1st Earl of Durham, 1840.

July 29th

died: Dr John Caius, scholar and
physician, 1573; Benjamin Robins,
mathematician, 1751; William
Wilberforce, philanthropist, 1833;
Dr Thomas Dick, scientific writer,
1857; John Prideaux, Bishop of
Worcester, 1650

July 30th

born: Samuel Rogers, poet, 1763.
died: Thomas Gray, poet, 1771.

July 31st

died: William T. Lowndes,
bibliographer, 1843.

August

Now swarthy summer, by rude health
    embrowned,
  Precedence takes of rosy-fingered spring;
And laughing joy, with wild flowers pranked and
    crowned,
  A wild and giddy thing,
And health robust, from every care unbound,
  Come on the zephyr's wing,
    And cheer the toiling clown.

Happy as holiday-enjoying face,
  Loud tongues, and 'merry as a marriage-bell,'
Thy lightsome step sheds joy in every place;
  And where the troubled dwell,
Thy witching smiles wean them of half their
    cares;
  And from thy sunny spell,
    They greet joy unawares.

Then with thy sultry locks all loose and rude,
  And mantle laced with gems of garish light,
Come as of wont; for I would fain intrude,
  And in the world's despite,
Share the rude mirth that thy own heart beguiles,
  If haply so I might
    Win pleasure from thy smiles.

I see the wild flowers, in their summer morn
  Of beauty, feeding on joy's luscious hours;
The gay convolvulus, wreathing round the thorn,
  Agape for honey showers;
And slender kingcup, burnished with the dew
  Of morning's early hours,
    Like gold yminted new;

And mark by rustic bridge, o'er shallow stream,
  Cow-tending boy, to toil unreconciled,
Absorbed as in some vagrant summer dream;
  Who now, in gestures wild,
Starts dancing to his shadow on the wall,
  Feeling self-gratified,
    Nor fearing human thrall:

Then thread the sunny valley laced with streams,
  Or forests rude, and the o'ershadowed brims
Of simple ponds, where idle shepherd dreams,
  And streaks his listless limbs;
Or trace hay-scented meadows, smooth and long,
  Where joy's wild impulse swims
    In one continued song.

JOHN CLARE

The eighth was August, being rich arrayed
  The garment all of gold, down to the ground:
Yet rode he not, but led a lovely maid
  Forth by the lily hand, the which was crowned
  With ears of corn, and full her hand was found.
That was the righteous Virgin, which of old
  Lived here on earth, and plenty made abound;
But after wrong was loved, and justice sold,
  She left the unrighteous world, and was to
    heaven extolled.

SPENSER

In height of mean temperature, August comes only second, and scarcely second to July.

In the old Roman calendar, August bore the name of *Sextilis*, as the sixth month of the series, and consisted but of twenty-nine days. Julius Caesar, in reforming the calendar of his nation, extended it to thirty days. When, not long after, Augustus conferred on it his own name, he took a day from February and added it to August, which has consequently ever since consisted of thirty-one days.

died: Queen Anne, Queen of England,
1714; Richard Savage, poet, 1743;
John Shebbeare, political writer,
1788; Mrs Elizabeth Inchbald,
novelist and dramatist and actress,
1821; Rev. Robert Morrison,
missionary in China, 1834;
Harriet Lee, novelist, 1851.

London Bridge – New and Old.

On the day when William IV and Queen Adelaide opened New London Bridge (1st of August, 1831), the vitality of the old bridge may be said to have ceased; a bridge which had had more commerce under and over it perhaps than any other in the world. Eight centuries at least had elapsed since the commencement of that bridge-traffic. There were

three or four bridges of wood successively built at this spot before A.D. 1176 in which year the stone structure was commenced; and this was the veritable 'Old London Bridge', which served the citizens for more than six hundred and fifty years. A curious fabric it was, containing an immense quantity of stone arches of various shapes and sizes, piers so bulky as to render the navigation between them very dangerous, and (until 1754) a row of buildings a-top. The bridge suffered by fire in 1212, again in 1666, and again in 1683. So many were the evils which accumulated upon, around, and under it, that a new bridge was resolved upon in 1823—against strong opposition on the part of the corporation. John Rennie furnished the plans, and his son, Sir John, carried them out. The foundation-stone was laid in 1825 by the Duke of York and the lord mayor; and the bridge took six years in building. The old bridge finally disappeared towards the end of 1832. Then began in earnest the career of that noble structure, the new bridge, which is now crossed every day by a number of persons equal to the whole population of some of our largest manufacturing towns.

Strictly, the Old London Bridge, for a water-way of 900 feet, had eighteen solid stone piers, varying from 25 to 34 feet in thickness; thus confining the flow of the river within less than half its natural channel. That this arose simply from bad engineering, is very probable; but it admitted of huge blocks of building being placed on the bridge, with only a few interspaces, from one end to the other. These formed houses of four storeys in height, spanning across the passageway for traffic, most of which was, of course, as dark as a railway-tunnel. Nestling about the basement-floors of these buildings were shops, some of which, as we learn from old title-pages, were devoted to the business of bookselling and publishing. About the centre, on a pier larger than the rest, was reared a chapel, of Gothic architecture of the twelfth century, 60 feet by 20, and of two floors, dedicated to St Thomas of Canterbury, and styled St Peter's of the Bridge.

In the earlier days of London Bridge, the gate at the end towards the city was that on which the heads of executed traitors were exhibited; but in the reign of Elizabeth, this grisly show was transferred to the gate at the Southwark end, which consequently became recognised as the Traitors' Gate.

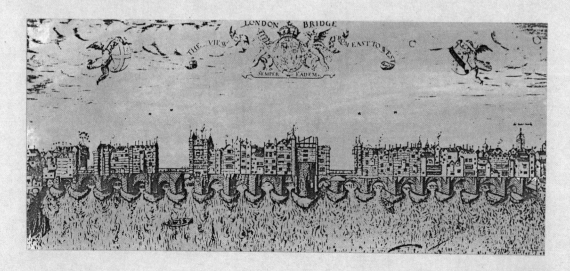

August 2nd

born: Cardinal Nicholas Wiseman, Archbishop of Westminster, 1802; John Manners, Marquis of Granby, soldier, 1721.
died: William II, King of England, 1100; Thomas Gainsborough, painter, 1788; Sidney Herbert, Baron Herbert of Lea, politician, 1861.

August 4th

born: Percy Bysshe Shelley, poet, 1792; died: William Cecil, Lord Burghley, minister of state, 1598; George Abbot, Archbishop of Canterbury, 1633; John Bacon, sculptor, 1799; Adam Duncan, Viscount Duncan, admiral, 1804.

August 3rd

born: John "Orator" Henley, preacher, 1692; Charles Stanhope, 3rd Earl Stanhope, politician, 1753.
died: Thomas Secker, Archbishop of Canterbury, 1768; Sir Richard Arkwright, inventor, 1792;

August 5th

died: Frederick North, Lord North, statesman, 1792; Richard Howe, Earl Howe, admiral of the fleet, 1799; Charles James Blomfield, Bishop of London, 1857.

August 6th ♌

Matthew Parker Ben Jonson

born: Matthew Parker, Archbishop of Canterbury, 1504; Bulstrode Whitelock, Keeper of the Great Seal, 1605; William Hyde Wollaston, chemist and physicist, 1766.
died: Ben Jonson, dramatist, 1637; James Petit Andrews, antiquary and historian 1797.

August 7th ♌

Caroline of Brunswick Princess Amelia

born: Princess Amelia, daughter of George III, 1783; John Ayrton Paris, physician, 1785; Robert Blake, admiral, 1657.
died: Caroline of Brunswick, Queen of England, 1821.

August 8th ♌

George Canning Mme Vestris Thomas Crofton Croker

born: Francis Hutcheson, philosopher, 1694.
died: Sir Richard Worsley, antiquary, 1805; George Canning, statesman, 1827; Thomas Crofton Croker, antiquary, 1854; Mrs Charles Mathews (Mme Vestris)

August 9th ♌

born: Isaak Walton, author of
"The Compleat Angler", 1593;
John Dryden, poet, 1631; John
Oldham, poet, 1653; Thomas
Telford, engineer, 1757.
died: Simon Ockley, orientalist,
1720; Robert Potter, poet and
publisher, 1804.

Queen Elizabeth at Tilbury Fort.

During the first week of August, in the eventful year 1588, there was doubt in England whether the much-dreaded Spanish Armada would or would not enter the Thames, in its attack upon the freedom and religion of England. Both sides of the Thames were hastily fortified, especially at Gravesend and Tilbury, where a chain of boats was established across the river to bar the passage. There was a great camp at Tilbury Fort, in which more than twenty thousand troops were assembled. After having reviewed the troops assembled in London, the queen went down to encourage those encamped at Tilbury, where her energetic demeanour filled the soldiery with enthusiasm. Riding on a war-charger, wearing armour on her back, and holding a marshal's truncheon in her hand—with the Earls of Essex and Leicester holding her bridle-rein, she harangued them thus: 'My loving people, we have been persuaded by some that are careful of our safety, to take heed how we commit ourselves to armed multitudes, for fear of treachery. But I assure you I do not desire to live to distrust my faithful and loving people. Let tyrants fear! I have always so behaved myself that, under God, I have placed my chiefest strength and safeguard in the loyal hearts and good-will of my subjects; and, therefore, I have come amongst you at this time, not as for my recreation and sport, but being resolved in the midst and heat of the battle to live or die amongst you all—to lay down for my God, for my kingdom, and for my people, my honour and my blood, even in the dust. I know that I have but the body of a weak and feeble woman; but I have the heart of a king, and of a king of England too, and think foul scorn that Parma, or Spain, or any prince of Europe, should dare to invade the borders of my realm! To which, rather than any dishonour shall grow by me, I myself will take up arms, I myself will be your general, the judge and rewarder of every one of your virtues in the field. I know already by your forwardness, that you have deserved rewards and crowns; and we do assure you, on the word of a prince, they shall be duly paid you. In the meantime, my lieutenant-general shall be in my stead, than whom never prince commanded more noble or more worthy subject. Nor will I suffer myself to doubt, but that by your obedience to my general, by the concord in the camp, and your valour in the field, we shall shortly have a famous victory over those enemies of my God, my kingdom, and my people.'

On the 10th of August 1675, a commencement was made of that structure which has done more for astronomy, perhaps, than any other building in the world—Greenwich Observatory. It was one of the few good deeds that marked the public career of Charles II. In about a year the building was completed; and then the king made Flamsteed his astronomer-royal, or 'astronomical observator', of the successive astronomers-royal—Flamsteed, Halley, Bradley, Bliss, Maskelyne, Pond, and Airy—it is the province of the historians of astronomy to tell. Flamsteed laboriously collected a catalogue of nearly three thousand stars; Halley directed his attention chiefly to observations of the moon; Bradley carried the methods of minute measurements of the heavenly bodies to a degree of perfection never before equalled; Bliss confined his attention chiefly to tabulating the relative positions of sun, moon, and planets; Maskelyne was the first to measure such minute portions of time as tenths of a second, in the passage of stars across the meridian; Pond was enabled to apply the wonderful powers of Troughton's instruments to the starry heavens; while Airy's name is associated with the very highest class of observations and registration in every department of astronomy.

born: Sir Charles James Napier, conqueror of Sind, 1782.
died: Dr Benjamin Hoadly, physician, 1757; John Wilson Croker, politician and essayist, 1857

CAMERAM STELLATAM.

August 11th ♌

born: Dr Richard Mead, physician, 1673; Joseph Nollekens, sculptor, 1737; Rowland Hill, 1st Viscount Hill, general, 1772;
died: James Wilson, politician and political economist, 1860.

August 12th ♌

George IV

Robert Stewart

Robert Southey

born: George IV, King of England,
1762; Robert Southey, poet, 1774.
died: Sir Thomas Smith, statesman
scholar and author, 1577; Robert
Stewart, Marquess of Londonderry,
Viscount Castlereagh, 1822.
Hawking in Olden Time

Of all the country sports appertaining to the upper classes during the Middle Ages, hawking may be fairly considered as the most distinctively aristocratic. It was attended with great expense; its practice was overlaid with a jargon of terms, all necessary to be learned by the gentleman who would fit himself for the company of others in the field; and thus hawking, in the course of centuries, became a semi-science, to be acquired by a considerable amount of patience and study.

To be seen bearing a hawk on the hand, was to be seen in the true character of a gentleman; and the grade of the hawk-bearer was known also by the bird he bore. Thus, the gerfalcon was appropriated to a king; the falcon-gentle, to a prince; the falcon of the rock, to a duke; the peregrine-falcon, to an earl; the merlin, to a lady; and so on through the various ranks. The goshawk was permitted to the yeoman; the nobby, to a young man; while the ordinary serving-men were allowed to practise with the kestrel. Priests were permitted the sparrow-hawk, but the higher clergy were, of course, allowed to use the birds pertaining to their rank; and their love of the sport, and pride of display, are satirised by many writers of their own era.

'A knowledge of hunting and hawking was an essential requisite in accomplishing the character of a knight,' says Warton; and a gentleman rarely appeared in public without his hawk on his fist. The custom was carried to the extreme; and a satirist of the fifteenth century very properly censures such as bring their birds to church with them:

> Into the church there comes another sot,
> Without devotion strutting up and down,
> For to be seen, and shew his braided coat;
> Upon his fist sits sparrow-hawk or falcon.

This constant connection of man and bird was in some degree necessitated, that it might know its master's voice, and be sufficiently familiar with, and obedient to him. It was laid down as a rule in all old manuals of falconry, that the sportsman constantly attend to the bird, feed him, and train him daily; and very minute are the rules laid down by authors who have, like Dame Juliana Berners, written on field-sports. To part with the hawk, even in circumstances of the utmost extremity, was deemed highly ignominious.

The dress of the hawk consisted of a close-fitting hood of leather or velvet, enriched with needle-work, and surmounted with a tuft of coloured feathers, for use as well as ornament, inasmuch as they assisted the hand in removing the hood when 'the quarry' (or birds for the hawk's attack) came in sight. A series of leathern and silken straps were affixed to the legs, to train the hawk in short flights, and bring him back to hand; or to hold him there, and free him entirely for a course at the game, by means of the jesses and tyrrits or rings. Othello uses a forcible simile from the practice of hawking, when speaking of his wife, he says:

> If I do prove her haggard,
> Though that her jesses were my dear heart strings,
> I'd whistle her off, and let her down the wind,
> To prey at fortune.

A small strap, fastened with rings of leather, passed round each leg of the hawk, just above the talons; they were termed bewets, and each of them had a bell attached. In a flight of hawks, it was so arranged that the different bells varied in tone, so that 'a consort of sweet sounds' might be produced.

August 13th ♌

Queen Adelaide

born: Dr William Wotton, scholar, 1666;
Adelaide, Queen of England, 1792.
died: Dr Gilbert Stuart, historian, 1786;
Robert Plumer Ward, novelist and
historian, 1846.

August 14th ♌

Edmund Law

died: Edmund Law, Bishop of Carlisle, 1787; Thomas Sheridan, actor, 1788; George Colman, dramatist, 1794; Henry Francis Cary, translator of Dante, 1844. George Combe, phrenologist 1858

August 15th ♌

Thomas de Quincey   Walter Scott

born: William Woollett, engraver, 1735; Sir Walter Scott, poet and novelist, 1771; Thomas de Quincey, author of
died: Dr Thomas Shaw, African traveller, 1751; Thomas Tyrwhitt, classical commentator, 1786.

August 16th ♌

Frederick, Duke of York

born: Ralph Thoresby, antiquary and topographer, 1658; Catherine Cockburn, dramatist and philosophical writer, 1679; Frederick, Duke of York, son of George III, 1763.
died: Thomas Fuller, divine, 1661; Dr Matthew Tindal, deist, 1733.

August 17th ♌

born: Thomas Stothard, painter and illustrator, 1755; William Carey, orientalist and missionary, 1761.
died: Edward Pearson, theologian, 1811

August 18th ♌

Andrew Marvell   John Russell

born: Henry Hammond, divine, 1605; Brook Taylor, mathematician, 1685; John Russell, Earl Russell, prime minister, 1792.
died: Andrew Marvell, poet 1628; William Boyd, 4th Earl of Kilmarnock, Jacobite, executed, 1746; Arthur Elphinstone, 6th Baron Balmerino, Jacobite, executed, 1746; Matthew Boulton, engineer, 1809

August 19th ♌

John Flamsteed   Elizabeth, Queen of Bohemia   Martin Archer Shee

born: Elizabeth, Queen of Bohemia, 1596. John Flamsteed, astronomer royal, 184
died: Robert Bloomfield, poet, 1823; Sir Martin Archer Shee, painter, 1850.

August 20th ♌

Edward Herbert

born: Thomas Simpson, mathematician, 1710.
died: Edward Herbert, 1st Baron Herbert of Cherbury, philosopher, 1648; Sir Charles Sedley, wit and dramatist, 1701; Joseph Spence, friend of Pope, 1768; James Thomas Quekett, histologist 1861

August 21st ♌

Henrietta Maria   Mary Wortley Montague

William IV

born: William IV, King of England, 1765.
died: Sir John Leake, admiral of the fleet, 1720; Henrietta Maria, Queen of England, 1669; Lady Mary Wortley Montague, writer, 1762; William Maginn, writer, 1842.

August 22nd ♌

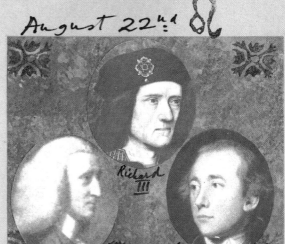

Richard III

George Lyttelton   Warren Hastings

born: Thomas Tredgold, engineer, 1788; Frank Stone, painter, 1800.
died: Richard III, King of England, 1485; Thomas Percy, 7th Earl of Northumberland, executed, 1572; George Lyttelton, Lord Lyttelton, politician, 1773; Warren Hastings, governor-general of India, 1818.

August 23rd ♌

William Warham   George Villiers

born: Rev. Rowland Hill, preacher, 1744.
died: William Warham, Archbishop of Canterbury, 1532; George Villiers, Duke of Buckingham, assassinated 1623.

August 24th ♍

Bartholomew Fair.

born: Robert Herrick, poet, (baptized) 1591; William Wilberforce, philanthropist, 1759.

died: Colonel Thomas Blood, adventurer, 1680; John Maitland, Duke of Lauderdale, 1682; John Owen, theologian, 1683; Anna Selina Storace, vocalist and actress, 1817; Theodore Hook, writer, 1841.

The great London Saturnalia—the Smithfield fair on the anniversary of St Bartholomew's Day—died a lingering death in 1855, after flourishing for seven centuries and a half. Originally established for useful trading purposes, it had long survived its claim to tolerance, and as London increased, had become a great public nuisance, with its scenes of riot and obstruction in the very heart of the city.

Hentzner, the German traveller, who visited England in 1598, tells us, 'that every year, upon St Bartholomew's Day, when the fair is held, it is usual for the mayor, attended by the twelve principal aldermen, to walk in a neighbouring field, dressed in his scarlet gown, and about his neck a golden chain.' A tent was pitched for their accommodation, and wrestling provided for their amusement. 'After this is over, a parcel of live rabbits are turned loose among the crowd, which are pursued by a number of boys, who endeavoured to catch them with all the noise they can make.' The next vivid picture of the fair we obtain from an eye-witness, shews how great was the change in its character during the progress of the reign of Elizabeth. This photograph of the fair in 1614, we obtain in Ben Jonson's comedy, which takes its title from, and is supposed to be chiefly enacted in, the precincts of the fair. There was hardly a trace now left of its old business character—it was all eating, drinking, and amusement.

In the reign of Charles II, the fair became a London carnival. The licence was extended from three to fourteen days, the theatres were closed during this time, and the actors brought to Smithfield. All classes, high and low, visited the place. Evelyn records his visit there, so does John Locke, and garrulous Pepys went often. On the 28th of August, 1667, he notes that he 'went twice round Bartholomew Fair, which I was glad to see again.' Two days afterwards, he writes: 'I went to Bartholomew Fair, to walk up and down; and there, among other things, find my Lady Castlemaine at a puppet-play (*Patient Grisel*), and a street full of people expecting her coming out.' This infamous woman divided her affections between the king, Charles II, and Jacob Hall, the rope-dancer, who was a great favourite at the fair, and salaried by her ladyship. In 1668, Pepys again notes two visits he paid to the fair, in company with Lord Brouncker and others, to see 'The mare that tells money, and many things to admiration—and then the dancing of the ropes, and also the little stage-play, which is very ridiculous.'

Virgo - the virgin of Mercury, and his signification, nature and property

August 24 to September 23

Manners when well placed

Being well dignified, he represents a man of a subtill and politick braine, intellect, and cogitation; an excellent disputant or Logician, arguing with learning and discretion, and using much eloquence in his speech, a searcher into all kinds of Mysteries and Learning, sharp and witty, learning almost anything without a Teacher; ambitious of being exquisite in every Science, desirous naturally of travell and seeing foraign parts: a man of an unwearied fancie, curious in the search of any occult knowledge; able by his owne *Genius* to produce wonders; given to Divination and the more secret knowledge; if he turne Merchant no man exceeds him in way of Trade or invention of new ways whereby to obtain wealth.

Manners when ill placed or dignified

A troublesome wit, a kinde of Phrenetick man, his tongue and Pen against every man, wholly bent to foole his estate and time in prating and trying nice conclusions to no purpose; a great lyar, boaster, pratler, busybody, false, a tale-carrier, given to wicked Arts, as Necromancy, and such like ungodly knowledges; easie of beleefe, an asse or very ideot, constant in no place or opinion, cheating and theeving every where; a newes-monger, pretending all manner of knowledge, but guilty of no true or solid learning; a trifler; a meere frantick fellow; if he prove a Divine, then a meer verball fellow, frothy, of no judgement, easily perverted, constant in nothing but idle words and bragging.

August 25ᵗʰ ♍

(portraits: William Herschel, James Watt, George Eden, David Hume)

born: George Eden, Earl of Auckland, governor general of India, 1784.
died: Thomas Chatterton, poet, 1770; David Hume, historian, 1776; James Watt, engineer, 1819; Sir William Herschel, astronomer, 1822.

August 26ᵗʰ ♍

(portraits: Robert Walpole, George Sackville, Albert Prince consort)

born: Robert Walpole, 1ˢᵗ Earl of Orford, statesman, 1676; Albert, Prince consort, 1819.
died: Lord George Sackville, 1ˢᵗ Viscount Sackville, 1785.

August 27ᵗʰ ♍

(portrait: James Thomson)

died: James Thomson, poet, 1748.
Louisa Brunton, Countess Craven, actress, 1860.

August 28ᵗʰ ♍

(portraits: James Henry Leigh Hunt, George Villiers)

born: George Villiers, 1ˢᵗ Duke of Buckingham, favourite 1592
died: Sir Francis Vere, general, 1609, Charles Boyle, 4ᵗʰ Earl of Orrery, 1731; John Hutchinson, author, 1737; James Henry Leigh Hunt, essayist, critic and poet, 1859

The Eglinton Tournament.

It was an idea not unworthy of a young nobleman of ancient lineage and ample possessions, to set forth a living picture, as it were, of the medieval tournament before the eyes of a modern generation. When the public learned that such an idea had occurred to the Earl of Eglinton, and that it was to be carried out in the beautiful park surrounding his castle in Ayrshire, it felt as if a new pleasure had been at length invented. And, undoubtedly, if only good weather could have been secured, the result could not have fallen short of the expectations which were formed.

Nearly two years were spent in making the necessary preparations, and on the 28th of August 1839, the proceedings commenced in the presence of an immense concourse of spectators, many of whom, in obedience to a hint previously given, had come in fancy-costumes. The spot chosen for the tourney was about a quarter of a mile eastward of the castle, surrounded by beautiful scenery; it comprised an arena of four acres, with a boarded fence all round. At convenient places, were galleries to hold 3000 persons, one for private friends of the earl and the knights who were to take part in the mimic contest, and the other for visitors of a less privileged kind. In the middle of the arena were barriers to regulate the jousts of the combatants. Each of the knights had a separate marquee or pavilion for himself and his attendants. The decorations everywhere were of the most costly character, being aided by many trappings which had recently been used at the Queen's coronation. Besides keeping 'open house' at the castle, the earl provided two temporary saloons, each 250 feet long, for banquets and balls. But the weather was unfavourable to the 'brave knights'; the rain fell heavily; spectators marred the medievalism of the scene by hoisting umbrellas; and the 'Queen of Beauty' and her ladies, who were to have ridden on elegantly-caparisoned palfreys, were forced to take refuge in carriages.

Some of the dresses were exceedingly gorgeous. The Marquis of Londonderry, as 'King of the Tournament', wore a magnificent train of green velvet, embroidered with gold, covered by a crimson-velvet cloak trimmed with gold and ermine, and having a crown covered in with crimson velvet; the Earl of Eglinton, as 'Lord of the Tournament', had a rich damasked suit of gilt armour, with a skirt of chain-mail; and Sir Charles Lamb, as 'Knight Marshal', had a suit of black armour, embossed and gilt, and covered by a richly-emblazoned surcoat. The esquires and pages were all gentlemen of fortune and position. Lady Seymour, as 'Queen of Beauty', wore a robe of crimson velvet, with the Seymour crest embroidered in silver on blue velvet, and a cloak of cerise velvet trimmed with gold and ermine. The ladies in the chief gallery were mostly attired in the costumes of the fourteenth and fifteenth centuries.

In every sense was the day's joyousness damped; for when the guests were quite ready for a grand banquet and ball in the evening, it was found that the two temporary pavilions, fitted up in the most splendid manner, were flooded with water from the heavy rains, and were quite useless for the purposes intended. On the 29th, the weather was nearly as bad. On the 30th, the skies were more favourable; the joustings were renewed, and were wound up by a tourney of eight knights armed with swords—used in some inoffensive way against each other's armour. Measures had been taken to render the banqueting-hall and ball-room available, and the day ended with a banquet for 300 persons and a ball for 1000. The 31st came, and with it weather so stormy and ungenial that any further proceedings with the tournament were abandoned. And thus ended this most costly affair.

August 29ᵗʰ ♍

William Brockedon

John Locke

Joseph Wright

born: John Locke, philosopher, 1632.
died: John Lilburne, political
agitator, 1657; Edmond Hoyle,
writer on card games, 1769;
Joseph Wright of Derby, painter,
1769; William Brockedon, painter,
1854.

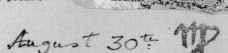

John Bunyan's
Meeting-House
in Zoar Street.

August 30ᵗʰ ♍

Mary Wollstonecraft Shelley

John Ross

born: Mary Wollstonecraft Shelley,
authoress, 1753.
died: Sir John Ross, Arctic
navigator, 1856; John Francis,
sculptor, 1861.

August 31ˢᵗ ♍

Henry V

John Bunyan

died: Henry V, King of England,
1422; John Bunyan, author
of the "Pilgrim's Progress", 1688;
William Borlase, antiquary, 1772;
Dr James Currie, physician, 1805;
Sir John Thomas Duckworth,
admiral, 1817.

JOHN · BVNYAN · JO

Everybody has heard of his birth at Elstow, about a mile from Bedford, in 1628; that he was bred a tinker; that his childhood was afflicted with remorse and dreams of fiends flying away with him; that, as he grew up, he 'danced, rang church-bells, played at tip-cat, and read *Sir Bevis of Southampton*', for which he suffered many stings of conscience; that his indulgence in profanity was such, that a woman of loose character told him 'he was the ungodliest fellow for swearing she had ever heard in all her life,' and that 'he made her tremble to hear him'; that he entered the Parliamentary army, and served against the king in the decisive campaign of 1645; that, after terrible mental conflicts, he became converted, a Baptist, and a preacher; that at the Restoration in 1660 he was cast into Bedford jail, where, with intervals of precarious liberty, he remained for twelve years, refusing to be set at large on the condition of silence, with the brave answer: 'If you let me out to-day, I'll preach again to-morrow'; that, on his release, the fame of his writings, and his ability as a speaker, drew about him large audiences in London and elsewhere, and that, a few months before the Revolution of 1688, he caught a fever in consequence of a long ride from Reading in the rain, and died at the house of his friend, Mr Strudwick, a grocer at the sign of the Star, on Snowhill, London.

Bunyan was buried in Bunhill Fields, called by Southey, 'the Campo Santo of the Dissenters'. There sleep Dr John Owen and Dr Thomas Goodwin, Cromwell's preachers; George Fox, the Quaker; Daniel Defoe, Dr Isaac Watts, Susannah Wesley, the mother of the Wesleys; Ritson, the antiquary; William Blake, the visionary poet and painter; Thomas Stothard, and a host of others of greater or lesser fame in their separate sects. A monument, with a recumbent statue of Bunyan, was erected over his grave in 1862.

'It is a significant fact,' observes Macaulay, 'that, till a recent period, all the numerous editions of the *Pilgrim's Progress* were evidently meant for the cottage and the servants' hall. The paper, the printing, the plates were of the meanest description. In general, when the educated minority differs [with the uneducated majority] about the merit of a book, the opinion of the educated minority finally prevails. The *Pilgrim's Progress* is perhaps the only book about which, after the lapse of a hundred years, the educated minority has come over to the opinion of the common people.'

September

Harvest awakes the morning still,
And toil's rude groups the valleys fill;
Deserted is each cottage hearth
To all life, save the cricket's mirth;
Each burring wheel its sabbeth meets,
Nor walks a gossip in the streets;
The bench beneath the eldern bough,
Lined o'er with grass, is empty now,
Where blackbirds, caged from out of the sun,
Would whistle while their mistress spun:
All haunt the thronged fields, to share
The harvest's lingering bounty there.

Anon the fields are getting clear,
And glad sounds hum in labour's ear;
When children halloo, 'Here they come!'
And run to meet the Harvest Home,
Covered with boughs, and thronged with
        boys,
Who mingle loud a merry noise,
And, when they meet the stacked-thronged
        yard
Cross-buns and pence their shouts reward.
Then comes the harvest-supper night,
Which rustics welcome with delight;
When merry game and tiresome tale,
And songs, increasing with the ale,
Their mingled uproar interpose,
To crown the harvest's happy close;
While Mirth, that at the scene abides,
Laughs, till she almost cracks her sides.

Thus harvest ends its busy reign,
And leaves the fields their peace again,
Where autumn's shadows idly muse
And tinge the trees in many hues:
Amid whose scenes I'm fain to dwell,
And sing of what I love so well.
But hollow winds, and tumbling floods,
And humming showers, and moaning woods,
All startle into sadden strife,
And wake a mighty lay to life,
Making, amid their strains divine,
Unheard a song so mean as mine.

JOHN CLARE

Next him September marched eke on foot,
    Yet he was hoary, laden with the spoil
Of harvest riches, which he made his boot,
    And him enriched with bounty of the soil;
    In his one hand, as fit for harvest's toil,
He held a knife-hook; and in th'other hand
    A pair of weights, with which he did assoil
Both more and less, where it in doubt did stand,
And equal gave to each as justice duly scanned.

SPENSER

SEPTEMBER

When the year began in March, this was the seventh of its months; consequently, was properly termed September. By the commencement of the year two months earlier, the name is now become inappropriate, as is likewise the case with its three followers—October, November and December. When Julius Caesar reformed the calendar, he gave this month a 31st day, which Augustus subsequently took from it; and it has since remained. Our Saxon ancestors called it *Gerst monath*, or barley month, because they then realised this crop; one of unusual importance to them, on account of the favourite beverage which they brewed from it.

On the 23rd, the sun enters the constellation Libra, and passes to the southward of the equator, thus producing the autumnal equinox: a period usually followed by a course of stormy weather. September, however, is often with us a month of steady and pleasant weather, notwithstanding that in the mornings and evenings the first chills of winter begin to be felt.

September 1st ♍

Richard Steele   Margaret, Countess of Blessington

born: Edward Alleyn, actor, 1566;
Margaret, Countess of Blessington,
authoress, 1789.
died: Henry More, theologian, 1687;
Sir Richard Steele, essayist, 1729;
William Yarrell, zoologist, 1856

September 2nd
born: John Howard, philanthropist,
1726.
died: Alice Lisle, victim of
judicial murder, 1685; John
Ireland, Dean of Westminster,
1842.
The Great Fire of London.

London was only a few months freed from a
desolating pestilence, it was suffering, with the
country generally, under a most imprudent and
ill-conducted war with Holland, when, on the
evening of the 2nd of September 1666, a fire
commenced by which about two-thirds of it were
burned down, including the cathedral, the Royal
Exchange, about a hundred parish churches, and a
vast number of other public buildings. The conflagration commenced in the house of a baker named
Farryner, at Pudding Lane, near the Tower, and,
being favoured by a high wind, it continued for three
nights and days, spreading gradually eastward, till it
ended at a spot called Pye Corner, in Giltspur Street.
Mr John Evelyn has left us a very interesting
description of the event, from his own observation, as
follows:

Old St Paul's after
the Great Fire.

'Sept. 2 1666—This fatal night, about ten, began
that deplorable fire near Fish Streete in London.
'Sept. 3—The fire continuing, after dinner I took
coach with my wife and sonn, and went to the Bank-
side in Southwark, where we beheld that dismal
spectacle, the whole Citty in dreadful flames neare ye
water side; all the houses from the Bridge, all
Thames Street, and upwards towards Cheapeside
downe to the Three Cranes, were now consum'd.
'The fire having continu'd all this night (if I may
call that night which was as light as day for ten miles
round about, after a dreadful manner) when conspir-
ing with a fierce eastern wind in a very drie season; I
went on foote to the same place, and saw the whole
South part of ye Citty burning from Cheapeside to ye
Thames, and all along Cornehill (for it kindl'd back
against ye wind as well as forward), Tower Streete,
Fenchurch Streete, Gracious Streete, and so along to
Bainard's Castle, and was now taking hold of St
Paule's Church, to which the scaffolds contributed
exceedingly. The conflagration was so universal, and
the people so astonish'd, that from the beginning, I
know not by what despondency or fate, they hardly
stirr'd to quench it, so that there was nothing heard
or seene but crying out and lamentation, running
about like distracted creatures, without at all
attempting to save even their goods, such a strange
consternation there was upon them, so as it burned
both in breadth and length, the Churches, Publiq
Halls, Exchange, Hospitals, Monuments, and ornaments, leaping after a prodigious manner from house
to house and streete to streete, at greate distances one
from ye other; for ye heate with a long set of faire and
warme weather, had even ignited the air, and
prepar'd the materials to conceive the fire, which
devour'd after an incredible manner, houses, furniture, and every thing. Here we saw the Thames
cover'd with goods floating, all the barges and boates
laden with what some had time and courage to save,
as, on ye other, ye carts, &c., carrying out to the
fields, which for many miles were strew'd with
moveables of all sorts, and tents erecting to shelter
both people and what goods they could get away. Oh
the miserable and calamitous spectacle! such as haply
the world had not seene the like since the foundation
of it, nor to be outdone till the universal conflagration. All the skie was of a fiery aspect, like the
top of a burning oven, the light seene above forty
miles round about for many nights. God grant my

eyes may never behold the like, now seeing above 10,000 houses all in one flame; the noise and cracking and thunder of the impetuous flames, ye shrieking of women and children, the hurry of people, the fall of Towers, Houses, and Churches, was like an hideous storme, and the aire all about so hot and inflam'd that at last one was not able to approach it, so that they were forc'd to stand still and let ye flames burn on, wch they did for neere two miles in length and one in bredth. The clouds of smoke were dismall, and reach'd upon computation neer fifty miles in length. Thus I left it this afternoone burning, a resemblance of Sodom, or the last day. London was, but is no more!

'Sept. 7—I went this morning on foote from Whitehall as far as London Bridge, thro' the late Fleete Streete, Ludgate Hill, by St Paules, Cheapeside, Exchange, Bishopsgate, Aldersgate, and out to Moorefields, thence thro' Cornehille, &c., with extraordinary difficulty, clambering over heaps of yet smoking rubbish, and frequently mistaking where I was. The ground under my feete was so hot, that it even burnt the soles of my shoes ... At my return I was infinitely concern'd to find that goodly Church St Paules now a sad ruine, and that beautifull portico (for structure comparable to any in Europe, as not long before repair'd by the King) now rent in pieces, flakes of vast stone split asunder, and nothing remaining intire but the inscription in the architrave, shewing by whom it was built, which had not one letter of it defac'd. It was astonishing to see what immense stones the heat had in a manner calcin'd, so that all ye ornaments, columns, freezes, and projectures of massie Portland stone flew off ... The lead, yron worke, bells, plate, &c. mealted; the exquisitely wrought Mercers Chapell, the sumptuous Exchange, ye august fabriq of Christ Church, all ye rest of the Companies Halls, sumptuous buildings, arches, all in dust; the fountaines dried up and ruin'd whilst the very waters remain'd boiling; the vorrago's of subterranean cellars, wells, and dungeons, formerly warehouses, still burning in stench and dark clouds of smoke, so that in five or six miles traversing about I did not see one load of timber unconsum'd, nor many stones but what were calcin'd white as snow. The people who now walk'd about ye ruines appear'd like men in a dismal desart, or rather in some great citty laid waste by a cruel enemy; to which was added the stench that came from some poore creatures bodies, beds, &c. Sir Tho. Gresham's statue, tho' fallen from its nich in the Royal Exchange, remain'd intire, when all those of ye Kings since ye Conquest were broken to pieces, also the standard in Cornehill, and Q. Elizabeth's effigies, with some armes on Ludgate, continued with but little detriment, whilst the vast yron chaines of the Cittie streetes, hinges, bars and gates of prisons, were many of them mealted and reduced to cinders by ye vehement heate. I was not able to passe through any of the narrow streetes, but kept the widest, the ground and aire, smoake and fiery vapour, continu'd so intense that my haire was almost sing'd, and my feete unsufferably surheated. The bie lanes and narrower streetes were quite fill'd up with rubbish, nor could one have knowne where he was, but by ye ruines of some Church or Hall, that had some remarkable tower or pinnacle remaining. I then went towards Islington and Highgate, where

one might have seene 200,000 people of all ranks and degrees dispers'd and lying along by their heapes of what they could save from the fire, deploring their losse, and tho' ready to perish for hunger and destitution, yet not asking one penny for relief, which to me appear'd a stranger sight than any I had yet beheld.'

September 3ʳᵈ ♍

born: Matthew Bolton, engineer 1728.
died; Sir Edward Coke, Judge and law writer, 1634; Oliver Cromwell, Lord Protector, 1658, George Lillo, dramatist, 1739; George Richardson Porter, statician, 1852.

September 4ᵗʰ ♍

died: Matthew Stewart, 4ᵗʰ Earl of Lennox, Regent of Scotland, 1571; Robert Dudley, Earl of Leicester, favourite of Elizabeth I, 1588; Charles Townshend, chancellor of the exchequer, 1767; James Wyatt, architect, 1813; William Macgillivray, naturalist, 1852.

September 5th ♍

Richard Tarleton

born: Robert Fergusson, poet, 1750;
Dr John Dalton, chemist and
natural philosopher, 1766.
died: Edmund Bonner, Bishop of
London, 1569; John James Heidegger,
manager of Opera, 1749;
Richard Tarleton, actor, 1588.

September 6th ♍

James
II
Edmund Gibson   John Bird Sumner

died: James II, King of England, 1701;
Edmund Gibson, Bishop of London, 1748;
John Bird Sumner, Archbishop of
Canterbury, 1862.
The Stratford Jubilee, or Shakespeare
commemoration Festival 1779.

On the morning of Wednesday, at five o'clock, the
proceedings were inaugurated by a serenade performed through the streets by a band of musicians and
singers from Drury Lane Theatre. Several guns were
then fired, and the magistrates assembled about eight
o'clock in one of the principal streets. A public
breakfast was prepared in the new town-hall at nine,
presided over by Mr Garrick as steward, who,
previous to the reception of the general company,
was formally waited on by the mayor and corporation
of Stratford, and presented with a medallion of
Shakespeare, carved on a piece of the famous
mulberry-tree, and richly set in gold. At breakfast,

favours in honour of the great dramatist were
universally worn by ladies as well as gentlemen, and
the assemblage numbered the most distinguished of
the aristocracy amid its guests. This entertainment
having been concluded, the company proceeded to
the church, where the oratorio of *Judith* was
performed under the superintendence of Dr Arne. A
procession, with music, led by Mr Garrick, was then
formed from the church to the amphitheatre, a
wooden building erected for the occasion on the bank
of the Avon, constructed after the manner of the
Rotunda at Ranelagh, in the form of an octagon, with
a roof supported by eight pillars, and elegantly
painted and gilded. Here dinner was served up at
three o'clock, and a suitable interval having elapsed a
musical performance took place, at which several
songs, chiefly written by Garrick, were received with
the greatest applause by the audience.

A grand ball commenced in the amphitheatre in
the evening, and was kept up till three o'clock next
morning. In front of the building, an ambitious
transparency was exhibited, representing Time
leading Shakspeare to immortality, with Tragedy on
one side, and Comedy on the other. A general
illumination took place in the town, along with a
brilliant display of fireworks, under the management
of Mr Angelo. The next morning was ushered in like
the former by firing of cannon, serenading, and
ringing of bells. A public breakfast was again served
in the town-hall, and at eleven o'clock the company
repaired to the amphitheatre, to hear performed
Garrick's *Shakespeare Ode*, which he had composed
for the dedication of the town-hall, and placing there
a statue of the great bard presented by Garrick to the
corporation.

The remainder of Thursday was, like the previous
day, spent in dining, listening to a concert, and
witnessing illuminations and fireworks. At midnight commenced a grand masquerade, said to have
been one of the finest entertainments of the kind
ever witnessed in Britain. Three ladies, we are informed, who personated Macbeth's witches, and
another, who appeared as Dame Quickly, excited
universal admiration. An Oxford gentleman assumed, with great effect, the character of Lord
Ogleby; but a person dressed as the Devil gave
inexpressible offence! One individual, whose costume attracted special attention, was James Boswell
in the character of an armed chief of Corsica, an
island of which he had published an account, and
regarding which he had, as his countrymen in the
north would say, 'a bee in his bonnet'.

Mr Garrick, reciting the Ode, in honour
Shakespeare at the jubilee.

On the masquerade revellers awaking from their slumbers on the following day (Friday), they found a deluge of rain, which had continued unintermittedly from the previous night, descending on the town of Stratford. All prospect, therefore, of carrying out the proposed Shakspeare pageant, in which the principal characters in his plays were to have been represented in a triumphal procession, *al fresco*, with chariots, banners, and all proper adjuncts, was rendered hopeless. There was, however, a jubilee horse-race, which was well attended, though the animals were up to their knees in water. In the evening another grand ball took place in the town-hall, in which the graceful minuet-dancing of Mrs Garrick, who in her youth had been a distinguished Terpsichorean performer on the London stage, won the highest encomiums. The assembly broke up at four o'clock on Saturday morning, and so ended the Stratford jubilee.

September 7th ♍

born: Elizabeth I, Queen of England, 1533.
died: Catherine Parr, Queen of England, 1548; Captain John Porteous, murdered, 1736; Hannah More, religious writer, 1833.

Old sayings as to clothes.

It is lucky to put on any article of dress, particularly stockings, inside out: but if you wish the omen to hold good, you must continue to wear the reversed portion of your attire in that condition, till the regular time comes for putting it off—that is, either bedtime or 'changing yourself'. If you set it right, you will 'change the luck'. It will be of no use to put on anything with the wrong side out *on purpose*.

The clothes of the dead will never wear long. When a person dies, and his or her clothes are given away to the poor, it is frequently remarked: 'Ah, they may look very well, but they won't wear; they belong to the dead.'

If a mother gives away *all* the baby's clothes she has (or the cradle), she will be sure to have another baby, though she may have thought herself above such vanities.

If a girl's petticoats are longer than her frock, that is a sign that her father loves her better than her mother does—perhaps because it is plain that her mother does not attend so much to her dress as she ought to do, whereas her father may love her as much as you please, and at the same time be very ignorant or unobservant of the rights and wrongs of female attire.

If you would have good-luck, you must wear something new on 'Whitsun-Sunday' (pronounced Wissun-Sunday). More generally, Easter Day is the one thus honoured, but a glance round a church or Sunday-school in Suffolk, on Whitsunday, shews very plainly that it is the one chosen for beginning to wear new 'things'.

While upon the subject of clothes, I may mention a ludicrous Suffolk phrase descriptive of a person not quite so sharp as he might be: he is spoken of as 'short of buttons', being, I suppose, considered an unfinished article.

September 8th ♍

born: John Leyden, physician and poet, 1775.
died: Princess Elizabeth, daughter of Charles I, 1650; Joseph Hall, Bishop of Norwich, 1656

September 9th ♍

died: James IV, King of Scotland, 1513; Robert Wood, traveller, 1771; Gilbert Wakefield, scholar, 1801.

September 10th ♍

John Soane

born: Sir John Soane, architect,
1753; Mungo Park, African
explorer, 1771.
died: Edward Pococke, orientalist,
1691.

September 11th ♍

James Harrington

born: Arthur Young, agriculturalist,
1741.
died: James Harrington, political
theorist, 1677; David Ricardo,
economist, 1823; Captain Basil
Hall, author, 1844.

September 12th ♍

William Dugdale

born: Sir William Dugdale, Garter
King-of-arms, 1605.
died: Griffith Jones, writer, 1786;

September 13th ♍

John Cheke   William Cecil

Charles James Fox   James Wolfe

born: William Cecil, Lord Burghley,
minister of state, 1520.
died: Sir John Cheke, tutor to Edward VI,
1557; James Wolfe, major-general, 1759;
Charles James Fox, statesman, 1806.

The death of General Wolfe.

September 14th ♍

Arthur Wellesley   James Stephen

born: Browne Willis, antiquary, 1682;
Lord William Cavendish Bentinck,
governor-general of India, 1774.
died: Robert Devereux, 3rd Earl of
Essex, 1646; Arthur Wellesley, 1st
Duke of Wellington, 1852; Augustus
W.N. Pugin, architect, 1852; James
Stephen, colonial under-secretary, 1859.

The Duke of Wellington.

On the 14th of September 1852, died Arthur, Duke of Wellington, the most illustrious Englishman of his time, at the age of eighty-three. He had performed the highest services to his country, and indeed to Europe, and the honours he had consequently received were such as would tire even a Spaniard. While so much honoured, the duke was a man of such simplicity of nature, that he never appeared in the slightest degree uplifted. His leading idea in life was the duty he owed to his country and its government, and with the performance of *that* he always appeared perfectly satisfied. He was the *truest* of men, and even in the dispatches and bulletins which he had occasion to compose amidst the excitements of victory, there is never to be traced a feeling in the slightest degree allied to vapouring or even self-complacency. It was not in respect of stricken fields alone, that he proved himself the superior of Napoleon. He was his superior in every moral attribute.

The death of this eminently great man was the result of natural decay, taking finally the form of a fit of epilepsy. He was interred with the highest public honours in St Pauls Cathedral.

September 15th

Richard Boyle

William Huskisson

I. K. Brunel

died: Richard Boyle, Earl of Cork, "the great earl", 1643; Sidney Godolphin, 1st Earl of Godolphin, 1712; William Huskisson, statesman, 1830; I. K. Brunel, civil engineer, 1859.

September 16th

Thomas Overbury

Allen Bathurst

died: Sir Thomas Overbury, poet, poisoned, 1613; Allen Bathurst, 1st Earl Bathurst, statesman, 1775.

September 17th

Tobias Smollett

Samuel Prout

born: Samuel Prout, painter, 1783.
died: Tobias Smollett, novelist, 1771;
Dr. John Kidd, physician, 1851.

September 18th ♍

Matthew Prior
Samuel Johnson
Gilbert Burnet
William Hazlitt

born: Gilbert Burnet, Bishop of
Salisbury, 1643; Dr Samuel Johnson,
lexicographer, 1709.
died: Matthew Prior, poet, 1721;
William Hazlitt, essayist, 1830;
Joseph Locke, civil engineer, 1860.

September 19th ♍

Prince Arthur

born: Prince Arthur, eldest son of
Henry VII, 1486; William Kirby,
entomologist, 1759; Henry Brougham,
Baron Brougham and Vaux, 1778.
died: Charles Edward Poulett
Thomson, baron Sydenham,
Governor general of Canada, 1841

The Battle of Poitiers.

On 19th September 1356, the second great battle fought by the English on French soil, in assertion of their chimerical claim to the crown of that country, was won by the Black Prince, in the face, as at Crécy, of an overwhelming superiority of numbers. Whilst the army of the French king mustered sixty thousand horse alone, besides foot soldiers, the whole force of Edward, horse and foot together, did not exceed ten thousand men.

The attack was commenced by the French, a body of whose cavalry came charging down a narrow lane with the view of dislodging the English from their position; but they encountered such a galling fire from the archers posted behind the hedges, that they turned and fled in dismay. It was now Edward's turn to assail, and six hundred of his bowmen suddenly appeared on the flank and rear of John's second division, which was thrown into irretrievable confusion by the discharge of arrows. The English knights, with the prince at their head, next charged across the open plain upon the main body of the French army. A division of cavalry, under the Constable of France, for a time stood firm, but ere long was broken and dispersed, their leader and most of his knights being slain. A body of reserve, under the Duke of Orleans, fled shamefully without striking a blow.

King John did his best to turn the fortune of the day, and, accompanied by his youngest son, Philip, a boy of sixteen, who fought by his side, he led up on foot a division of troops to the encounter. After having received two wounds in the face, and been thrown to the ground, he rose, and for a time defended himself manfully with his battle-axe against the crowd of assailants by whom he was surrounded. The brave monarch would certainly have been slain had not a French knight, named Sir Denis, who had been banished for killing a man in a fray, and in consequence joined the English service, burst through the press of combatants, and exclaimed to John in French: 'Sire, surrender.' The king, who now felt that his position was desperate, replied: 'To whom shall I surrender? Where is my cousin, the Prince of Wales?' 'He is not here,' answered Sir Denis; 'but surrender to me, and I will conduct you to him.' 'But who are you?' rejoined the king. 'Denis de Morbecque,' was the reply; 'a knight of Artois; but I serve the king of England because I cannot belong to France, having forfeited all I had there.' 'I surrender to you,' said John, extending his right-hand glove; but this submission was almost too late to save his life, for the English were disputing with Sir Denis and the Gascons the honour of his capture, and the French king was in the utmost danger from their violence. At last, Earl Warwick and Lord Cobham came up, and with every demonstration of respect conducted John and his son Philip to the Black Prince, who received them with the utmost courtesy. He invited them to supper, waited himself at table on John, as his superior in age and rank, praised his valour and endeavoured by every means in his power to diminish the humiliation of the royal captive.

The Great Plague of London.

The week ending the 19th of September 1665, was that in which this memorable calamity reached its greatest destructiveness. It was on the 26th of the previous April that the first official notice announcing that the plague had established itself in the parish of St Giles-in-the-Fields, appeared in the form of an order of council, directing the precautions to be taken to arrest its progress. The evil had at this time been gradually gaining head during several weeks. Vague suspicions of danger had existed during the latter part of the previous year, and serious alarm was felt, which however gradually abated. But the suspicions proved to be too true; the infection, believed to have been brought over from Holland, had established itself in the parish of St Giles, remained concealed during the winter, and began to shew itself in that and the adjoining parishes at the approach of spring, by the increase in their usual bills of mortality. At the date of the order of council just alluded to, there could be no longer any doubt that the parishes of St Giles, St Andrews, Holborn, and one or two others adjoining, were infected by the plague.

During the months of May and June, the infection spread in spite of all the precautions to arrest its progress, but, towards the end of the latter month, the general alarm was increased by the certainty that it had not only spread into the other parishes outside the walls, but that several fatal cases had occurred in the city. People now began to hurry out of town in great numbers, while it was yet easy to escape, for as soon as the infection had become general, the strictest measures were enforced to prevent any of the inhabitants leaving London, lest they might communicate the dreadful pestilence.

The alarm in London was increased when, in July, the king with the court also fled, and took refuge in Salisbury, leaving the care of the capital to the Duke of Albemarle. The circumstance of the summer being unusually hot and calm, nourished and increased the disease. An extract or two from Defoe's narrative will give the best notion of the internal state of London at this melancholy period. Speaking of the month in which the court departed for Salisbury, he tells us that already 'the face of London was strangely altered—I mean the whole mass of buildings, city, liberties, suburbs, Westminster, Southwark, and altogether; for, as to the particular part called the City, or within the walls, that was not yet much infected; but, in the whole, the face of things, I say, was much altered; sorrow and sadness sat upon every face, and though some parts were not yet overwhelmed, yet all looked deeply concerned, and as we saw it apparently coming on, so every one looked on himself and his family as in the utmost danger: were it possible to represent those times exactly, to those that did not see them, and give the reader due ideas of the horror that everywhere presented itself, it must make just impressions upon their minds, and fill them with surprise. London might well be said to be all in tears; the mourners did not go about the streets indeed, for nobody put on black, or made a formal dress of mourning for their nearest friends; but the voice of mourning was truly heard in the streets; the shrieks of women and children at the windows and doors of their houses, where their nearest relations were perhaps dying, or just dead, were so frequent to be heard, as we passed the streets, that it was enough to pierce the stoutest heart in the world to hear them.

Tears and lamentations were seen almost in every house, especially in the first part of the visitation; for towards the latter end, men's hearts were hardened, and death was so always before their eyes, that they did not so much concern themselves for the loss of their friends, expecting that themselves should be summoned the next hour.'

September 20th ♍

Lucius Cary   John Garden

died: Lucius Cary, 2nd Viscount Falkland, royalist, 1643. John Garden, Bishop of Worcester, 1662; William Hutton, topographer, 1815; William Finden, engraver, 1852

September 21st ♍

Edward II

died: Edward II, King of England, 1327; Col. James Gardiner, of dragoons, 1745; John Balguy, divine, 1748.

Princess Augusta

Philip Dormer Stanhope

Theodore Edward Hook

born: Richard Busby, headmaster of Westminster School, 1606; Philip Dormer Stanhope, 4th Earl of Chesterfield, politician, wit and letter writer, 1694; Theodore Edward Hook, novelist and writer 1788.
died: Princess Augusta of England, daughter of George III, 1840.

The Battle of Zutphen.

It was in this skirmish that the gallant and lamented Sir Philip Sidney, the boast of his age, and the hope of many admiring friends, received the fatal wound which cut short the thread of a brief but brilliant existence. During the whole day he had been one of the foremost in action, and once rushed to the assistance of his friend, Lord Willoughby, on observing him 'nearly surrounded by the enemy', and in imminent peril: after seeing him in safety, he continued the combat with great spirit, until he received a shot in the thigh, as he was remounting a second horse, the first having been killed under him.

John Jewel

born: Jeremy Collier, non-juror, 1650.
died: John Jewel, Bishop of Salisbury, 1571; Matthew Baillie, morbid anatomist, 1823; Joseph Ritson, antiquary, 1803; William Upcott, antiquary, 1845; Edward Wedlake Brayley, topographer and archaeologist, 1854.

Henry Hardinge

born: Sharon Turner, historian, 1768.
died: Henry Hardinge, 1st Viscount Hardinge, field Marshal, 1856

The Feast of Ingathering

Wherever, throughout the earth, there is such a thing as a formal harvest, there also appears an inclination to mark it with a festive celebration. In England, this festival passes generally under the endeared name of *Harvest-Home*. In Scotland, where that term is unknown, the festival is hailed under the name of the *Kirn*. In the north of England, its ordinary designation is the *Mell-Supper*. And there are perhaps other local names. But everywhere there is a thankful joy, a feeling which pervades all ranks and conditions of the rural people, and for once in the year brings all upon a level.

Most of our old harvest-customs were connected with the ingathering of the crops, but some of them began with the commencement of harvest-work. Thus, in the southern counties, it was customary for the labourers to elect, from among themselves, a leader, whom they denominated their 'lord'. To him all the rest were required to give precedence, and to leave all transactions respecting their work. He made the terms with the farmers for mowing, for reaping, and for all the rest of the harvest-work; he took the lead with the scythe, with the sickle, and on the 'carrying days'; he was to be the first to eat and the first to drink, at all their refreshments; his mandate

Libra -the scales of the planet Venus and her severall significations and nature

September 24 to October 23

Manners and quality when well placed.

Shee signifies a quiet man, not given to Law, Quarrel or Wrangling; not Vitious, Pleasant, Neat and Spruce, Loving Mirth in his words and actions, cleanly in Apparel, rather Drinking much than Gluttonous, prone to Venery, oft entangled in love-matters, Zealous in their affections, Musicall, delighting in Baths, and all honest merry Meetings, or Maskes and Stage-playes, easie of Beliefe, and not given to Labour, or take any Pains, a Company keeper, Cheerful, nothing Mistrustful, a right vertuous Man or Woman, oft had in some Jealousie, yet no cause for it.

When ill

Then he is Riotous, Expensive, wholly given to Loosenesse and Lewd companies of Women, nothing regarding his Reputation, coveting unlawful Beds, Incestuous, an Adulterer, Fantastical, a meer Skip-jack, of no Faith, no Repute, no Credit; spending his Meanes in Ale Houses, Taverns, and amongst Scandalous, Loose people; a meer Lazy companion, nothing careful of the things of this Life, or any thing Religious; a meer Atheist and natural man.

was to be law to all the rest, who were bound to address him as 'My Lord', and to shew him all due honour and respect. Disobedience in any of these particulars was punished by imposing fines according to a scale previously agreed on by 'the lord' and all his vassals. In some instances, if any of his men swore or told a lie in his presence, a fine was inflicted. In Buckinghamshire and other counties, 'a lady' was elected as well as 'a lord', which often added much merriment to the harvest-season. For, while the lady was to receive all honours due to the lord from the rest of the labourers, he (for the lady was one of the workmen) was required to pass it on to the lord. For instance, at drinking-time, the vassals were to give the horn first to the lady, who passed it to the lord, and when he had drunk, *she* drank next, and then the others indiscriminately. Every departure from this rule incurred a fine. The blunders which led to fines, of course, were frequent, and produced great merriment.

In the old simple days of England the grain last cut was brought home in its wagon—called the *Hock Cart*—surmounted by a figure formed of a sheaf with gay dressings—a presumable representation of the goddess Ceres—while a pipe and tabor went merrily sounding in front, and the reapers tripped around in a hand-in-hand ring, singing appropriate songs, or simply by shouts and cries giving vent to the excitement of the day.

> Harvest-home, harvest-home,
> We have ploughed, we have sowed,
> We have reaped, we have mowed,
> We have brought home every load,
> Hip, hip, hip, harvest-home!

So they sang or shouted. In Lincolnshire and other districts, hand-bells were carried by those riding on the last load, and the following rhymes were sung:

> The boughs do shake, and the bells do ring,
> So merrily comes our harvest in,
> Our harvest in, our harvest in,
> So merrily comes our harvest in!
> Hurrah!

Troops of village children, who had contributed in various ways to the great labour, joined the throng, solaced with plum-cake in requital of their little services. Sometimes, the image on the cart, instead of being a mere dressed-up bundle of grain, was a pretty girl of the reaping-band, crowned with flowers, and hailed as *the Maiden*. Of this we have a description in a ballad of Bloomfield's:

> Home came the jovial Hockey load,
> Last of the whole year's crop,
> And Grace among the green boughs rode,
> Right plump upon the top.
>
> This way and that the wagon reeled,
> And never queen rode higher;
> Her cheeks were coloured in the field,
> And ours before the fire.

In the north, there seem to have been some differences in the observance. It was common there for the reapers, on the last day of their business, to have a contention for superiority in quickness of dispatch, groups of three or four taking each a ridge, and striving which should soonest get to its termination. In Scotland, this was called a *kemping*, which simply means a striving. In the north of England, it was a *mell*, which, I suspect, means the same thing (from Fr. *mêlée*). As the reapers went on during the last day, they took care to leave a good handful of the grain uncut, but laid down flat, and covered over; and, when the field was done, the 'bonniest lass' was allowed to cut this final handful, which was presently dressed up with various sewings, tyings, and trimmings, like a doll, and hailed as a *Corn Baby*. It was brought home in triumph, with music of fiddles and bagpipes, was set up conspicuously that night at supper, and was usually preserved in the farmer's parlour for the remainder of the year. The bonny lass who cut this handful of grain, was deemed the *Har'st Queen*. In Hertfordshire, and probably other districts of England, there was the same custom of reserving a final handful; but it was tied up and erected, under the name of a *Mare*, and the reapers then, one after another, threw their sickles at it, to cut it down. The successful individual called out: 'I have her!' 'What have you?' cried the rest. 'A mare, a mare, a mare!' he replied. 'What will you do with her?' was then asked. 'We'll send her to John Snooks,' or whatever other name, referring to some neighbouring farmer who had not yet got all his grain cut down.

In the evening of harvest-home, the supper takes place in the barn, or some other suitable place, the master and mistress generally presiding. This feast is always composed of substantial viands, with an abundance of good ale, and human nature insures that it should be a scene of intense enjoyment. Some one, with better voice than his neighbours, leads off a song of thanks to the host and hostess, in something like the following strain:

> Here's a health to our master,
> The lord of the feast;
> God bless his endeavours,
> And send him increase!
>
> May prosper his crops, boys,
> And we reap next year;
> Here's our master's good health, boys,
> Come, drink off your beer!
>
> Now harvest is ended,
> And supper is past;
> Here's our mistress's health, boys,
> Come, drink a full glass.

One of the rustic assemblage, being chosen to act as 'lord', goes out, puts on a sort of disguise, and comes in again, crying in a prolonged note, *Lar-gess!* He and some companions then go about with a plate among the company, and collect a little money with a view to further regalements at the village ale-house. With these, protracted usually to a late hour, the harvest-feast ends.

September 25th

Arabella Stuart

Samuel Butler

Richard Porson

born: William Romaine, divine, 1714.
died: Lady Arabella Stuart, 1615;
Samuel Butler, poet, 1680;
Richard Porson, Greek Scholar, 1808

September 26th

Launcelot Andrews

Richard Wellesley

Cuthbert Collingwood

born: Cuthbert Collingwood, vice-
admiral, 1750.
died: Launcelot Andrews, Bishop of
Winchester, 1626; Richard
Wellesley, Marquès Wellesley, governor-
general of India, 1842.

September 27th

William of Wykeham

died: William of Wykeham, Bishop
of Winchester and Lord Chancellor, 1404;
Thomas Burnet, master of the Charterhouse,
1715.

September 28th

born: Sir William Jones, oriental
scholar, 1746.
died: William Julius Mickle, poet, 1734;
Thomas Day, author, 1789; Granville
Penn, author, 1844; Thomas Amyot,
antiquary, 1815.

September 29th

Thomas Chubb

Robert Clive

Horatio Nelson

born: Thomas Chubb, deist, 1679;
Robert Clive, Lord Clive governor of Bengal
1725; Horatio Nelson, Viscount Nelson,
vice-admiral, 1758

Michaelmas Day.

Michaelmas Day, the 29th of September, properly
named the day of St Michael and All Angels, is a great
festival of the Church of Rome, and also observed as a
feast by the Church of England. In England, it is one
of the four quarterly terms, or quarter-days, on
which rents are paid, and in that and other divisions
of the United Kingdom, as well as perhaps in other
countries, it is the day on which burgal magistracies
and councils are re-elected. The only other remarkable thing connected with the day is a widely
prevalent custom of marking it with a goose at
dinner.

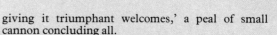

Sir Hugh Myddelton, and the Water Supply of Old London.

Michaelmas Day, 1613, is remarkable in the annals of London, as the day when the citizens assembled to witness, and celebrate by a public pageant, the entrance of the New River waters to the metropolis.

There were present Sir John Swinnerton the lord mayor, Sir Henry Montague the recorder, and many of the aldermen and citizens; and a speech was written by Thomas Middleton the dramatist, who had before been employed by the citizens to design pageants and write speeches for their Lord Mayors' Shows, and other public celebrations. On this occasion, as we are told in the pamphlet descriptive of the day's proceedings, 'warlike music of drums and trumpets liberally beat the air' at the approach of the civic magnates; then 'a troop of labourers, to the number of threescore or upwards, all in green caps alike, bearing in their hands the symbols of their several employments in so great a business, with drums before them, marching twice or thrice about the cistern, orderly present themselves before the mount, and after their obeisance, the speech is pronounced.'

Now for the fruits then: flow forth, precious
    spring,
So long and dearly sought for, and now bring,
Comfort to all that love thee: loudly sing,
And with thy crystal murmur struck together,
Bid all thy true well-wishers welcome hither!

'At which words,' we are told, 'the flood-gate opens, the stream let into the cistern, drums and trumpets giving it triumphant welcomes,' a peal of small cannon concluding all.

This important work, of the utmost sanitary value to London, was commenced and completed by the indomitable energy of one individual, after it had been declined by the corporate body, and opposed by many upholders of 'good old usages', the bane of all improvements. The bold man, who came prominently forward when all others had timidly retired, was a simple London tradesman, a goldsmith, dwelling in Basinghall Street, named Hugh Myddelton. Many projects had been brought before the citizens to convey a stream toward London, but the expense and difficulty had deterred them from using the powers with which they had been invested by the legislature; when Myddelton declared himself ready to carry out the great work, and in May 1609 'the dauntless Welshman' began his work at Chadwell, near Ware. Myddelton sought new strength, and found it effectually in the king. James I joined the spirited contractor, agreed to pay one-half of the expenses in consideration of one-half share in its ultimate profits, and to repay Myddelton one-half of what he had already disbursed. This spirited act of the king silenced all opposition, the work went steadily forward, and in about fifteen months after this new contract, the assembly took place at the New River Head, in the fields between Islington and London, to witness the completion of the great work, as we have already described it.

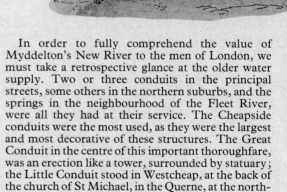

In order to fully comprehend the value of Myddelton's New River to the men of London, we must take a retrospective glance at the older water supply. Two or three conduits in the principal streets, some others in the northern suburbs, and the springs in the neighbourhood of the Fleet River, were all they had at their service. The Cheapside conduits were the most used, as they were the largest and most decorative of these structures. The Great Conduit in the centre of this important thoroughfare, was an erection like a tower, surrounded by statuary; the Little Conduit stood in Westcheap, at the back of the church of St Michael, in the Querne, at the north-east end of Paternoster Row. Leaden pipes ran all

The Little Conduit in Cheapside

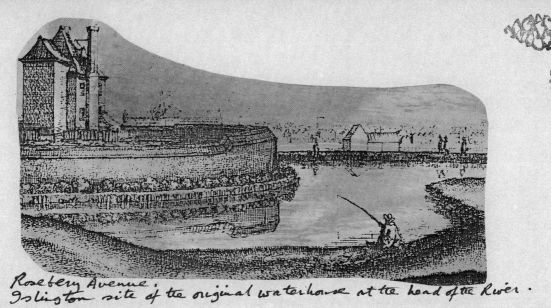

Rosebery Avenue. Islington site of the original waterhouse at the head of the River.

along Cheapside, to convey the water to various points; and the City Records tell of the punishment awarded one dishonest resident, who tapped the pipe where it passed his door, and secretly conveyed the water to his own well. Except where conveyed to some public building, water had to be fetched for domestic use from these ever-flowing reservoirs. Large tankards, holding from two to three gallons, were constructed for this use; and may be seen ranged round the conduit in the cut opposite. Many poor men lived by supplying water to the householders; 'a tankard-bearer' was hence a well-known London character. His dress is protected by coarse aprons hung from his neck, and the weight of his large tankard when empty, partially relieved from the left shoulder, by the aid of the staff in his right hand. He wears the 'city flat-cap', his dress altogether of the old fashion, such as belonged to the time of 'bluff King Hal'. When water was required in smaller

quantities, apprentices and servant-girls were sent to the conduits. Hence they were not only gossiping-places, but spots where quarrels constantly arose. A curious print in the British Museum—published about the time of Elizabeth—entitled *Tittle Tattle*, is a satire on these customs, and tells us in homely rhyme:

> At the conduit striving for their turn,
>   The quarrel it grows great,
> That up in arms they are at last,
>   And one another beat.

Oliver Cob, the water-bearer, is one of the characters in Ben Jonson's play, *Every Man in his Humour*, and the sort of coarse repartee he indulges in, may be taken as a fair sample of that used at the London conduits. It was not till a considerable time after the opening of the New River that their utility ceased.

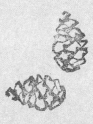

Nature now spreads around, in dreary hue,
A pall to cover all that summer knew;
Yet, in the poet's solitary way,
Some pleasing objects for his praise delay,
Something that makes him pause and turn again,
As every trifle will his eye detain:
The free horse rustling through the stubble field,
And cows at lair in rushes, half conceal'd,
With groups of restless sheep who feed their fill,
O'er clear'd fields rambling wheresoe'er they will;
The hedger stopping gaps, amid the leaves,
Which time, o'erhead, in every colour weaves;
The milkmaid stepping with a timid look,
From stone to stone, across the brimming brook;
The cotter journeying with his noisy swine,
Along the wood-side where the brambles twine,
Shaking from mossy oaks the acorns brown,
Or from the hedges red haws dashing down;
The nutters, rustling in the yellow woods,
Who tease the wild things in their solitudes;
The hunters, from the thicket's avenue,
In scarlet jackets, startling on the view,
Skimming a moment o'er the russet plain,
Then hiding in the motley woods again;
The plopping guns' sharp, momentary shock,
Which Echo bustles from her cave to mock;
The bawling song of solitary boys,
Journeying in rapture o'er their dreaming joys,
Haunting the hedges in their reveries,
For wilding fruit that shines upon the trees;
The wild wood music from the lonely dell,
Where merry gipsies o'er their raptures dwell,
Haunting each common's wild and lonely nook,
Where hedges run as crooked as the brook,
Shielding their camps beneath some spreading
        oak,
And but discovered by the circling smoke

Puffing, and peeping up, as wills the breeze,
Between the branches of the coloured trees:
Such are the pictures that October yields,
To please the poet as he walks the fields;
While Nature—like fair woman in decay,
Whom pale consumption hourly wastes away—
Upon her waning features, winter chill,
Wears dreams of beauty that seem lovely still.

JOHN CLARE

Then came October full of merry glee;
    For yet his noule was totty of the must,
Which he was treading in the wine-fat's see,
    And of the joyous oyle, whose gentle gust
Made him so frolic and so full of lust:
    Upon a dreadful Scorpion he did ride,
The same which by Dianae's doom unjust
    Slew great Orion; and eeke by his side
He had his ploughing-share and coutler ready
        tied.

SPENSER

This month, so called from being the eighth in the year according to the old Alban or Latin calendar, was, by our Saxon ancestors, styled *Wyn monath*, or the wine month. In some of the ancient Saxon calendars, this month is allegorised by the figure of a husbandman carrying a sack on his shoulders and sowing corn, in allusion to the practice of sowing the winter grain, which takes place in October. In other old almanacs, the sport of hawking has been adopted as emblematical of this, the last month of autumn.

 OCTOBER

On the 23rd of the month, the sun enters the sign of Scorpio, an astronomical emblem said to typify, in the form of a destructive insect, the increasing power of cold over nature, in the same manner as the equal influence of cold and heat is represented by Libra, or the balance, the sign of the preceding month of September. Though a melancholy feeling is associated with October, from the general decay of nature by which it is characterised, there occurs, nevertheless, not infrequently in it, some of the finest and most exhilarating weather of the year. Frosts in the mornings and evenings are common, whilst the middle of the day is often enlivened by all the sunshine of July without its oppressiveness.

October 1st

John Blow

died: John Blow, composer, 1708.

October 2nd

Richard III Augustus Keppel

born: Richard III, King of England, 1452; Joseph Ritson, antiquary, 1752.
died: Augustus Keppel, Viscount Keppel, admiral, 1786.

October 3rd

died: Robert Barclay, quaker apologist, 1690; A.E. Chalon, painter, 1860.

Watching and lighting old London

Civilisation, in its slowest progress, may be well illustrated by a glance at the past modes of guarding and lighting the tortuous and dangerous streets of old cities. From the year 1253, when Henry III established night-watchmen, until 1830, when Sir Robert Peel's police act established a new kind of guardian, the watchman was little better than a person who 'Disturbed your rest to tell you what's o'clock.'

The watchman of the olden time carried a fire-pot, called a cresset, on the top of a long pole, and thus marched on, giving light as he bawled the hour, and at the same time, notification of his approach to all thieves, who had thus timeous warning to escape.

The London watchman of the time of James I, differed in no essential point from his predecessors in that of Elizabeth. He carried a halbert and a horn-lantern, was well secured in a frieze gabardine, leathern-girdled; and wore a serviceable hat, like a pent-house, to guard against weather. Such 'ancient and most quiet watchmen' would naturally prefer being out of harm's way, and warn thieves to depart in peace by ringing the bell, that the wether of their flock carried; 'then presently call the rest of the watch together, and thank God you are rid of a knave,' as honest Dogberry advises. Above the head of the man is inscribed the cry he uttered as he walked the round of his parish. It is this: 'Lanthorne and a whole candell light, hange out your lights heare!' This was in accordance with the old local rule of London, as established by the mayor in 1416, that all house-holders of the better class, rated above a low rate in the books of their respective parishes, should hang a lantern, lighted with a fresh and whole candle, nightly outside their houses for the accommodation of foot-passengers, from Allhallows evening to Candlemas day.

The honest men had, however, need to be abed betimes, for total darkness fell early on the streets when the rush-candle burned in its socket; and was dispelled only by the occasional appearance of the watchman with his horn lantern; or that more important and noisier official, the bellman. One of these was appointed to each ward, and acted as a sort of inspector to the watchmen and the parish, going round, says, Stow, 'all night with a bell, and at every lane's end, and at the ward's end, gave warning of fire and candle, and to help the poor, and pray for the dead.' He was a regular parish official, visible by day also, advertising sales, crying losses, or summoning

to weddings or funerals by ringing his bell. It was the duty of the bellman of St Sepulchre's parish, near Newgate, to rouse the unfortunates condemned to death in that prison, the night before their execution, and solemnly exhort them to repentance with good words in bad rhyme, ending with:

When Sepulchre's bell to-morrow tolls,
The Lord above have mercy on your souls!

The watchman was a more prosaic individual, never attempting a rhyme; he restricted himself to news of the weather, such as: 'Past eleven, and a starlight night'; or 'Past one o'clock, and a windy morning'.

October 4th

Richard Cromwell   Samuel Horsley

born: Richard Cromwell, son of Oliver Cromwell, 1626; Edmund Malone, critic and author, 1741.
died: John Campbell, 2nd Duke of Argyll and Duke of Greenwich, 1743; Henry Carey, poet, 1743; Samuel Horsley, Bishop of St Asaph, 1806.

October 5th ♎

Charles Cornwallis   Lloyd Kenyon

born: William Wilkie, "the
Scottish Homer", 1721;
Lloyd Kenyon, 1st Baron Kenyon,
Master of the Rolls, 1732.
died: Charles Cornwallis, 1st
Marquis Cornwallis, governor-
general of India, 1805.

October 7th ♎

William Laud   George Gascoigne

born: William Laud, Archbishop
of Canterbury, 1573.
died: George Gascoigne, poet,
1577; Thomas Reid, philosopher,
1796.

October 6th ♎

Nevil Maskelyne

born: John Caius, scholar and
physician, 1510; Nevil
Maskelyne, astronomer royal, 1732.

October 8th ♎

born: John Hoadly, poet and
dramatist, 1711.
died: Andrew Kippis,
nonconformist divine, 1795.

October 9th ♎

Barbara Villiers

died: Barbara Villiers,
Duchess of Cleveland, mistress
of Charles II, 1709; Sir Richard
Blackmore, physician and writer,
1729; Michael Kelly, actor, 1826

October 11th ♎

Thomas Wyatt

James Barry

born: Samuel Clarke, divine, 1675;
James Barry, painter, 1741.
died: Sir Thomas Wyatt, poet, 1542;
Thomas Stackhouse, theologian,
1752; Samuel Wesley, musician,
1837.

October 12th ♎

Edward VI

Elizabeth Fry

born: Edward VI, King of England,
1537.
died: Elizabeth Fry, prison
reformer, 1845; Robert
Stephenson, engineer, 1859.

October 10th ♎

John Potter

born: John Campbell, 2nd Duke of Argyll
and Duke of Greenwich, 1678. Henry
Cavendish, natural philosopher, 1731;
died: Thomas Sheridan, schoolmaster, 1738;
John Potter, Archbishop of Canterbury, 1747.

Richard Boyle

born: Edward, Prince of Wales,
only son of Henry VI, 1453;
Richard Boyle, 1st Earl of
Cork, the "Great Earl" 1566.
died: Thomas Harrison,
regicide, 1660.

Notes from Aubrey: on English Manners in old times.

'There were very few free-schools in England before the Reformation. Youths were generally taught Latin in the monasteries, and young women had their education, not at Hackney, as now A.D. 1678, but at nunneries, where they learned needlework, confectionary, surgery, physic, writing, drawing, &c. Anciently, before the Reformation, ordinary men's houses had no chimneys, but flues like louvre-holes. In the halls and parlours of great houses were written texts of Scripture, on painted cloths.

'Before the late civil wars, at Christmas, the first dish that was brought to table was a boar's head, with a lemon in his mouth. At Queen's College, in Oxford, they still retain this custom; the bearer of it brings it into the hall, singing to an old tune an old Latin rhyme—*Caput apri defero, &c.* [The boar's head in bring I.] The first dish that was brought to table on Easter-day, was a red herring riding away on horseback—*i.e.*, a herring arranged by the cook, something after the manner of a man on horseback, set in a corn-salad. The custom of eating a gammon of bacon at Easter was this—namely, to shew their abhorrence of Judaism at that solemn commemoration of our Lord's resurrection.

'The use of "Your humble servant", came first into England on the marriage of Queen Mary, daughter of Henry IV of France [to King Charles I]. The usual salutation before that time was, "God keep you!" "God be with you!" and, among the vulgar, "How dost do?" with a thump on the shoulder. Until this time, the court itself was unpolished and unmannered. King James's court was so far from being civil to women, that the ladies, nay, the queen herself, could hardly pass by the king's apartment without receiving some affront.

'In days of yore, lords and gentlemen lived in the country like petty kings: had their castles and their boroughs, and gallows within their liberties, where they could try, condemn, and execute. They never went to London but in parliament time, or once a year, to do their homage to their king. They always ate in Gothic halls, at the high table or oriel (a little room at the upper end of the hall, where stands a table), with the folks at the side-tables. The meat was served up by watchwords. Jacks are but of late invention; the poor boys did turn the spits, and licked the dripping for their pains. The beds of the men-servants and retainers were in the hall, as now in the grand or privy chamber. The hearth was commonly in the middle, whence the saying, "Round about our coal-fire."

'The halls of the justices of the peace were dreadful to behold; the screen was garnished with corslets and helmets gaping with open mouths, with coats of mail, lances, pikes, halberts, brownbills, and bucklers. Public inns were rare. Travellers were entertained at religious houses for three days together, if occasion served. The meetings of the gentry were not at taverns, but in the fields or forests, with hawks and hounds, and their bugle-horns in silken baldrics.

'In the last age, every gentleman-like man kept a sparrow-hawk, and a priest kept a bobby, as Dame Julian Berners teaches us (who wrote a treatise on field-sports, *temp.* Henry VI); it was also a diversion for young gentlewomen to man, sparrow-hawks and merlins.

'Before the Reformation, there were no poor-rates; the charitable doles given at religious houses, and the church-ale in every parish, did the business. In every parish there was a church-house, to which belonged spits, pots, crocks, &c., for dressing provisions. Here the housekeepers met and were merry, and gave their charity. The young people came there too, and had dancing, bowling, and shooting at butts. Mr Antony Wood assures me, there were few or no alms-houses before the time of King Henry VIII; that at Oxford, opposite Christ Church, is one of the most ancient in England. In every church was a poor-man's box, and the like at great inns.

'Before the wake, or feast of the dedication of the church, they sat up all night fasting and praying—that is to say, on the eve of the wake. In the Easter-holidays was the clerk's "ale", for his private benefit and the solace of the neighbourhood.

'Glass windows, except in churches and gentlemen's houses, were rare before the time of Henry VIII. In my own remembrance, before the civil wars, copyholders and poor people had none in Herefordshire, Monmouthshire, and Salop: it is so still [A.D. 1678].'

October 14th

James II

William Penn

Thomas Chaloner

Charles Abbot

William the Conqueror.

born: James II, King of England, 1633; William Penn, founder of Pennsylvania, 1644; Charles Abbot, 1st Baron Colchester, speaker of the House of Commons 1757.

died: Harold, last Saxon King of England, 1066; Sir Thomas Chaloner, diplomatist and author, 1565.

Battle of Hastings.

an inadequate army to repel the invaders, waited a little while to gather strength from the reinforcements which were every day pouring in to his standard. But the signal success which, only a few days previous, he had gained over the Norwegians in the north of England, made him over-confident in his own powers, and the very promptitude and rapidity which formed one of his leading characteristics proved the principal cause of his overthrow.

On the 28th of September, sixteen days before the battle, the Normans, with their leader William, had disembarked, totally unopposed, from their ships at a place called Bulverhithe, between Pevensey and Hastings. The future Conqueror of England was the last to land, and as he placed his foot on shore, he made a false step, and fell on his face. A murmur of consternation ran through the troops at this incident as a bad omen, but with great presence of mind William sprang immediately up, and shewing his troops his hand filled with English sand, exclaimed: 'What now? What astonishes you? I have taken seisin of this land with my hands, and by the splendour of God, as far as it extends it is mine—it is yours!'

The Battle of Hastings, fought on Saturday, the 14th of October 1066, was one of those decisive engagements which at various periods have marked the commencement of a new epoch or chapter in the world's history. Gained by the Duke of Normandy, mainly through superiority of numbers, and several well-directed feints, the conduct of the Saxons and their monarch Harold was such as to command the highest admiration on the part of their enemies, and the result might have been very different had Harold, instead of marching impetuously from London with

The invading army then marched to Hastings, pitching their camp near the town, and sallying out from this intrenchment to burn and plunder the surrounding country. Landed on a hostile shore, with a brave and vigorous foe to contend with, all William's prospects of success lay in striking a decisive blow before Harold could properly muster his forces or organise his means of resistance. The impetuosity of the Saxon king, as already mentioned, soon furnished him with such an opportunity.

English, and on the last occasion Harold, struck by a random arrow which entered his left eye and penetrated to the brain, was instantaneously killed. This still further increased the disorder of his followers, who, however, bravely maintained the fight round their standard for a time. This at last was grasped by the Normans, who then raised in its stead the consecrated banner, which the Pope had sent William from Rome, as a sanction to his expedition. At sunset the combat terminated, and the Normans remained masters of the field.

Arriving at *Senlac*, which the bloody engagement a few days subsequently was destined to rechristen by the appellation of *Battle*, Harold pitched his camp, and then received a message from William, demanding that he should either resign his crown in favour of the Norman, submit the question at issue to the decision of the Pope, or finally maintain his right to the English crown by single combat with his challenger. All these proposals were declined by Harold, as was also a last offer made by William to resign to his opponent all the country to the north of the Humber, on condition of the provinces south of that river being ceded to him in sovereignty.

On Friday the 13th, the Normans quitted Hastings, and took up their position on an eminence opposite to the English, for the purpose of giving battle on the following day. A singular contrast was noticeable in the manner that the respective armies passed the intervening night. Whilst the Saxons, according to their old convivial custom, spent the time in feasting and rejoicing, singing songs, and quaffing bumpers of ale and wine, the Normans, after finishing their warlike preparations, betook themselves to the offices of devotion, confessed, and received the holy sacrament by thousands at a time.

At early dawn next day, the Normans were marshalled by William and his brother Odo, the warlike Bishop of Bayeux, who wore a coat of mail beneath his episcopal robes. They advanced towards the English, who remained firmly intrenched in their position, and for many hours repulsed steadily with their battle-axes the charge of the enemy's cavalry, and with their closed shields rendered his arrows almost inoperative. Great ability was shewn by William and his brother in rallying their soldiers after these reverses, and the attacks on the English line were again and again renewed. Up to three o'clock in the afternoon, the superiority in the conflict remained with the latter. Then, however, William ordered a thousand horse to advance, and then take to flight, as if routed. This stratagem proved fatal to the Saxons, who, leaving their position to pursue the retreating foe, were astounded by the latter suddenly facing about, and falling into disorder, were struck down on every side. The same manoeuvre was twice again repeated with the same calamitous results to the

October 15th

born: Allan Ramsay, poet, 1686; Alexander Fraser Tytler, Lord Woodhouslee, 1747.
died: James Anderson, economi[st] 1808; Letitia Elizabeth Macleo[d] poetess, 1838.

October 16th

died: Nicholas Ridley, Bishop of London, burnt, 1555; Hugh Latimer, Bishop of Worcester, burnt, 1555. John Hunter, anatomist and surgeon, 1793.

October 17th

born: John Wilkes, politician, 1727; Sir Philip Sidney, poet, 1586.
died: John Ward, biographer, 175[?] John Brown, physician, 1788.

October 18th

born: Mathew Henry, non conformist divine, 1662; Richard "Beau" Nash, 1674; Thomas Phillips, painter, 1770.
died: Sarah Jennings, Duchess of Marlborough 1744.

October 19th

born: Sir Thomas Browne, physician and author, 1605; James Henry Leigh Hunt, essayist, poet & critic, 1784.
died: John, King of England, 1216; Sir Thomas Browne, physician and author 1682; Jonathan Swift, satirist, 1745; Sir Godfrey, Kneller painter, 1723

October 20th

born, Sir Christopher Wren, architect, 1632. Henry John Temple, 3rd Viscount Palmerston, statesman, 1784.
Michael Dahl, painter, 1743.

October 21st

born: George Colman the younger, dramatist, 1762; Samuel Taylor Coleridge, poet and philosopher, 1772.
died: Edmund Waller, poet, 1687; Samuel Foote, actor and dramatist, 1777; Alexander Runciman, painter, 1785; Horatio Nelson, Viscount Nelson, vice-admiral, 1805.

October 22nd

born: Sir Philip Francis, author, 1740.
died: Sir Cloudisley Shovell, admiral of the Fleet, 1707; Henry Richard Vassall Fox, 3rd Baron, Holland, 1840.

October 23rd

died: Anne Oldfield, actress 1730.

October 24th ♏

born: Sir James Mackintosh, philosopher, 1765.
died: Jane Seymour, Queen of England, 1537.

Fox Hunting

Now that the cornfields have been thoroughly cleared of their produce, that the woods are strewed with fallen leaves, and the shortened days bespeak the near approach of winter, when the fields in the mornings are crisp with the glittering rime which soon dissolves beneath the autumn sunbeams, when angling for the season has fairly closed, and even the sportsman's ardour has begun to languish, then commences the most renowned and exhilarating of all rural pastimes—the thoroughly British sport of fox-hunting. The period over which it extends comprises nearly six months, from the latter part of October to the beginning of April. Much of that space of course, however, wholly unavailable for hunting-purposes, whilst the ground is either bound by hard frost or covered with snow.

Though this sport requires, for its exercise, the possession both of a considerable amount of physical courage and activity, and of pecuniary means to sustain the expenses which it entails, there is, nevertheless, no amusement which engages so large and universal a sympathy with all classes of the community. No Briton, however unable he may be from the circumstances of his position to take an active part in the chase, can refrain from experiencing a mingled feeling alike of envy and admiration as he witnesses the gallant array of horsemen assemble at the 'meet'; see the grand 'burst' when the fox has been started, and the cry of 'Tallyho! Gone away!' breaks forth; and then follow with his eye the cavalcade in its exciting pursuit, as it sweeps o'er hill and dale, with the hounds in full cry; till the outlines of the figures, becoming rapidly less and less distinct, are fairly lost in the distance. A scene like this stirs the blood in the veins of the most sluggish, whilst with the devotees of the exciting sport, the enthusiasm felt is such as frequently remains unimpaired by the progress of years or the chills of age, and the grayheaded fox-hunter of threescore may often be seen following the hounds with the same ardour as the stripling of eighteen.

As is well-known, much of the success of a 'run' in hunting depends on the condition of the atmosphere. When this is very dry, or when a sharp northerly breeze prevails, the scent or exhalation from the hunted animal is rarefied and dissipated, and becomes consequently impossible to be traced and followed up by the dogs. When, on the other hand, the air is moist, but without the presence of actual rain, and a gentle gale blows from the south or west, then the scent clings to the adjoining soil and vegetation; and a more favourable condition still is, when it is suspended in the air at a certain height from the earth, and the dogs are enabled to follow it *breast high*, at full speed, without putting their heads to the ground.

The leaps taken by fox-hunters during the chase form alike the most exciting and perilous part of the pastime. In Leicestershire, which is generally regarded *par excellence* as the hunting-county of England, two specially formidable descriptions of fences require frequently to be surmounted. These are the *ox-fence* and the *bullfinch-fence*. In the former, which is rendered necessary in the locality as an effectual barrier to the roaming of cattle from their pastures during the season of the *œstrus*, or gadfly, the adventurous votary of Diana finds himself confronted by a wide ditch, bordered by a strong blackthorn-hedge, and beyond that by a railing four feet in height, all of which obstacles must be cleared by him and his steed. The bullfinch-fence, on the other hand, of still more frequent occurrence, is a thick and lofty quickset-hedge, of perhaps half a century's growth, with a ditch on one side, and requiring to be charged at full speed by the horseman, who manages to push through.

Scorpio - the scorpion ♏ October 24 to November 22
Of the Planet Mars,
and his severall significations

♏

♏

♏

Manners when well dignified

In feats of Warre and Courage invincible, scorning any should exceed him, subject to no Reason, Bold Confident immoveable, Contentious, challenging all Honour to themselves, Valiant, lovers of Warre and things pertaining thereunto, hazarding himselfe to all Perils, willingly will obey no body, or submit to any; a large Reporter of his owne Acts, one that slights all things in comparison of Victory, and yet of prudent behaviour in his owne affaires.

When ill placed.

Then he is a Pratler without modesty or honesty, a lover of Slaughter and Quarrels, Murder, Theevery, a promoter of Sedition, Frayes and Commotions, an Highway-Theefe, as wavering as the Wind, a Traytor, of turbulent Spirit, Perjured, Obscene, Rash, Inhumane, neither fearing God or caring for man, Unthankful, Trecherous, Oppressors, Ravenous, Cheaters, Furious, Violent.

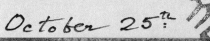
October 25th ♏

King Stephen; Geoffrey Chaucer; William Hogarth; George II

died: Stephen, King of England, 1154; Geoffrey Chaucer, poet 1400; William Elphinstone, Bishop of Aberdeen, 1514; Charles Mordaunt, 3rd Earl of Peterborough, admiral, general, and diplomatist, 1735; George II King of England, 1760; William Hogarth, painter, 1764.

The Battle of Agincourt.

The reader of the *Spectator* may recollect Sir Roger de Coverley declining, with thanks, a hound which had been sent him as a present, informing the sender with all courtesy that the dog in question was an excellent *bass*, but that at present he wanted only a *counter-tenor*. Fox-hunters dilate with rapture on the cry of a pack of hounds, more grateful, doubtless, to their ears than the most ethereal warblings of a Lind or a Grisi. A whimsical anecdote is often related of the Cockney, who, when the ardent fox-hunter exclaimed, in reference to the baying of the pack: 'What glorious music! don't you hear it?' replied: 'Music! I can hear nothing of it for the yelping of these confounded dogs!'

Till the end of the seventeenth century, fox-hunting can scarcely be said to have existed as a sport, the stag, the buck, and the hare taking the precedence with our ancestors as objects of the chase, which, at an earlier period, included the wolf and the boar. The county of Leicester, at the present day, constitutes the head-quarters of the sport; a pre-eminence which it owes partly to the nature of the ground, more pastoral than arable, partly to the circumstance of the covers being separated by considerable intervals, preventing the fox from readily getting to earth, and thus securing a good 'run'. The town of Melton-Mowbray, which may be regarded as the fox-hunting metropolis, is thronged during the season by sporting-visitors, who benefit the place to the extent, it is said, of £50,000 a year, and indeed form its main support. The vicinity is the country of the celebrated Quorn or Quorndon pack of hounds, so called from Quorndon Hall, the residence of the great hunter, Mr Meynell, and subsequently of the successive masters of 'the Quorn', which takes the first place amid the fox-hunting associations of the United Kingdom.

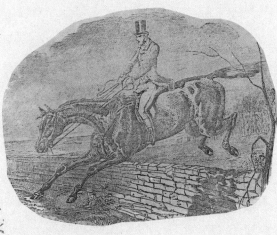

In connection with St Crispin's Day occurs one of the most brilliant events of English history—the celebrated battle of Azincourt, gained, like those of Crécy and Poitiers, under an immense disparity in point of numbers on the side of the victors, and also under the most disadvantageous circumstances from the effect of fatigue and privations. The chivalrous Henry V, after proclaiming what can only be designated a most unjustifiable war with France, had embarked on an expedition for its conquest at Southampton, in August 1415, and landed near Harfleur, which he invested and captured after a siege of thirty-six days. So great, however, was the loss sustained by the English army, owing to a terrible dysentery which had broken out in the camp, that the project of re-embarking for England was

But we in it shall be remembered—
We few, we happy few, we band of brothers;
For he to-day that sheds his blood with me
Shall be my brother; be he ne'er so vile,
This day shall gentle his condition:
And gentlemen in England, now a-bed,
Shall think themselves accurs'd they were not
    here;
And hold their manhoods cheap whiles any speaks
That fought with us upon St Crispin's day.

As in the two previous great battles between the English and French, the success of the former was mainly owing to their bowmen, whose arrows threw the French cavalry into confusion, and who themselves afterwards broke into the enemy's ranks, and did terrible execution with their hatchets and billhooks. The chivalry of France was fearfully thinned, upwards of 7000 knights and gentlemen, and 120 great lords perishing on the field, whilst the loss of the English did not exceed 1600 men. An immense amount of plunder was obtained by the victors, the weakness of whose army, however, prevented them from improving their advantages, and they accordingly continued their march to Calais. From this Henry embarked for England, landed at Dover, and marching in triumph from thence to London, entered that city with a long array of captives, and a pageant of imposing splendour such as had been wholly unprecedented in the case of any previous English monarch.

seriously deliberated in a council of war. The idea was indignantly rejected by Henry, who declared that he must first see a little more of 'this good land of France'. With a greatly reduced army, he accordingly commenced a march through Normandy and Picardy to Calais; and after surmounting numerous difficulties, was engaged on 25th October, near the village of Azincourt or Agincourt, by L Albret, the Constable of France, at the head of an army which outnumbered that of the English monarch in the proportion of at least six to one. In immediate prospect of the conflict, and in reference to the day on which it was to be fought, Shakspeare represents Henry delivering himself as follows:

This day is call'd the feast of Crispian:
He that outlives this day, and comes safe home,
Will stand a tip-toe when this day is nam'd,
And rouse him at the name of Crispian.
He that shall live this day, and see old age,
Will yearly on the vigil feast his neighbours,
And say, To-morrow is Saint Crispian:
Then will he strip his sleeve and shew his scars,
And say, These wounds I had on Crispian's day.
Old men forget; yet all shall be forgot,
But he'll remember, with advantages,
What feats he did that day: then shall our names
Familiar in their mouths as household words—
Harry the king, Bedford and Exeter,
Warwick and Talbot, Salisbury and Gloster—
Be in their flowing cups freshly remember'd:
This story shall the good man teach his son;
And Crispin Crispian shall ne'er go by,
From this day to the ending of the world,

St Crispin's Day.

From time immemorial, Crispin and Crispinian have been regarded as the patron-saints of shoemakers, who used to observe, and still in many places celebrate, their day with great festivity and rejoicings. One special ceremony was a grand procession of the brethren of the craft with banners and music, whilst various characters representing King Crispin and his court were sustained by different members.

St Crispin and his brother Crispinian were natives of Rome, and having become converts to Christianity, travelled northwards into France, to propagate the faith. They fixed their residence at Soissons, where they preached to the people during the day, and at night earned their subsistence by the making of shoes. They furnished the poor with shoes, it is said, at a very low price, and the legend adds that an angel supplied them with leather. In the persecution under the Emperor Maximian, they suffered martyrdom, and according to a Kentish tradition, their relics, after being cast into the sea, were washed ashore at Romney Marsh. In medieval art, the two brothers are represented as two men at work in a shoemaker's shop, and the emblem for their day in the Clog Almanacs is a pair of shoes.

certainly brought up there. His words are these:
'Also in the citie of London, that is to mee soe deare
and sweete, in which I was foorth growne; and more
kindely love have I to that place than to any other in
yerth (as every kindely creature hath full appetite to
that place of his kindly engendure).'

Apropos of the poet's origin, Stowe records that
'Richard Chawcer, vintner, gave,' to the church of St
Mary Aldermary, 'his tenement and tavern, with the
appurtenance, in the Royal Streete the corner of
Kerion Lane, and was there buried, 1348.'

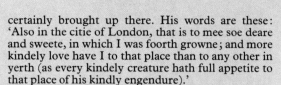

Chaucer.

To decide where Chaucer was born, is a still more
puzzling question. Fuller inclines to think that his
native place was Woodstock, in Oxfordshire. When
Queen Elizabeth 'passed a fair stone house next to her
palace in that town' to some tenant or other, this same
building was described as *Chaucer's House*, and
retained the name long afterwards. But as we find the
poet living at Woodstock in Edward III's time, and
dying there in his old age, the name of the house is
accounted for. Another authority (Leland) leans to
Berkshire, where Dunnington Castle, near
Newbury, is said to have been Chaucer's family
property. An oak in the park there, went by the name
of *Chaucer's Oak*. But we afterwards find this same
property in the possession of a certain Thomas
Chaucer—whether he were Chaucer's son or not
makes no matter—and thus the place need not by any
means have been the poet's birthplace, so far as the
name of the oak is concerned. Others maintain that
London can justly claim the honours; and it appears
from Chaucer's own words, in his *Testament of Love*,
that, whether he were born there or not, he was

From an old folio edition of his works, dated 1602, presented to the British Museum by Tyrwhitt in 1786, we have gleaned a little tribute to the poet, not unworthy to be recovered from the grasp of oblivion:

A BALLADE IN THE PRAISE AND COMMENDACION
OF MASTER GEFFRAY CHAUCER FOR HIS
GOLDEN ELOQUENCE.

Maister Geffray Chaucer, that now lithe in grave,
The noble rhetoricion, and poet of Great Britaine,
That worthy was, the laurer (*sic*) of poetry to have
For this his labour, and the palme to attaine,
Which first made to distil, and reine,
The gold dewe dropes, of spech and eloquence,
Into English tonge, through his excellence.

October 26th ♏

died: Philip Doddridge, nonconformist divine, 1751

October 27th ♏

born: Andrew Combe, physiologist and phrenologist, 1797.
died: George Morland, painter, 1804.

October 28th ♏

born: Sir David Dalrymple, Lord Hailes, judge, 1659.
died: John Locke, philosopher, 1704; Prince George of Denmark, consort of Queen Anne, 1708.

October 29th ♏

born: George Abbot, Archbishop of Canterbury, 1562
died: Sir Walter Raleigh, writer, executed, 1618; James Shirley, dramatic poet, buried, 1666.

October 30th ♏

Edward Vernon
Richard Brinsley Sheridan

born: Richard Brinsley Sheridan, statesman and dramatist, 1751.
James Perry, journalist, 1756.
died: Edward Vernon, admiral, 1757.
John Whitaker, historian, 1808;
Edward Cartwright, inventor, 1823;
Allan Cunningham, miscellaneous writer, 1842.

October 31st ♏

John Bradshaw
William Augustus, Duke of Cumberland
John Keats
John Evelyn

born: John Evelyn, diarist, 1620;
John Keats, poet, 1795;
John Bradshaw, regicide, 1659.
died: William Augustus, Duke of
Cumberland, military commander,
1765.

Halloween.

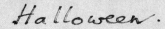

There is perhaps no night in the year which the popular imagination has stamped with a more peculiar character than the evening of the 31st of October, known as All Hallow's Eve, or Halloween. It is clearly a relic of pagan times, for there is nothing in the church-observance of the ensuing day of All Saints to have originated such extraordinary notions as are connected with this celebrated festival, or such remarkable practices as those by which it is distinguished.

The leading idea respecting Halloween is that it is the time, of all others, when supernatural influences prevail. It is the night set apart for a universal walking abroad of spirits, both of the visible and invisible world; for, as will be afterwards seen, one of the special characteristics attributed to this mystic evening, is the faculty conferred on the immaterial principle in humanity to detach itself from its corporeal tenement and wander abroad through the realms of space. Divination is then believed to attain its highest power, and the gift asserted by Glendower of calling spirits 'from the vasty deep', becomes available to all who choose to avail themselves of the privileges of the occasion.

There is a remarkable uniformity in the fireside-customs of this night all over the United Kingdom. Nuts and apples are everywhere in requisition, and consumed in immense numbers. Indeed the name of *Nutcrack Night*, by which Halloween is known in the north of England, indicates the predominance of the former of these articles in making up the entertainments of the evening. They are not only cracked and eaten, but made the means of vaticination in love-affairs. And here we quote from Burns's poem of *Halloween*:

The auld guidwife's well-hoordit nits
　Are round and round divided,
And mony lads' and lasses' fates
　Are there that night decided:
Some kindle, couthie, side by side,
　And burn thegither trimly;
Some start awa wi saucy pride,
　And jump out-owre the chimly
　　　　Fu' high that night.
Jean slips in twa wi' tentie e'e;
　Wha 'twas, she wadna tell;
But this is Jock, and this is me,
　She says in to hersel':
He bleezed owre her, and she owre him,
　As they wad never mair part;
Till, fuff! he started up the lum,
　And Jean had e'en a sair heart
　　　　To see 't that night.

As to apples, there is an old custom, perhaps still observed in some localities on this merry night, of hanging up a stick horizontally by a string from the ceiling, and putting a candle on the one end, and an apple on the other. The stick being made to twirl rapidly, the merry-makers in succession leap up and snatch at the apple with their teeth (no use of the hands being allowed), but it very frequently happens that the candle comes round before they are aware, and scorches them in the face, or anoints them with grease. The disappointments and misadventures occasion, of course, abundance of laughter. But the grand sport with apples on Halloween, is to set them afloat in a tub of water, into which the juveniles, by turns, duck their heads with the view of catching an apple. Great fun goes on in watching the attempts of the youngster in the pursuit of the swimming fruit, which wriggles from side to side of the tub, and evades all attempts to capture it; whilst the disappointed aspirant is obliged to abandon the chase in favour of another whose turn has now arrived. The apples provided with stalks are generally caught first, and then comes the tug of war to win those which possess no such appendages. Some competitors will deftly *suck up* the apple, if a small one, into their mouths. Others plunge manfully overhead in pursuit of a particular apple, and having forced it to the bottom of the tub, seize it firmly with their teeth, and emerge, dripping and triumphant, with their prize. This venturous procedure is generally rewarded with a hurrah! by the lookers-on, and is recommended, by those versed in Halloween-aquatics, as the only sure method of attaining success. In recent years, a practice has been introduced, probably by some tender mammas, timorous on the subject of their offspring catching cold, of dropping a fork from a height into the tub among the apples, and thus turning the sport into a display of marksmanship. It forms, however, but a very indifferent substitute for the joyous merriment of ducking and diving.

Another ceremony much practised on Halloween, is that of the Three Dishes or *Luggies*. Two of these are respectively filled with clean and foul water, and one is empty. They are ranged on the hearth, when the parties, blindfolded, advance in succession, and dip their fingers into one. If they dip into the clean water, they are to marry a maiden; if into the foul water, a widow; if into the empty dish, the party so dipping is destined to be either a bachelor or an old maid. As each person takes his turn, the position of the dishes is changed. Burns thus describes the custom:

In order, on the clean hearth-stane,
　The luggies three are ranged,
And every time great care is ta'en
　To see them duly changed:
Auld uncle John, wha wedlock's joys
　Sin' Mar's year did desire,
Because he gat the toom dish thrice,
　He heaved them on the fire
　　　　In wrath that night

The ceremonies above described are all of a light sportive description, but there are others of a more weird-like and fearful character, which in this enlightened incredulous age have fallen very much into desuetude. One of these is the celebrated spell of eating an apple before a looking-glass, with the view of discovering the inquirer's future husband, who it is believed will be seen peeping over her shoulder. A curious, and withal, cautious, little maiden, who desires to try this spell, is thus represented by Burns:

Wee Jenny to her granny says:
　'Will ye go wi' me, granny?
I'll eat the apple at the glass,
　I gat frae uncle Johnny.

Another of these, what may perhaps be termed *unhallowed*, rites of All Hallows' Eve, is to wet a shirt-sleeve, hang it up to the fire to dry, and lie in bed watching it till midnight, when the apparition of the individual's future partner for life will come in and turn the sleeve.

Other rites for the invocation of spirits might be referred to, such as the sowing of hemp-seed, and the winnowing of three *wechts* of nothing, i.e., repeating three times the action of exposing corn to the wind. In all of these the effect sought to be produced is the same—the appearance of the future husband or wife of the experimenter.

The landscape sleeps in mist from morn till noon;
And, if the sun looks through, 'tis with a face
Beamless and pale and round, as if the moon,
When done the journey of her nightly race,
Had found him sleeping, and supplied his place.
For days the shepherds in the fields may be,
Nor mark a patch of sky—blindfold they trace
The plains, that seem without a bush or tree,
Whistling aloud by guess to flocks they cannot see.

The timid hare seems half its fears to lose,
Crouching and sleeping 'neath its grassy lair,
And scarcely startles, tho' the shepherd goes
Close by its home, and dogs are barking there;
The wild colt only turns around to stare
At passer by, then knaps his hide again;
And moody crows besides the road, forbear
To fly, tho' pelted by the passing swain;
Thus day seems turn'd to night, and tries to wake in
vain.

The owlet leaves her hiding-place at noon
And flaps her grey wings in the doubting light;
The hoarse jay screams to see her out so soon,
And small birds chirp and startle with affright;
Much doth it scare the superstitious wight,
Who dreams of sorry luck, and sore dismay;
While cow-boys think the day a dream of night,
And oft grow fearful on their lonely way,
Fancying that ghosts may wake, and leave their
graves by day.

Yet but awhile the slumbering weather flings
Its murky prison round—then winds wake loud;
With sudden stir the startled forest sings
Winter's returning song—cloud races cloud,
And the horizon throws away its shroud,
Sweeping a stretching circle from the eye;
Storms upon storms in quick succession crowd,
And o'er the sameness of the purple sky
Heaven paints, with hurried hand, wild hues of
every dye.

At length the stir of rural labour's still,
And Industry her care awhile forgoes;
When Winter comes in earnest to fulfil
His yearly task, at bleak November's close,
And stops the plough, and hides the field in
snows;
When frost locks up the stream in chill delay,
And mellows on the hedge the jetty sloes
For little birds—then Toil hath time for play,
And naught but threshers' flails awake the dreary
day.

JOHN CLARE

Next was November; he full grosse and fat
As fed with lard, and that right well might
seeme;
For he had been a fatting hogs of late
That yet his browes with sweat did reek and
steem,
And yet the season was full sharp and breem;
In planting eeke he took no small delight:
Whereon he rode, not easie was to deeme;
For it a dreadful Centaure was in sight,
The seed of Saturne and fair Nais, Chiron hight.

SPENSER

November was styled by the ancient Saxons *Wint
monath*, or the wind month, from the gales of wind
which are so prevalent at this season of the year,
obliging our Scandinavian ancestors to lay up their
keels on shore, and refrain from exposing themselves
on the ocean till the advent of more genial weather in
the ensuing year. It bore also the name of *Blot
monath*, or the bloody month, from the circumstance
of its being customary then to slaughter great
numbers of cattle, to be salted for winter use.

NOVEMBER

On the 22nd of this month, the sun enters the sign of
Sagittarius or the Archer, an emblem said to express
the growing predominance of cold which now shoots
into the substance of the earth, and suspends the
vegetative powers of nature. November is generally
regarded as the gloomiest month of the year, and it is
perhaps true that less enjoyment is derivable in it
from external objects than in any other of the twelve
divisions of the calendar. It is popularly regarded as
the month of blue devils and suicides.

November 1ˢᵗ ♏

born: Sir Mathew Hale, judge, 1609.
died: Dr John Radcliffe, physician, 1714; Humphrey Prideaux, orientalist, 1724; Alexander Cruden, author of the "Concordance", 1770; Lord George Gordon, agitator, 1793.

All Saints.

This festival takes its origin from the conversion, in the seventh century, of the Pantheon at Rome into a Christian place of worship, and its dedication by Pope Boniface IV to the Virgin and all the martyrs. The anniversary of this event was at first celebrated on the 1st of May, but the day was subsequently altered to the 1st of November, which was thenceforth, under the designation of the Feast of All Saints, set apart as a general commemoration in their honour. The festival has been retained by the Anglican Church.

November 2ⁿᵈ ♏

Richard Hooker   Richard Bancroft
Princess Amelia   Edward, Duke of Kent

born: William Vincent, Dean of Westminster 1739; Edward, Duke of Kent, father of Queen Victoria 1767.
died: Dr Richard Hooker, author of the Ecclesiastical Polity, 1600; Richard Bancroft, Archbishop of Canterbury 1610; Princess Amelia, daughter of George III, 1810; Sir Samuel Romilly, law reformer, 1818.

November 3rd ♏

died: Robert Lowth, bishop
of London, 1787.

November 4th ♏

William III   Charles Churchill

born: William III, King of England,
1650; James Montgomery, poet
1771.
died: John Benbow, vice-admiral,
1702; Charles Churchill, poet,
1764; Josiah Tucker, economist
and divine, 1799.

November 5th ♏

Angelica Kauffmann *Princess Charlotte*

born: Dr John Brown, author,
1715.
died: Angelica Kauffmann,
painter, 1807; Princess Charlotte,
daughter of George IV, 1817.

The Gunpowder Plot.

The 5th of November marks the anniversary of two prominent events in English history—the discovery and prevention of the gunpowder treason, and the inauguration of William III in Torbay. The originator of the Gunpowder Plot was Robert Catesby, a gentleman of ancient family, who at one period of his life had become a Protestant, but having been reconverted to the Catholic religion, had endeavoured to atone for his apostasy by the fervour of a new zeal. Having resolved in his own mind a project for destroying, at one blow, the King, Lords, and Commons, he communicated it to Thomas Winter, a Catholic gentleman of Worcestershire. He it was who procured the co-adjutorship of the celebrated Guido or Guy Fawkes who was not, as has sometimes been represented, a low mercenary ruffian, but a gentleman of good family, actuated by a spirit of ferocious fanaticism. Other confederates were gradually assumed and it was resolved to effect the purpose of blowing the legislature into the air.

The Gunpowder Plotters.

The preparations were completed about the month of May 1605, and the confederates then separated till the final blow could be struck. The time fixed for this was at first the 3rd of October, the day on which the legislature should meet; but the opening of parliament having been prorogued by the king to the 5th of November, the latter date was finally resolved on. By this time several dissensions had arisen among the conspirators on the question of giving warning to some special friends to absent themselves from the next meeting of parliament. Great mystery attaches to the celebrated anonymous letter received on the evening of the 26th of October by Lord Monteagle, a Roman Catholic nobleman, and brother-in-law of Francis Tresham, one of the conspirators. Be this as it may, the communication in question was the only avowal or ascertained method whereby the king's ministers received intelligence of the schemes under preparation. Though the conspirators were made aware, through a servant of Lord Monteagle, of the discovery which had been made, they nevertheless, by a singular infatuation, continued their preparations, in the hope that the true nature of their scheme had not been unfolded. In this delusion it seems to have been the policy of the government to maintain them to the last. Even after Suffolk, the lord chamberlain, and Lord Monteagle had actually, on the afternoon of Monday the 4th of November, visited the cellar beneath the House of Lords, and there discovered in a corner Guy Fawkes, who pretended to be a servant of Mr Percy the tenant of the vault, it was still determined to persist in the undertaking. At two o'clock the following morning, a party of soldiers under the command of Sir Thomas Knyvett, a Westminster magistrate, visited the cellar, seized Fawkes at the door, and carried him off to Whitehall, where, in the royal bedchamber, he was interrogated by the king and council, and from thence was conveyed to the Tower. It is needless to pursue further in detail the history of the Gunpowder Plot.

Fawkes interrogated by James I

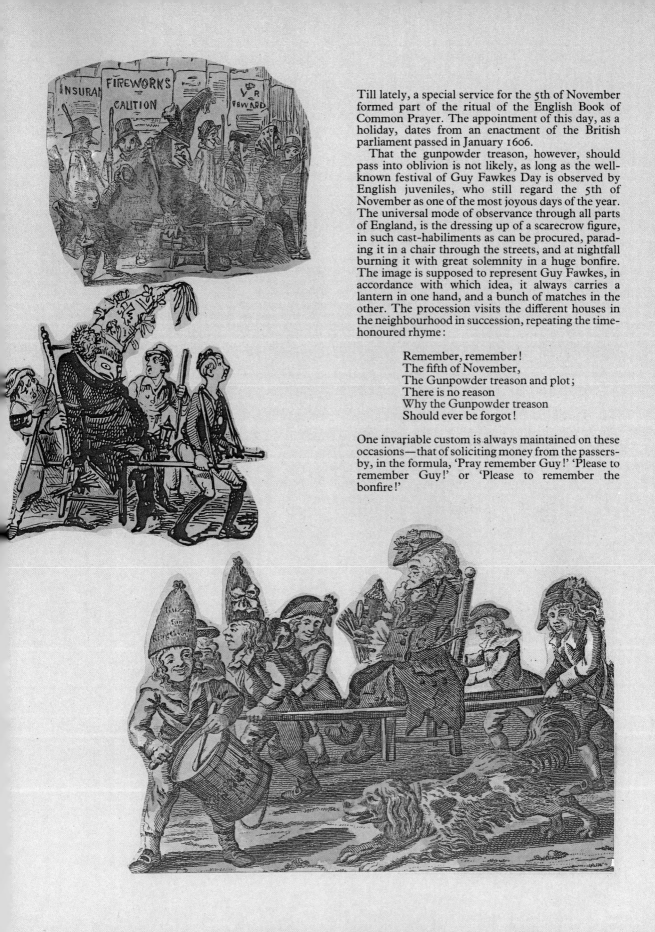

Till lately, a special service for the 5th of November formed part of the ritual of the English Book of Common Prayer. The appointment of this day, as a holiday, dates from an enactment of the British parliament passed in January 1606.

That the gunpowder treason, however, should pass into oblivion is not likely, as long as the well-known festival of Guy Fawkes Day is observed by English juveniles, who still regard the 5th of November as one of the most joyous days of the year. The universal mode of observance through all parts of England, is the dressing up of a scarecrow figure, in such cast-habiliments as can be procured, parading it in a chair through the streets, and at nightfall burning it with great solemnity in a huge bonfire. The image is supposed to represent Guy Fawkes, in accordance with which idea, it always carries a lantern in one hand, and a bunch of matches in the other. The procession visits the different houses in the neighbourhood in succession, repeating the time-honoured rhyme:

> Remember, remember!
> The fifth of November,
> The Gunpowder treason and plot;
> There is no reason
> Why the Gunpowder treason
> Should ever be forgot!

One invariable custom is always maintained on these occasions—that of soliciting money from the passers-by, in the formula, 'Pray remember Guy!' 'Please to remember Guy!' or 'Please to remember the bonfire!'

November 6th ♏

Prince Henry   Colley Cibber

born : Colley Cibber, dramatist, 1671.
died : Prince Henry, son of James I, 1612

November 7th ♏

William Stukeley

born : William Stukeley, antiquarian, 1687.
died : John Kyrle, "The Man of Ross" 1724; Paul Sandby, painter, 1809.

November 8th ♏

Thomas Bewick   John Milton

born : Captain John Byron, vice-admiral, 1723.
died : John Milton, poet, 1674; Thomas Bewick, woodengraver, 1828 ; George Peacock, Dean of Ely, 1858.

November 9th ♏

Gilbert Sheldon   William Camden

died : William Camden, author of "Britannia", 1623; Gilbert Sheldon, Archbishop of Canterbury, 1677.

The Lord Mayor's Show.

The earliest printed description of the shows on Lord Mayor's Day, is that by George Peele, 1585. The pageants were then occupied by children, appropriately dressed, to personate London, the Thames, Magnanimity, Loyalty, &c.; who complimented the mayor as he passed. One 'apparelled like a Moor', at the conclusion of his speech, very sensibly reminded him of his duties in these words:

This now remains, right honourable lord,
That carefully you do attend and keep
This lovely lady, rich and beautiful,
The jewel wherewithal your sovereign queen
Hath put your honour lovingly to trust,
That you may add to London's dignity,
And London's dignity may add to yours.

A very good idea of these annual pageants may be obtained from that concocted by Anthony Munday in 1616, for the mayoralty of Sir John Leman, of the Fishmongers' Company. The first pageant was a fishing-boat, with fishermen 'seriously at labour, drawing up their nets, laden with living fish, and bestowing them bountifully upon the people.' This ship was followed by a crowned dolphin, in allusion to the mayor's arms, and those of the company, in which dolphins appear; and 'because it is a fish inclined much by nature to musique, Arion, a famous musician and poet, rideth on his backe.' Then followed the king of the Moors, attended by six tributary kings on horseback. They were succeeded by 'a lemon-tree richly laden with fruit and flowers,' in punning allusion to the name of the mayor; a fashion observed whenever the name allowed it to become practicable. Then came a bower adorned with the names and arms of all members of the Fishmongers' Company who had served the office of mayor; with their great hero, Sir William Walworth,

inside; an armed officer, with the head of Wat Tyler, on one side, and the Genius of London, 'a crowned angel with golden wings,' on the other. Lastly, came the grand pageant drawn by mermen and mermaids, 'memorizing London's great day of deliverance,' when Tyler was slain; on the top sat a victorious angel, and King Richard was represented beneath, surrounded by impersonations of royal and kingly virtues. There is still preserved, in Fishmongers' hall, a very curious contemporary drawing of this show.

When the great civil war broke out, men's minds became too seriously occupied to favour such displays; and the gloomy puritanism of the Cromwellian era put a stop to them entirely. With the Restoration came back the old city-shows in all their splendour. In 1660, the Royal Oak was the principal feature in compliment to Charles II, and no expense was spared to make a good display of other inventions, 'there being twice as many pageants and speeches as have formerly shewn', says the author, John Tatham, who was for many years afterwards employed in this capacity. He was succeeded by Thomas Jordan, who enlivened his pageantry with humorous songs and merry interludes, suited to Cavalier tastes.

In 1691, Elkanah Settle succeeded to the post of city-laureate, and contributed the yearly pageants until 1708, when printed descriptions cease.

Shorn of its antique pageantry, and bereft of its ancient significance, the procession that passes through London to Westminster every 9th of November, when the mayor of London is 'sworn into' office, becomes in the eyes of many simply ludicrous. It is so, if we do not cast a retrospective glance at the olden glories of the mayoralty, the original importance of the mayor, and the utility of the civic companies, when the law of trading was little understood and ill defined. These companies guarded and enforced the best interests of the traders who composed their fraternities. The Guildhall was their grand rendezvous. The mayor was king of the city, and poets of no mean fame celebrated his election, and invented pageantry for exhibition in the streets and halls, rivalling the court masques in costly splendour.

November 10th ♏

born: Oliver Goldsmith, poet and dramatist, 1728; Granville Sharp, philanthropist, 1734.

November 11th ♏

born: Francis Henry, 8th Earl of Bridgewater, founder of the "Bridgewater Treatises", 1756.

November 12th ♏

born: Richard Baxter, nonconformist divine, 1615; Edward Vernon, admiral, 1684; Mrs Amelia Opie, novelist, 1769.
died: Thomas Fairfax, 3rd Baron Fairfax, general, 1671; Sir John Hawkins, naval commander, 1595; William Hayley, poet, 1820; Charles Kemble, actor, 1854

November 13th ♏

Edward III / Sophia Dorothea / William Etty

born: Edward III, King of England, 1312.
died: Sophia Dorothea, consort of George I, 1726; William Etty, painter, 1849; Sir John Forbes, physician, 1801.

November 14th ♏

Louise Kerovaille / Benjamin Hoadly / Charles Lyell

born: Benjamin Hoadley, Bishop of Bangor, 1676; Sir Charles Lyell, geologist, 1797.
died: Louise Kerovaille, Duchess of Portsmouth, mistress of Charles II, 1734.

November 15th ♏

William Pitt / William Herschel / William Cowper

born: William Pitt, Earl of Chatham, statesman, 1708; William Cowper, poet, 1731; Sir William Herschel, astronomer, 1738.
died: James Hamilton, 4th Duke of Hamilton, 1712.

November 16th ♏

Henry III

born: Francis Danby, painter, 1793.
died: Henry III, King of England 1272; James Ferguson, astronomer, 1776; George Wombwell, managerie proprietor, 1850

November 17th ♍

died: Mary I, Queen of England, 1558; John Earle, Bishop of Salisbury, 1665; Thomas Pelham-Holles, Duke of Newcastle, statesman, 1768; Charlotte, Queen of George III, 1818; Thomas Erskine, Baron Erskine, Lord Chancellor, 1823.

Queen Elizabeth's Day.

Violent political and religious excitement characterised the close of the reign of King Charles II. It had been usual to observe the anniversary of the accession of Queen Elizabeth with rejoicings; and hence the 17th of November was popularly known as 'Queen Elizabeth's Day'; but after the Great Fire, these rejoicings were converted into a satirical saturnalia of the most turbulent kind. The Popish Plot, the Meal-tub Plot, and the murder of Sir Edmundbury Godfrey, had excited the populace to anti-papistical demonstrations, which were fostered by many men of the higher class, who were members of political and Protestant clubs.

From the rare pamphlet, *London's Defence to Rome*, which describes 'the magnificent procession and solemn burning of the pope at Temple Bar, November 17, 1679', we learn that 'the bells generally about the town began to ring about three o'clock in the morning'; but the great procession was deferred till night, when 'the whole was attended with one hundred and fifty flambeaus and lights, by order; but so many more came in volunteers, as made up some thousands ... At the approach of evening (all things being in readiness), the solemn procession began, setting forth from Moorgate, and so passing first to Aldgate, and thence through Leadenhall Street, by the Royal Exchange through Cheapside, and so to Temple Bar. Never were the balconies, windows, and houses more numerously lined, or the streets closer thronged, with multitudes of people, all expressing their abhorrence of popery with continued shouts and exclamations, so that 'tis modestly computed that, in the whole progress, there could not be fewer than two hundred thousand spectators.'

The way was cleared by six pioneers in caps and red waistcoats, followed by a bellman bearing his lantern and staff, and ringing his bell, crying out all the way in a loud and dolesome voice: 'Remember Justice Godfrey!' He was followed by a man on horseback, dressed like a Jesuit, carrying a dead body before him, 'representing Justice Godfrey, in like manner as he was carried by the assassins to Primrose Hill'. Godfrey was a London magistrate, before whom the notorious Titus Oates had made his first deposition; he was found murdered in the fields at the back of Primrose Hill, with a sword run through his body, to make it appear that by falling upon it intentionally, he had committed suicide; but wounds in other parts of his person, and undeniable marks of strangulation, testified the truth. There was little need for a bellman to recall this dark deed to the remembrance of the Londoners. The excitement was increased by another performer in the procession, habited as a priest, 'giving pardons very plentifully to all those that should murder Protestants, and proclaiming it meritorious.' He was followed by a long array of Catholic church dignitaries, ending with 'the pope, in a lofty glorious pageant, representing a chair of state, covered with scarlet, richly embroidered and fringed, and bedecked with golden balls and crosses.' When the procession reached the foot of Chancery Lane, in Fleet Street, it came to a stop; 'then having entertained the thronging spectators for some time with ingenious fireworks, a vast bonfire being prepared just over against the Inner Temple gate, his holiness, after some compliments and reluctances, was decently toppled from all his grandeur into the flames.'

This show proved so immensely popular, that it was reproduced next year, with additional political pageantry. The following year it was announced that the pageantry should be grander than ever, but the mayor was now the nominee of the king, and effectually suppressed the display, patrolling all the streets with officers till midnight, and having the City trained-bands in reserve in the Exchange, and a company of Horse Guards on the other side of Temple Bar. 'Thus ended these *Diavolarias*,' says Roger North.

November 18th ♏

born: Sir David Wilkie, painter, 1785.
died: Cardinal Reginald Pole, 1558; Cuthbert Tunstall, Bishop of Durham, 1559; Charles Heath, engraver, 1848; George Manby, inventor, 1854; Charles Forbes, naturalist, 1854; Frank Stone, painter, 1859.

November 19th ♏

born: Robert Devereux, 2nd Earl of Essex, favourite of Queen Elizabeth I, 1567; Charles I, King of England, 1600.
died: Thomas Shadwell, poet, 1692; John Wilkins, Bishop of Chester, 1672.

Relics of Queen Elizabeth I

November 20th ♏

Christopher Hatton

Queen Caroline

born: Thomas Chatterton,
poet, 1752.
died: Sir Christopher Hatton,
lord chancellor, 1591;
Caroline, Queen of England,
1737; Abraham Tucker,
philosopher, 1774; Roger Payne,
bookbinder.

November 21st ♏

Thomas Gresham

Henry Purcell

died: Sir Thomas Gresham,
founder of the Royal Exchange 1579;
Henry Purcell, composer, 1695;

November 22nd ♏

John Tillotson

Robert Clive

died: John Tillotson,
Archbishop of Canterbury, 1694;
Robert Clive, Lord Clive,
Governor of Bengal, 1774;
John Stackhouse, botanist,
1819.

November 23rd ↑

Thomas Tallis

Thomas Birch

born: Dr Thomas Birch, historian,
1705 & John Wallis, mathematician,
1616.
died: Perkin Warbeck, pretender, 1499;
Thomas Tallis, composer, 1585.

Sagittarius - the centaur November 23 to December 22
of the Planet Jupiter, and his signification

Manners and actions when well placed

Then he is Magnanimous, Faithfull, Bashfull, Aspiring in an honourable way at high matters, in all his actions a Lover of faire Dealing, desiring to benefit all men, doing Glorious things, Honourable and Religious, of sweet and affable Conversation, wonderfully indulgent to his Wife and Children, reverencing Aged men, a great Reliever of the Poore, full of Charity and Godlinesse, Liberal, hating all Sordid actions, Just, Wise, Prudent, Thankfull, Vertuous : so that when you find ♃ the Significator of any man in a Question, or Lord of his Ascendant in a Nativity, and well dignified, you may judge him qualified as abovesaid.

When ill

When ♃ is unfortunate, then he wastes his Patrimony, suffers every one to cozen him, is Hypocritically Religious, Tenacious, and stiffe in maintaining false Tenents in Religion; he is Ignorant, Carelesse, nothing Delightfull in the love of his Friends; of a grosse, dull Capacity, Schismaticall, abasing himselfe in all Companies, crooching and stooping where no necessity is.

November 24th

John Knox   William Sancroft

Laurence Sterne   William Lamb

born: Laurence Sterne, writer and novelist, 1713; John Bacon, sculptor, 1740; Grace Darling, heroine, 1815.
died: John Knox, reformer, 1572; William Sancroft, archbishop of Canterbury, 1693; William Lamb, 2nd Viscount Melbourne, 1848.

November 25th

Isaac Watts

born: Charles Kemble, actor, 1775.
died: Edward Alleyn, actor 1626; Dr Isaac Watts, hymn writer, 1748; Henry Baker, naturalist and poet, 1774

November 26th

Henry Ireton

born: Sir James Ware, antiquary, 1594; William Derham, divine, 1657.
died: Henry Ireton, son-in-law of Oliver Cromwell, 1651; John London McAdam, improver of roads, 1836; George Nugent Grenville, Baron Nugent, author, 1856

November 27th

John Watts   Robert Lowth

born: Robert Lowth, Bishop of London, 1710; John Murray, publisher, 1778;
died: Basil Montagu, writer & philanthropist, 1851.

The four weeks immediately preceeding Christmas are collectively styled *Advent*, a term denoting *approach* or *arrival*, and are so called in reference to the coming of the birth of our Saviour. With this period, the ecclesiastical or Christian year is held to commence, and the first Sunday of these four weeks is termed Advent Sunday, or the first Sunday in Advent. It is always the *nearest* Sunday to the feast of St Andrew, November 30th, whether before or after that day; so that in all cases the season of Advent shall contain the uniform number of four Sundays.

November 28th

born: George William Manby, inventor, 1765.
died: Eleanor, Queen of Edward I, 1291; Edward Plantagenet, Earl of Warwick, executed, 1499.

November 29th

Margaret, Queen of Scotland

Brian Walton

John Ray

Prince Rupert

Thomas Wolsey

born: Margaret, daughter of Henry VII
& Queen of Scotland, 1489;
John Ray, Naturalist, 1627;
Edmund Lyons, 1st Baron Lyons,
admiral, 1790.
died: Cardinal Thomas Wolsey,
minister of Henry VIII, 1530; Brian
Walton, Bishop of Chester, 1661;
Prince Rupert, Cavalier general,
1682; Anthony à Wood, antiquarian,
1695; Charles Buller, liberal
politician, 1848.

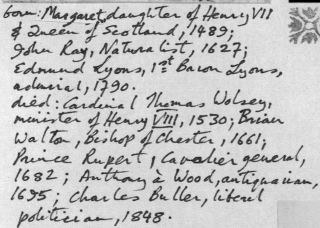

November 30th

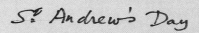

St Andrew's Day

St Andrew has been regarded since time immemorial as the patron saint of Scotland; and his day, the 30th of November, is a favourite occasion of social and national reunion, amid Scotchmen residing in England and other places abroad.

born: Sir Henry Savile, scholar, 1549; Sir Philip Sidney, soldier and poet, 1554; Jonathan Swift, satirist, 1667; John Toland, deist, 1670.
died: William Gilbert, physician, 1603; John Selden, jurist, 1654; James Sheridan Knowles, dramatist, 1862.

December

Glad Christmas comes, and every hearth
   Makes room to give him welcome now,
E'en want will dry its tears in mirth,
   And crown him with a holly bough;
Though tramping 'neath a winter sky,
   O'er snowy paths and rimy stiles,
The housewife sets her spinning by
   To bid him welcome with her smiles.

Each house is swept the day before,
   And windows stuck with evergreens,
The snow is besom'd from the door,
   And comfort crowns the cottage scenes.
Gilt holly, with its thorny pricks,
   And yew and box, with berries small,
These deck the unused candlesticks,
   And pictures hanging by the wall.

Neighbours resume their annual cheer,
   Wishing, with smiles and spirits high,
Glad Christmas and a happy year
   To every morning passer-by;
Milkmaids their Christmas journeys go,
   Accompanied with favour'd swain;
And children pace the crumping snow,
   To taste their granny's cake again.

Around the glowing hearth at night,
   The harmless laughter and winter tale
Go round, while parting friends delight
   To toast each other o'er their ale;
The cotter oft with quiet zeal
   Will musing o'er his Bible lean;
While in the dark the lovers steal
   To kiss and toy behind the screen.

Old customs! Oh! I love the sound
   However simple they may be:
Whate'er with time hath sanction found,
   Is welcome and is dear to me.
Pride grows above simplicity,
   And spurns them from her haughty mind,
And soon the poet's song will be
   The only refuge they can find.

JOHN CLARE

And after him came next the chill December;
Yet he through merry feasting which he made,
And great bonfires, did not the cold remember;
His Saviour's birth his mind so much did glad.
Upon a shaggy-bearded goat he rode,
The same wherewith Dan Jove on tender yeares,
They say, was nourish by th'Idean mayd;
And in his hand a broad deepe bowle he beares,
Of which he freely drinks an health to all his
   peeres.

SPENSER

December, like the three preceding months, derives its name from the place which it held in the old Roman calendar, where the year was divided, nominally, only into ten months, with the insertion of supplementary days, to complete the period required for a revolution of the earth round the sun. In allusion to the practice of lighting fires in this month for the purpose of warmth, Martial applies to it the epithet of *fumosus* or smoky. He also characterises it as *canus* or hoary, from the snows which then overspread the high grounds. By the ancient Saxons, December was styled *Winter-monath* or winter-month; a term which, after their conversion to Christianity, was changed to *Heligh monath* or holy month from the anniversary which occurs in it, of the birth of Christ.

DECEMBER

On the 22nd of December, the sun enters the sign of
Capricornus or the Goat. The idea thus allegorised
by a climbing animal is said to be the ascent of the
sun, which, after reaching its lowest declination at
the winter-solstice, on the 21st of this month,
recommences its upward path, and continues to do so
from that date until it attains its highest altitude at
the summer-solstice, on the 21st of June.

As regards meteorological characteristics,
December bears in its earlier portion a considerable
resemblance to the preceding month of November.
Heavy falls of snow and hard frosts used to be of
normal occurrence at the season of Christmas.

December 1st

Henry I

born: John Keill, mathematician
and astronomer, 1671.
died: Henry I, King of England,
1135; Sir James Ware,
antiquary, 1666; Dr George
Birkbeck, founder of
mechanics institutions, 1841

December 2nd
born: Henry Gally Knight,
writer on architecture 1786.
died: Mrs Amelia Opie,
novelist, 1853.

December 3rd
born: Samuel Compton,
inventor, 1753; Robert
Bloomfield, poet, 1766.

December 4th

Thomas Hobbes

Robert Jenkinson

Thomas Carlyle

William Drummond

born: Thomas Carlyle, historian, 1795;
died: William Drummond of Hawthornden,
poet, 1649; Thomas Hobbes, philosopher,
1679; Robert Jenkinson, 2nd Earl
of Liverpool.

December 5th

Sir Henry Wotton

Robert Harley

born: Robert Harley, 1st Earl of
Oxford, 1661.
died: Sir Henry Wotton, diplomatic
and poet, 1639; John Bewick,
wood-engraver, 1795; Capt.
S. A. Warner, inventor, 1853.

December 6th

George Monk

King Henry VI

Nicholas Rowe

born: Henry VI, King of England,
1421; General George Monk,
Duke of Albermarle, 1608;
Rev. Richard Harris Barham,
author, 1788.
died: Nicholas Rowe, poet
laureate and dramatist, 1718;
Catherine Clive, actress, 1788.

The Boy Bishop: Eton Montem

On St Nicholas's Day, in ancient times, a singular ceremony used to take place. This was the election of the *Boy-Bishop*, or *Episcopus Puerorum*, who, from this date to Innocents', or Childermas Day, on the 28th December, exercised a burlesque episcopal jurisdiction, and, with his juvenile dean and prebendaries, parodied the various ecclesiastical functions and ceremonies.

The election of the Boy-bishop seems to have prevailed generally throughout the English cathedrals, and also in many of the grammar-schools, but the place where, of all others, it appears to have specially obtained, was the episcopal diocese of Salisbury or Sarum. A full description of the mock-ceremonies enacted on the occasion is preserved in the *Processional of Salisbury Cathedral*, where also the service of the Boy-bishop is printed and set to music. It seems to have constituted literally a mimic transcript of the regular episcopal functions; and we do not discover any trace of parody or burlesque, beyond the inevitable one—the ludicrous contrast presented by the diminutive bishop and his chapter to the grave and canonical figures of the ordinary clergy of the cathedral. The actors in this solemn farce were composed of the choristers of the church, and must have been well drilled in the parts which they were to perform.

With the establishment of Protestantism in England, the pastime of the Boy-bishop disappeared; but the well-known festivity of the *Eton Montem* appears to have originated in, and been a continuance under another form, of the medieval custom above detailed. The Eton celebration, now abolished, consisted, as is well-known, in a march of the scholars attending that seminary to Salt Hill, in the neighbourhood (*ad montem*—'To the Mount'—whence the name of the festivity), where they dined, and afterwards returned in procession to Eton in the evening. It was of a thoroughly military character, the mitre and ecclesiastical vestments of the Boy-bishop and his clergy of former times being exchanged for the uniforms of a company of soldiers and their captain. Certain boys, denominated *salt-bearers*, and their *scouts* or deputies, attired in fancy-dresses, thronged the roads in the neighbourhood, and levied from the passers-by tribute money for the benefit of

Eton College Chapel

Mitre of Bishop Wren

December 7th
born: Richard Valpy,
schoolmaster, 1754;
died: Algernon Sidney,
republican, executed
1683.

December 8th

Mary Queen of Scots

Thomas de Quincey

their captain. This was supposed to afford the latter the means of maintaining himself at the university, and amounted sometimes to a considerable sum, occasionally reaching as high as £1000. According to ancient practice, the salt-bearers were accustomed to carry with them a handkerchief filled with salt, of which they bestowed a small quantity on every individual who contributed his quota to the subsidy. The origin of this custom of distributing salt is obscure, but it would appear to have reference to those ceremonies so frequently practised at schools and colleges in former times, when a new-comer or *freshman* arrived, and, by being *salted*, was, by a variety of ceremonies admitted to a participation with the other scholars in their pastimes and privileges.

The Eton-Montem was abolished in January 1847. This step, however, was not taken without a considerable amount of opposition.

born: Mary Queen of Scots, 1542;
Charles Wentworth Dilke,
antiquary and critic, 1789.
died: Richard Baxter,
nonconformist divine, 1691.
Thomas de Quincey, writer
and author, 1859.

December 9th

born: John Milton, poet, 1608;
William Whiston, divine, 1667.
died: Sir Anthony van Dyck,
painter, 1641; Edward Hyde,
Earl of Clarendon, statesman and
historian, 1674.

December 10th
born: Thomas Holcroft, dramatist,
novelist and translator, 1745.
died: Edward Gunter, mathematician,
1626; William Empson, editor, 1852.

December 11th
born: Charles Wesley,
musician, 1757.
died: Sir Roger L'Estrange,
journalist and pamphleteer,
1737.

December 12th

born: Samuel Hood, Viscount Hood,
admiral, 1724; Erasmus Darwin,
physician, 1731.
died: Henry St. John, Viscount
Bolingbroke, 1751; Colley Cibber,
dramatist, 1757; Sir Mark Isambard
Brunel, civil engineer, 1849.

born: William Drummond of
Hawthornden, poet, 1585;
Arthur Penrhyn Stanley, Dean of
Westminster, 1815.
died: Dr Samuel Johnson,
Lexicographer, 1784.

The Tradescants.

The following lines are inscribed upon a tomb in
Lambeth churchyard:

Know, stranger, ere thou pass; beneath this
    stone,
Lye John Tradescant, grandsire, father, son;
The Last dy'd in his spring; the other two
Lived till they had travelled Art and Nature
    through,
As by their choice collections may appear,
Of what is rare, in land, in sea, in air;
Whilst they (As Homer's Iliad in a nut)
A world of wonders in one closet shut.
These famous antiquarians that had been
Both gardeners to the Rose and Lily Queen,
Transplanted now themselves, sleep here;
    and when
Angels shall with their trumpets waken men,
And fire shall purge the world, these hence
    shall rise
And change this garden for a paradise.

The grandsire of the above epitaph was of Flemish
origin. After travelling through Europe and in the
East, he settled in England; and was at one time
gardener to the Duke of Buckingham, and afterwards
to Charles I. He formed a large 'physic garden' at
South Lambeth, and was the means of introducing
many plants into this country. He was also an
enthusiastic collector of curiosities, with which he
filled his house, and earned for it the popular name of
'Tradeskin's Ark'. He died at an advanced age in
1652 or 1653. His son, another John Tradescant,
followed in his father's footsteps. In 1656, he
published a catalogue of his collection under the title
of *Museum Tradescantianum*. From this we learn that
it was indeed a multifarious assemblage of strange
things—stuffed animals and birds, chemicals, dyeing
materials, idols, weapons, clothes, coins, medals,
musical instruments, and relics of all sorts.

In Ashmole's diary, under the date 12th December
1659, occurs the entry: 'Mr Tradescant and his wife
told me they had long been considering upon whom
to bestow their closet of curiosities when they died,
and at last resolved to give it unto me.' Tradescant
died in 1672, and bequeathed his house to Ashmole,
who, after some litigation with his friend's widow,
took possession of the ark in 1674. The collection was
left by Ashmole to the university of Oxford, and was
the nucleus of the museum bearing his name.

December 14th

born: Daniel Neal, historian, 1678;
James Bruce, African traveller, 1730;
Charles Wolfe, poet, 1791.
died: Henry Aldrich, divine and scholar
1710; Thomas Tenison, Archbishop of
Canterbury, 1715; J.C. Loudon, landscape
gardner, 1843; George Hamilton-Gordon,
4th Earl of Aberdeen, statesman, 1860;
Prince Albert, Consort of Queen Victoria, 1861.

December 16th

born: John Selden, jurist, 1584;
George Whitefield, evangelist, 1714;
Elizabeth Carter, poet, 1717;
Jane Austen, novelist, 1775.
died: James V, King of Scotland, 15
Sir William Petty, political economist
1687.

December 15th

born: George Romney, painter,
1734.
died: Izaak Walton, author,
1683; John Shute-Barrington,
1st Viscount Barrington, lawyer, 1683.

December 17th

born: Prince Rupert, cavalier
general, 1619; Anthony à Wood,
antiquary, 1632; Sir Humphry Davy,
natural philosopher, 1779.

December 18th

Thomas Graham

died: Heneage Finch, 1st Earl of
Nottingham, lord Chancellor, 1682;
Dr Alex Adam, writer on
antiquities, 1809; Thomas
Dunham Whitaker, topographer,
1821; Thomas Graham, Baron
Lynedoch, general, 1843;
Samuel Rogers, poet, 1855.

December 19th

James Dalhousie
J. M. W. Turner

born: Sir William Edward Parry,
artic explorer, 1790.
died: Augustus Pugin, architect,
1832; Joseph Mallard Turner, painter,
1851; James, 1st Marquess of
Dalhousie, governor general of India, 1860.

December 20th

born: John Wilson Croker,
politician and essayist, 1780.
died: Thomas Hill, book-
collector, 1840; Paul
Whitehead, satirist, 1774.

December 21st

born: Thomas à Becket,
Archbishop of Canterbury,
probably 1118.
died: John Harris, principal of
New College, London, 1856.

December 22nd

died: Richard Alleine, nonconformist divine, 1681; James Harris, author of "Hermes", 1780; Martin Joseph Routh, president of Magdalen College, 1854

December 23rd

Matthew Wren

born: Matthew Wren, Bishop of Ely, 1585; Heneage Finch, 1st Earl of Nottingham, lord chancellor, 1621; Robert Barclay, Quaker, 1648
died: Sir Philip Francais, author, 1818; Hugh Miller, man of letters and geologist, 1856

December 24th

William Warburton

born: William Warburton, Bishop of Gloucester, 1698; George Crabbe, poet, 1754;
died: Henry John Todd, author, 1845

Christmas Eve.

With Christmas Eve, the Christmas holidays may practically be said to commence, though according to ecclesiastical computation, the festival really begins on the 16th of December, or the day which is distinguished in the calendar as *O Sapientia*, from the name of an anthem, sung during Advent. The season is held to terminate on 1st of February, or the evening before the Purification of the Virgin (Candlemas Day), by which date, according to the ecclesiastical canons, all the Christmas decorations must be removed from the churches. In common *parlance*, certainly, the Christmas holidays comprehend a period of nearly a fortnight, commencing on Christmans Eve, and ending on Twelfth Day. The whole of this season is still a jovial one, abounding in entertainments and merry-makings of all sorts, but is very changed from what it used to be with our ancestors in feudal times, when it was an almost unintermitted round of feasting and jollity.

For a picture of Christmas Eve, in the olden time, we can desire none more graphic than that furnished by Sir Walter Scott in *Marmion*.

> On Christmas Eve the bells were rung;
> On Christmas Eve the mass was sung;
> That only night, in all the year,
> Saw the stoled priest the chalice rear.
> The damsel donned her kirtle sheen;
> The hall was dressed with holly green;
> Forth to the wood did merry-men go,
> To gather in the mistletoe.
> Then opened wide the baron's hall;
> Power laid his rod of rule aside,
> And ceremony doffed his pride.
> The heir, with roses in his shoes,
> That night might village partner choose.
> The lord, underogating, share
> The vulgar game of 'post and pair'.
> All hailed, with uncontrolled delight,
> And general voice, the happy night,
> That to the cottage, as the crown,
> Brought tidings of salvation down!

Capricorn — the goat ♑
Of the Planet Saturne,
and his signification.

December 23 to January 20

Manners and Actions, when well dignified.

Then he is profound in Imagination, in his Acts severe, in his words reserved, in speaking and giving very spare, in labour patient, in arguing or disputing grave, in obtaining the goods of this life studious and solicitous, in all manners of actions austere.

When ill.

Then he is envious, covetous, jealous and mistrustful, timorus, sordid, outwardly dissembling, sluggish, suspitious, stubborne, a contemner of women, a close lyar, malicious, murmuring, never contented, ever repining.

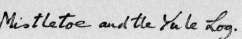

Mistletoe and the Yule Log.

Two popular observances belonging to Christmas are more especially derived from the worship of our pagan ancestors—the hanging up of the mistletoe, and the burning of the Yule log.

As regards the former of these practices, it is well known that, in the religion of the Druids, the mistletoe was regarded with the utmost veneration, though the reverence which they paid to it seems to have been restricted to the plant when found growing on the oak—the favourite tree of their divinity Tutanes. The growth of the mistletoe on the oak is now of extremely rare occurrence, but in the orchards of the west-midland counties of England, such as the shires of Gloucester and Worcester, the plant flourishes in great frequency and luxuriance on the apple-trees. Large quantities are annually cut at the Christmas season, and despatched to London and other places, where they are extensively used for the decoration of houses and shops. The special custom connected with the mistletoe on Christmas Eve, and an indubitable relic of the days of Druidism, handed down through a long course of centuries, must be familiar to all our readers. A branch of the mystic plant is suspended from the wall or ceiling, and any one of the fair sex, who, either from inadvertence, or, as possibly may be insinuated, *on purpose*, passes beneath the sacred spray, incurs the penalty of being then and there kissed by any lord of creation who chooses to avail himself of the privilege.

The burning of the Yule log is an ancient Christmas ceremony, transmitted to us from our Scandinavian ancestors, who, at their feast of *Juul*, at the winter-solstice, used to kindle huge bonfires in honour of their god Thor. The custom, though sadly shorn of the 'pomp and circumstance' which formerly attended it, is still maintained in various parts of the country. The bringing in and placing of the ponderous block on the hearth of the wide chimney in the baronial hall was the most joyous of the ceremonies observed on Christmas Eve in feudal times. The venerable log, destined to crackle a welcome to all-comers, was drawn in triumph from its resting-place at the feet of its living brethren of the woods. Each wayfarer raised his hat as it passed, for he well knew that it was full of good promises, and that its flames would burn out old wrongs and heartburnings, and cause the liquor to bubble in the wassail-bowl, that was quaffed to the drowning of ancient feuds and animosities. So the Yule-log was worthily honoured, and the ancient bards welcomed its entrance with their minstrelsy. And here, in connection with the festivities on Christmas Eve, we may quote Herrick's inspiriting stanzas :

> Come bring with a noise,
> My merry, merry boys,
>   The Christmas log to the firing,
> While may good dame she
> Bids ye all be free,
>   And drink to your heart's desiring.

The Lord of Misrule.

The Christmas Tree.

The functionary with the above whimsical title played an important part in the festivities of Christmas in the olden time. His duties were to lead and direct the multifarious revels of the season, or, as we should say at the present day, to act as Master of the Ceremonies. The following account of him is given by Stow: 'In the feast of Christmas, there was in the king's house, wheresoever he lodged, a *Lord of Misrule*, or Master of Merry Disports, and the like had ye in the house of every nobleman of honour or good worship, were he spiritual or temporal. The Mayor of London, and either of the Sheriffs, had their several *Lords of Misrule*, ever contending, without quarrel or offence, who should make the rarest pastime to delight the beholders. These lords beginning their rule at Allhallows Eve, continued the same till the morrow after the Feast of the Purification, commonly called Candlemas Day, in which space there were fine and subtle disguisings, masks and mummeries, with playing at cards for counters, nayles and points, in every house, more for pastimes than for game.'

The Christmas-tree seems to be a very ancient custom in Germany, and is probably a remnant of the splendid and fanciful pageants of the Middle Ages. Within the last twenty years, and apparently since the marriage of Queen Victoria and Prince Albert, previous to which time it was almost unknown in this country, the custom has been introduced into England with the greatest success. Though thoroughly an innovation on our old Christmas customs, and partaking, indeed, somewhat of a prosiac character, rather at variance with the beautiful poetry of many of our Christmas usages, he would be a cynic indeed, who could derive no pleasure from contemplating the group of young and happy faces who cluster round the Christmas-tree.

Christmas Games: Snapdragon.

One favourite Christmas sport, very generally played on Christmas Eve, has been handed down to us from time immemorial under the name of 'Snapdragon'. A quantity of raisins are deposited in a large dish or bowl (the broader and shallower this is, the better), and brandy or some other spirit is poured over the fruit and ignited. The bystanders now endeavour, by turns, to grasp a raisin, by plunging their hands through the flames; and as this is somewhat of an arduous feat, requiring both courage and rapidity of action, a considerable amount of laughter and merriment is evoked at the expense of the unsuccessful competitors. As an appropriate accompaniment we introduce here:

The Song of Snapdragon
Here he comes with flaming bowl,
Don't he mean to take his toll,
    Snip! Snap! Dragon!
Take care you don't take too much,
Be not greedy in your clutch,
    Snip! Snap! Dragon!

Christmas Eve — The Mummers.

The mummers, or, as they are styled in Scotland, the *guisers* or *guizards*, occupied a prominent place in the Christmas revels of the olden time, and their performances, though falling, like the other old customs of the season, into desuetude, are still kept up in several parts of the country. The term *mummer* is synonymous with *masker*, and is derived from the Danish, *mumme*, or Dutch, *momme*. The custom of mumming at the present day, such as it is, prevails only at the Christmas season, the favourite and commencing night for the pastime being generally Christmas Eve. Formerly, however, it seems to have been practised also at other times throughout the year, and Stow, in his *Survey of London*, has preserved to us an account of a splendid 'mummerie', which, in 1377, was performed shortly before Candlemas by the citizens of London, for the amusement of Prince Richard, son of the Black Prince, and afterward the unfortunate monarch Richard II.

The grand and special performance of the mummers from time immemorial, has been the representation of a species of drama, which embodies the time-honoured legend of St George and the dragon, with sundry whimsical adjuncts, which contribute to give the whole affair an aspect of 'a very tragical mirth'. The actors, chiefly young lads, having arrayed themselves in the costumes proper to the allegorical characters they are to support, sally forth in company on Christmas Eve, to commence their round of visits to the houses of the principal inhabitants of the parish. Arriving at the first residence in their way, they knock at the door, and claim the privilege of Christmas in the admission of St George and his 'merrymen'. First is seen Old Father Christmas, bearing, as emblematic devices, the holly bough, wassail-bowl, &c. Beside him stands a pretty girl, carrying a branch of mistletoe. Then come the Grand Turk, the gallant knight, St George, and the latter's antagonist, the devouring dragon. A doctor is also present with a large box of pills to cure the wounded. Drums and other music accompany the procession.

Christmas Day:
December 25th

Matthew Hale

Isaac Newton

born: Sir Isaac Newton, natural philosopher,
1642; William Collins, poet, 1721;
Richard Porson, Greek Scholar, 1759.
died: Sir Matthew Hale, judge, 1679;
James Hervey, devotional writer, 1758;
John Logan, divine and poet, 1788.

The festival of Christmas is regarded as the greatest
celebration throughout the ecclesiastical year, and so
important and joyous a solemnity is it deemed, that a
special exception is made in its favour, whereby, in
the event of the anniversary falling on a Friday, that
day of the week, under all circumstances a fast, is
transformed to a festival.

The geniality and joyousness of the Christmas
season in England has long been a national charac-
teristic. The following poem or carol, by George
Wither, who belongs to the first half of the seventeenth century, describes with hilarious animation
the mode of keeping Christmas in the poet's day:

So now is come our joyfulst feast;
    Let every man be jolly;
Each room with ivy leaves is drest,
    And every post with holly,
Though some churls at our mirth repine,
Round your foreheads garlands twine;
Drown sorrow in a cup of wine,
    And let us all be merry.

Now all our neighbours' chimneys smoke,
    And Christmas blocks are burning;
Their ovens they with baked meat choke,
    And all their spits are turning.
Without the door let sorrow lye;
    And if for cold it hap to die;
We'll bury't in a Christmas-pie,
    And evermore be merry.

Christmas Fare.

During the Christmas holidays, open-house was kept by the barons and knights, and for a fortnight and upwards, nothing was heard of but revelry and feasting. The grand feast, however, given by the feudal chieftain to his friends and retainers, took place with great pomp and circumstance on Christmas-day. Among the dishes served up on this important occasion, the boar's head was first at the feast and foremost on the board. Heralded by a jubilant flourish of trumpets, and accompanied by strains of merry minstrelsy, it was carried—on a dish of gold or silver, no meaner metal would suffice— into the banqueting-hall by the server; who, as he advanced at the head of the stately procession of nobles, knights, and ladies, sang:

> The boar's head in hand bring I
> With garlands gay and rosemary;
> I pray you all sing merrily,
> *Qui estis in convivio.*

Mince-pies were popular under the name of 'mutton-pies' as early as 1596, later authorities all agreeing in substituting neats-tongue in the place of mutton, the remaining ingredients being much the same as those recommended in modern recipes. In Herrick's time it was customary to set a watch upon the pies, on the night before Christmas, lest sweet-toothed thieves should lay felonious fingers on them; the jovial vicar sings:

> Come guard the Christmas-pie,
> That the thief, though n'er so sly,
> With his flesh-hooks don't come nigh,
>   To catch it
> From him, who all alone sits there,
> Having his eyes still in his ear,
> And a deal of nightly fear,
>   To watch it.

Geese, capons, pheasants drenched with amber-grease, and pies of carps-tongues, helped to furnish the table in bygone Christmasses, but there was one national dish—neither flesh, fowl, nor good red herring—which was held indispensable. This was furmente, frumenty or furmety, concocted— according to the most ancient formula extant—in this wise: 'Take clean wheat, and bray it in a mortar, that the hulls be all gone off, and seethe it till it burst, and take it up and let it cool; and take clean fresh broth, and sweet milk of almonds, or sweet milk of kine, and temper it all; and take the yolks of eggs. Boil it a little, and set it down and mess it forth with fat venison or fresh mutton.'

Plum-porridge was the progenitor of the pride and glory of an English Christmas. In old times, plum-pottage was always served with the first course of a Christmas-dinner. It was made by boiling beef or mutton with broth, thickened with brown bread; when half-boiled, raisins, currants, prunes, cloves, mace and ginger were added, and when the mess had been thoroughly boiled it was sent to the table with the best meats. Sir Roger de Coverley thought there was some hope of a dissenter, when he saw him enjoy his porridge at the hall on Christmas-day. Plum-broth figures in *Poor Robin's Almanac* for 1750, among the items of Christmas fare, and Mrs Frazer, 'sole teacher of the art of cookery in Edinburgh, and several years' colleague, and afterwards successor to Mrs McIver', who published a cookery-book in 1791, thought it necessary to include plum-pottage among her soups. Brand partook of a tureenful of 'luscious plum-porridge' at the table of the royal chaplain in 1801, but that is the latest appearance of this once indispensable dish of which we have any record.

Christmas Carols.

Amid so many popular customs at Christmas, full of so much sweet and simple poetry, there is perhaps none more charming than that of the Christmas carols, which celebrate in joyous and yet devout strains the Nativity of the Saviour. The term is believed to be derived from the Latin *cantare* (to sing) and *rola* an interjection expressive of joy. The practice appears to be as ancient as the celebration of Christmas itself, and we are informed that in the early ages of the church, the bishops were accustomed to sing carols on Christmas-day among their clergy. It will be recollected that Goldsmith's *Vicar of Wakefield*, describing the unsophisticated character of his parishioners, says: 'They kept up the Christmas carol.' Such a composition as the following might have been sung by these simple swains.

God rest you merry, gentlemen,
  Let nothing you dismay,
For Jesus Christ our Savour
  Was born upon this day,
To save us all from Satan's power,
  When we were gone astray.
    O tidings of comfort and joy!
    For Jesus Christ our Saviour
    Was born on Christmas-day.

Christmas carols are sung on Christmas Eve as well as on the morning of Christmas-day, and indeed the former is regarded by many as the more appropriate occasion. Then the choristers, attached to the village-church, make their rounds to the principal houses throughout the parish, and sing some of those simple and touching hymns. The airs to which they are sung are frequently no less plaintive and melodious than the words, and are often accompanied by instruments.

Christmas Decorations.

Stow, that invaluable chronicler, informs us in his *Survey of London*, that 'against the feast of Christmas every man's house, as also their parish churches, were decked with holme (the evergreen oak), ivy, bayes, and whatsoever the season of the year afforded to be green. The conduits and standards in the streets were likewise garnished.' The favourite plants for church decorations at Christmas are holly, bay, rosemary, and laurel. A quaint old writer thus spiritualises the practice of Christmas decorations. 'So our churches and houses decked with bayes and rosemary, holly and ivy, and other plants which are always green, winter and summer, signify and put us in mind of His Diety, that the child that now was born was God and man, who should spring up like a tender plant, should always be green and flourishing, and live for evermore.'

Aubrey informs us that in several parts of Oxfordshire, it was the custom for the maidservant to ask the man for ivy to decorate the house; and if he refused or neglected to fetch in a supply, the maids stole a pair of his breeches, and nailed them up to the gate in the yard or highway.

December 26th ♍

born; D. John Wilkes, politician, 1797.

St Stephen's Day.

To St Stephen, the Proto-martyr, as he is generally styled, the honour has been accorded by the church of being placed in her calendar immediately after Christmas-day, in recognition of his having been the first to seal with his blood the testimony of fidelity to his Lord and Master. The year in which he was stoned to death, as recorded in the Acts of the Apostles, is supposed to have been A.D. 33. The festival commemorative of him has been retained in the Anglican calendar.

Christmas Boxes.

St Stephen's day, being the customary day for the claimants of Christmas-boxes going their rounds, it has received popularly the designation of *Boxing-day.*

Christmas Pantomimes.

Pantomimic acting had its place in the ancient drama, but the grotesque performances associated with our English Christmas, are peculiar to this country. Cibber says that they originated in an attempt to make stage-dancing something more than motion without meaning. In the early part of the last century, a ballet was produced at Drury Lane, called the *Loves of Mars and Venus,* 'wherein the passions were so happily expressed, and the whole story so intelligibly told by a mute narration of gesture only, that even thinking-spectators allowed it both a pleasing and rational entertainment. From this sprung forth that succession of monstrous medleys that have so long infested the stage, and which arise upon one another alternately at both houses, outvying in expense, like contending bribes at both sides at an election, to secure a majority of the multitude.' Cibber's managerial rival, Rich, found himself unable, with the Lincoln's-Inn-Fields' company, to compete with Drury Lane in the legitimate drama, and struck out a path of his own, by the invention of the comic pantomine. By the help of gay scenes, fine habits, grand dances, appropriate music, and other decorations, he exhibited a story from Ovid's *Metamorphoses,* or some other mythological work. Between the pauses or acts of this serious representation, he interwove a comic fable, consisting chiefly of Harlequin and Columbine, with a variety of surprising adventures and tricks, which were produced by the magic wand of Harlequin; such as the sudden transformation of palaces and temples to huts and cottages; of men and women into wheel-barrows and joint-stools; of trees turned to houses; colonnades to beds of tulips; and mechanics' shops into serpents and ostriches.

Baron Munchausen

Pantaloon   Harlquin   Columbine   Clown

Villagers

Crockodile

Fairy

Lion

Corkscrew

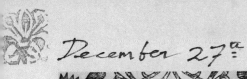

December 27th ♑

Charles Lamb

born: Arthur Murphy, author
and actor, 1727.
died: Thomas Cartwright,
puritan divine, 1603;
Thomas Guy, founder of Guy's
Hospital, 1724. Henry Home
Lord Kames, judge, 1782.
Charles Lamb, essayist, 1834.

December 28th ♑

Mary II   Thomas Babington Macaulay

born: Thomas Henderson,
astronomer, 1798.
died: Mary II, Queen of England
1694; Thomas Babington Macaulay,
historian, 1858.

December 29th ♑

Thomas Sydenham

William Crotch

Thomas à Becket

died: Thomas à Becket, Archbishop of
Canterbury, murdered, 1170; Thomas
Sydenham, physician, 1689; William
Crotch, composer, 1847.

December 30th ♑

John Philips   John Holt

born: Sir John Holt, judge, 1642;
John Philips, poet, 1676.
died: Roger Ascham, educationalist,
1568.

December 31st ♑

Catherine of Braganza
Charles Cornwallis
Robert Boyle
Charles Edward Stuart

born: Charles Edward Stuart, the Young Pretender, 1721; Charles, 1st Marquis Cornwallis, Governor general of India, 1738. died: Robert Boyle, natural philosopher and chemist, 1691; Catherine of Braganza, Queen of England, 1705; John Flamstead, astronomer, 1719; William Gifford, editor, 1826.

To the community at large, the passing away of the Old Year and the arrival of his successor is heralded by peals of bells, which, after twelve o'clock has struck, burst forth from every steeple, warning us that another year has commenced.

> Ring out wild bells to the wild sky,
>   The flying cloud, the frosty light:
>   The Year is dying in the night;
> Ring out, wild bells, and let him die.
>
> Ring out the old, ring in the new,
>   Ring, happy bells, across the snow:
>   The Year is going, let him go;
> Ring out the false, ring in the true.
>
> Ring out the grief that saps the mind,
>   For those that here we see no more;
>   Ring out the feud of rich and poor,
> Ring in redress to all mankind.
>
> Ring out a slowly-dying cause,
>   And ancient forms of party strife;
>   Ring in the nobler modes of life,
> With sweeter manners, purer laws.
>
> Ring out the want, the care, the sin,
>   The faithless coldness of the times;
>   Ring out, ring out my mournful rhymes,
> And ring the fuller minstrel in.
>
> Ring out false pride in place and blood,
>   The civic slander and the spite;
>   Ring in the love of truth and right,
> Ring in the common love of good.
>
> Ring out old shapes of foul disease;
>   Ring out the narrowing lust of gold;
>   Ring out the thousand wars of old,
> Ring in the thousand years of peace.
>
> Ring in the valiant man and free,
>   The larger heart, the kindlier hand;
>   Ring out the darkness of the land,
> Ring in the Christ that is to be.
>   TENNYSON

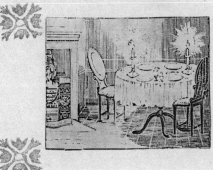

New Year's Eve, or Hogmany

The epithet of the *Daft* (mad) *Days*, applied to the season of the New Year in Scotland, indicates very expressively the uproarious joviality which characterised the period in question. The exuberance of joyousness—which, it must be admitted, sometimes led to great excesses—has now much declined, but New-year's Eve and New-year's Day constitute still the great national holiday in Scotland.

Acknowledgements

The Author and Publishers would like to thank the following for their permission to reproduce illustrations, many of which came from private collections:

Reproduced by Gracious Permission of Her Majesty The Queen; Lord Aberdare; Albertina Museum, Vienna; the Warden and Fellows of All Souls College, Oxford; Society of Antiquaries of London; Apsley House, London; Ashmolean Museum, Oxford; the Lord Auckland; Avon County Council; the Earl Bathurst; Bayeux Museum; the Duke of Bedford; the Trustees of the late Earl Berkeley; Bodleian Library, Oxford; the British Library, London; the Trustees of the British Museum, London; the Marquess of Bute; the Syndics of Cambridge University Library; Castle Museum, Nottingham; Chatsworth Settlement Trustees (Devonshire Collection); Chevening Estate; the Marquess and Dowager Marchioness of Cholmondeley; Christie's, London; the Earl of Clarendon; Viscount Cobham; Thomas Coram Foundation for Children, London; the Master, Fellows and Scholars of Corpus Christi College, Cambridge; the Earl of Craven; Lord Croft; Crown Copyright – reproduced with permission of the Controller of Her Majesty's Stationery Office; Sir William Dugdale; the Governors of Dulwich Picture Library; Lord Dynevor; Bishop's Palace, Ely; Emmanuel College, Cambridge; the Provost and Fellows of Eton College; P. Evelyn; Examination Schools, Oxford; Fitzwilliam Museum, Cambridge; the Frick Collection, New York; the Church Commissioners, Fulham Palace; Garrick Club, London; Goodwood House by courtesy of the Trustees; the Gresham Committee; Guildhall Art Gallery, City of London; the Earl of Haddington; the Duke of Hamilton; the Prince of Hanover; Lord Hesketh; Kunsthistorisches Museum, Vienna; Laing Art Gallery, Newcastle; Lambeth Palace, London; A.C.F. Lambton; Viscount de L'Isle; the Louvre, Paris; the Earl of Malmesbury; City of Manchester Art Galleries; the Duke of Marlborough; Lord Methuen; Midland Bank Limited; the Viscount Montgomery of Alamein; the Museum of London; National Gallery, Cape Town; National Gallery of Ireland, Dublin; the Trustees of the National Gallery, London; National Gallery of Victoria, Melbourne; National Portrait Gallery, London; National Theatre, London (Maugham Collection); The National Trust; New College, Oxford; the Marquess of Northampton; the Earl of Pembroke; the Master and Fellows of Pembroke College, Cambridge; the Bishop of Peterborough; City of Plymouth Museum and Art Gallery; Princeton University, New Jersey; Lord Romsey, Broadlands, Romsey, Hampshire; the Earl of Rosebery; Royal Albert Memorial Museum, Exeter; Royal College of Physicians, London; The Royal Society, London; Lord Sackville; the Earl of St Germans; St John's College, Cambridge; the Dean and Chapter, St Paul's Cathedral; Scottish National Portrait Gallery; Lord Shelburne; the Trustees of Sir John Soane's Museum, London; Somerset Archaeological and Natural History Society; Stoneleigh Abbey Preservation Trust Limited; L.G. Stopford Sackville; Colin Tennant; the Lord Tollemache; Toronto Art Gallery; Lord Tweedmouth; Trinity College, Cambridge; Trinity College, Dublin; Trinity College, Oxford; Trinity House, Edinburgh; Madam Tussauds, London; Uffizi Gallery, Florence; Victoria and Albert Museum, London; the Earl Waldegrave; Walters Art Gallery, Baltimore; the Dean and Chapter of Westminster; the Warden and Fellows of Winchester College; Wrightsman Collection; Yale Gallery of Fine Arts, New Haven, Conn.; the Marquess of Zetland. Reproduced by kind permission of the Lord Bishop of London and the Church Commissioners for England; copyright reserved to the Courtauld Institute of Art.